# Computer Programming
## An Advanced Course

Noel Kalicharan
*Senior Lecturer, Computer Science*
*The University of the West Indies*
*St. Augustine, Trinidad*

Published September 2006



noel.kalicharan@sta.uwi.edu
noelk@hotmail.com

# Preface

This book takes up where *C Programming – A Beginner's Course* leaves off. It assumes you have a working knowledge of basic programming concepts such as variables, constants, assignment, selection (**if...else**) and looping (**while**, **for**). It also assumes you are comfortable with writing functions and working with arrays. If you are not, it is recommended that you study *A Beginner's Course* before tackling the material in this book.

As in the first book, the emphasis is not on teaching the C language, per se, but rather, on using C to teach concepts that any budding programmer should know. The major topics covered are sorting, searching, merging, structures, pointers, linked lists, stacks, queues, recursion and random numbers.

Chapter 1 deals with sorting a list, searching a list and merging two ordered lists.

Chapter 2 introduces an important concept—the structure. Structures allow you to group a set of related data and manipulate them as one. This chapter shows you how to search and sort an array of structures and how to create useful user-defined types using **typedef** and **struct**s.

Chapter 3 covers that elusive but very powerful concept—pointers. Many programmers will tell you that this is probably the most difficult concept to grasp and the one that gives them the most headache. We hope that, after reading this chapter, you will agree that it does not have to be so.

Chapter 4 deals with linked lists—an important data structure in its own right but also the foundation for more advanced structures such as trees and graphs.

Chapter 5 is devoted specifically to stacks and queues, perhaps the most useful kinds of linear lists. They have important applications in Computer Science.

Chapter 6 introduces a powerful programming methodology—recursion. There is no doubt that recursion takes a bit of getting used to. But, once mastered, you would be able to solve a whole new world of problems that would be difficult to solve using traditional techniques.

We all like to play games. But what lurks inside these game-playing programs? Random numbers. Chapter 7 shows you how to use random numbers to play some simple games and simulate real-life situations.

Almost anything we need to store on a computer must be stored in a file. We use text files for storing the kinds of documents we create with a text editor or word processor. We use binary files for storing photographic image files, sound files, video files and files of 'records'. Chapter 8 shows how to create and manipulate text and binary files. And it also explains how to work with that most versatile kind of file—a random access file.

I wish to express my thanks to Anisa Sawh-Ramdhan for her careful reading of the manuscript. Any errors that remain are all mine.

Noel Kalicharan

# Contents

# 1 Sorting, searching and merging

**In this chapter, we will explain:**

- how to sort a list of items using insertion sort
- how to add a new item to a sorted list so that the list remains sorted
- how to sort an array of strings
- how to sort related (parallel) arrays
- how to search a sorted list using *binary search*
- how to write a program to do a frequency count of words in a passage
- how to merge two sorted lists to create one sorted list

## 1.1 Sorting an array - insertion sort

*Sorting* is the process by which a set of values are arranged in ascending or descending order. There are many reasons to sort. Sometimes we sort in order to produce more readable output (for example, to produce an alphabetical listing). A teacher may need to sort her students in order by name or by average score. If we have a large set of values and we want to identify duplicates, we can do so by sorting; the repeated values will come together in the sorted list. There are many ways to sort. We will discuss a method known as *insertion sort.*

Consider the following array:

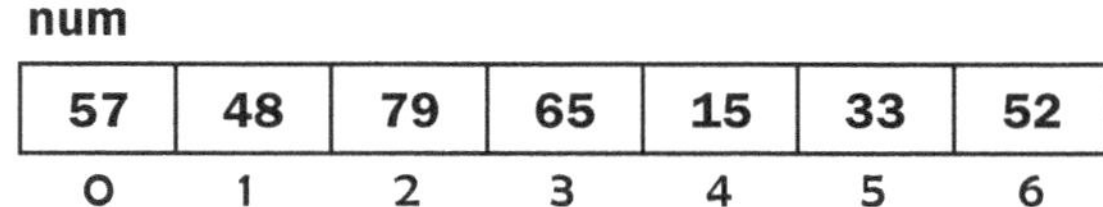


Think of the numbers as cards on a table and picked up one at a time in the order in which they appear in the array. Thus, we first pick up 57, then 48, then 79, and so on, until we pick up 52. However, as we pick up each new number, we add it to our hand in such a way that the numbers in our hand are all sorted.

When we pick up 57, we have just one number in our hand. We consider one number to be sorted.

When we pick up 48, we add it in front of 57 so our hand contains

```
48 57
```

When we pick up 79, we place it after 57 so our hand contains

```
48 57 79
```

When we pick up 65, we place it after 57 so our hand contains

```
48 57 65 79
```

At this stage, four numbers have been picked up and our hand contains them in sorted order.

When we pick up 15, we place it before 48 so our hand contains

```
15 48 57 65 79
```

When we pick up 33, we place it after 15 so our hand contains

```
15 33 48 57 65 79
```

Finally, when we pick up 52, we place it after 48 so our hand contains

```
15 33 48 52 57 65 79
```

The numbers have been sorted in ascending order.

The method described illustrates the idea behind *insertion sort*. The numbers in the array will be processed one at a time, from left to right. This is equivalent to picking up the numbers from the table, one at a time. Since the first number, by itself, is sorted, we will process the numbers in the array starting from the second.

When we come to process **num[j]**, we can assume that **num[0]** to **num[j-1]** are sorted. We then attempt to insert **num[j]** among **num[0]** to **num[j-1]** so that **num[0]** to **num[j]** are sorted. We will then go on to process **num[j+1]**. When we do so, our assumption that **num[0]** to **num[j]** are sorted will be true.

Sorting **num** in ascending order using insertion sort proceeds as follows:

**1st pass**

- Process **num[1]**, that is, 48. This involves placing 48 so that the first two numbers are sorted; **num[0]** and **num[1]** now contain

  **num**

  | 48 | 57 |
  |---|---|
  | 0 | 1 |

  and the rest of the array remains unchanged.

**2nd pass**

- Process **num[2]**, that is, 79. This involves placing 79 so that the first three numbers are sorted; **num[0]** to **num[2]** now contain

  **num**

  | 48 | 57 | 79 |
  |---|---|---|
  | 0 | 1 | 2 |

  and the rest of the array remains unchanged.

**3rd pass**

- Process **num[3]**, that is, 65. This involves placing 65 so that the first four numbers are sorted; **num[0]** to **num[3]** now contain

  **num**

  | 48 | 57 | 65 | 79 |
  |---|---|---|---|
  | 0 | 1 | 2 | 3 |

and the rest of the array remains unchanged.

**4th pass**

- Process **num[4]**, that is, 15. This involves placing 15 so that the first five numbers are sorted. To simplify the explanation, think of 15 as being taken out and stored in a simple variable (**key**, say) leaving a 'hole' in **num[4]**. We can picture this as follows:

**key** 15

**num**

| 48 | 57 | 65 | 79 |  | 33 | 52 |
|---|---|---|---|---|---|---|
| 0 | 1 | 2 | 3 | 4 | 5 | 6 |

The insertion of 15 in its correct position proceeds as follows:

- Compare 15 with 79; it is smaller so move 79 to location 4, leaving location 3 free. This gives:

**key** 15

**num**

| 48 | 57 | 65 |  | 79 | 33 | 52 |
|---|---|---|---|---|---|---|
| 0 | 1 | 2 | 3 | 4 | 5 | 6 |

- Compare 15 with 65; it is smaller so move 65 to location 3, leaving location 2 free. This gives:

**key** 15

**num**

| 48 | 57 |  | 65 | 79 | 33 | 52 |
|---|---|---|---|---|---|---|
| 0 | 1 | 2 | 3 | 4 | 5 | 6 |

- Compare 15 with 57; it is smaller so move 57 to location 2, leaving location 1 free. This gives:

**key** 15

**num**

| 48 |  | 57 | 65 | 79 | 33 | 52 |
|---|---|---|---|---|---|---|
| 0 | 1 | 2 | 3 | 4 | 5 | 6 |

- Compare 15 with 48; it is smaller so move 48 to location 1, leaving location 0 free. This gives:

**key** 15

**num**

|  | 48 | 57 | 65 | 79 | 33 | 52 |
|---|---|---|---|---|---|---|
| 0 | 1 | 2 | 3 | 4 | 5 | 6 |

- There are no more numbers to compare with 15 so it is inserted in location 0, giving

**key** 15

**num**

| 15 | 48 | 57 | 65 | 79 | 33 | 52 |
|---|---|---|---|---|---|---|
| 0 | 1 | 2 | 3 | 4 | 5 | 6 |

- We can express the logic of placing 15 by saying that as long as **key** is less than **num[k]**, for some **k**, we move **num[k]** to position **num[k + 1]** and move on to consider **num[k - 1]**, providing it exists. It won't exist when **k** is actually 0. In this case, the process stops and **key** is inserted in position 0.

**5th pass**

- Process **num[5]**, that is, 33. This involves placing 33 so that the first six numbers are sorted. This is done as follows:
- Store 33 in **key**, leaving location 5 free;
- Compare 33 with 79; it is smaller so move 79 to location 5, leaving location 4 free;
- Compare 33 with 65; it is smaller so move 65 to location 4, leaving location 3 free;
- Compare 33 with 57; it is smaller so move 57 to location 3, leaving location 2 free;
- Compare 33 with 48; it is smaller so move 48 to location 2, leaving location 1 free;
- Compare 33 with 15; it is bigger; insert 33 in location 1. This gives:

**key**

| 33 |
|---|

**num**

| 0 | 1 | 2 | 3 | 4 | 5 | 6 |
|---|---|---|---|---|---|---|
| 15 | 33 | 48 | 57 | 65 | 79 | 52 |

- We can express the logic of placing 33 by saying that as long as **key** is less than **num[k]**, for some **k**, we move **num[k]** to position **num[k + 1]** and move on to consider **num[k - 1]**, providing it exists. If **key** is greater than or equal to **num[k]** for some **k**, then key is inserted in position **k + 1**. Here, 33 is greater than **num[0]** and so is inserted into **num[1]**.

**6th pass**

- Process **num[6]**, that is, 52. This involves placing 52 so that the first seven (all) numbers are sorted. This is done as follows:
- Store 52 in **key**, leaving location 6 free;
- Compare 52 with 79; it is smaller so move 79 to location 6, leaving location 5 free;
- Compare 52 with 65; it is smaller so move 65 to location 5, leaving location 4 free;
- Compare 52 with 57; it is smaller so move 57 to location 4, leaving location 3 free;
- Compare 52 with 48; it is bigger; insert 52 in location 3. This gives:

**key**

| 52 |
|---|

**num**

| 0 | 1 | 2 | 3 | 4 | 5 | 6 |
|---|---|---|---|---|---|---|
| 15 | 33 | 48 | 52 | 57 | 65 | 79 |

The array is now completely sorted.

The following is an outline to sort the first **n** elements of an array, **num**, using insertion sort:

```
for j = 1 to n - 1 do
  insert num[j] among num[0] to num[j-1] so that
  num[0] to num[j] are sorted
endfor
```

Using this outline, we write the function **insertionSort** using the parameter **list**.

```
void insertionSort(int list[], int n) {
//sort list[0] to list[n-1] in ascending order
  int j, k, key;
  for (j = 1; j < n; j++) {
    key = list[j];
    k = j - 1; //start comparing with previous item
    while (k >= 0 && key < list[k]) {
      list[k + 1] = list[k];
      --k;
    }
    list[k + 1] = key;
  } //end for
} //end insertionSort
```

The **while** statement is at the heart of the sort. It states that as long as we are within the array (**k >= 0**) and the current number (**key**) is less than the one in the array (**key < list[k]**), we move **list[k]** to the right (**list[k + 1] = list[k]**) and move on to the next number on the left (**--k**).

We exit the **while** loop if **k** is equal to -1 or if **key** is greater than or equal to **list[k]**, for some **k**. In either case, **key** is inserted into **list[k + 1]**.

If **k** is -1, it means that the current number is smaller than all the previous numbers in the list and must be inserted in **list[0]**. But **list[k + 1]** *is* **list[0]** when **k** is -1, so **key** is inserted correctly in this case.

The function sorts in ascending order. To sort in descending order, all we have to do is change **<** to **>** in the **while** condition, thus:

```
while (k >= 0 && key > list[k])
```

Now, a key moves to the left if it is *bigger*.

We write Program P1.1 to test whether **insertionSort** works correctly. Only **main** is shown in the box below. Adding the function completes the program.

**Program P1.1**

```
#include <stdio.h>
main() {
  void insertionSort(int [], int);
  int n, v, num[10];
  printf("Type up to 10 numbers followed by 0\n");
  n = 0;
  scanf("%d", &v);
  while (v != 0) {
    num[n++] = v;
    scanf("%d", &v);
  }
  //n numbers are stored from num[0] to num[n-1]
  insertionSort(num, n);
  printf("\nThe sorted numbers are\n");
  for (v = 0; v < n; v++) printf("%d ", num[v]);
  printf("\n");
} //end main
```

The program requests up to 10 numbers (since the array is declared to be of size 10), stores them in the array **num**, calls **insertionSort**, then prints the sorted list.

The following is a sample run of the program:

```
Type up to 10 numbers followed by 0
57 48 79 65 15 33 52 0

The sorted numbers are
15 33 48 52 57 65 79
```

We could easily generalize **insertionSort** to sort a *portion* of a list. To illustrate, we re-write **insertionSort** (next page) to sort **list[lo]** to **list[hi]** where **lo** and **hi** are passed as arguments to the function.

Since element **lo** is the first one, we start processing elements from **lo + 1** until element **hi**. This is reflected in the **for** statement. Also now, the lowest subscript is **lo**, rather than 0. This is reflected in the **while** condition **k >= lo**. Everything else remains the same as before.

## 1.2 Inserting an element in place

Insertion sort uses the idea of adding a new element to an already sorted list so that the list remains sorted. We can treat this as a problem in its own right (nothing to do with insertion sort). Specifically, given a sorted list of items from **list[m]** to **list[n]**, we want to add a new item (**newItem**, say) to the list so that **list[m]** to **list[n + 1]** are sorted.

```
void insertionSort(int list[], int lo, int hi) {
//sort list[lo] to list[hi] in ascending order
  int j, k, key;
  for (j = lo + 1; j <= hi; j++) {
    key = list[j];
    k = j - 1; //start comparing with previous item
    while (k >= lo && key < list[k]) {
      list[k + 1] = list[k];
      --k;
    }
    list[k + 1] = key;
  } //end for
} //end insertionSort
```

Adding a new item increases the size of the list by 1. We assume that the array has room to hold the new item. We write the function **insertInPlace** to solve this problem.

```
void insertInPlace(int newItem, int list[], int m, int n) {
//list[m] to list[n] are sorted
//insert newItem so that list[m] to list[n+1] are sorted
  int k = n;
  while (k >= m && newItem < list[k]) {
    list[k + 1] = list[k];
    --k;
  }
  list[k + 1] = newItem;
} //end insertInPlace
```

Using **insertInPlace**, we can re-write **insertionSort**, above, as follows:

```
void insertionSort(int list[], int lo, int hi) {
//sort list[lo] to list[hi] in ascending order
  void insertInPlace(int, int [], int, int);
  int j;
  for (j = lo + 1; j <= hi; j++)
    insertInPlace(list[j], list, lo, j - 1);
} //end insertionSort
```

## 1.3 Sorting an array of strings

Consider the problem of sorting a list of names in alphabetical order. In C, each name is stored in a character array. To store several names, we need a two-dimensional character array. For example, we can store 8 names as follows:

| | 0 | 1 | 2 | 3 | 4 | 5 | 6 | 7 | 8 | 9 | 10 | 11 | 12 | 13 | 14 |
|---|---|---|---|---|---|---|---|---|---|---|---|---|---|---|---|
| **0** | T | a | y | l | o | r | , | | V | i | c | t | o | r | \0 |
| **1** | D | u | n | c | a | n | , | | D | e | n | i | s | e | \0 |
| **2** | R | a | m | d | h | a | n | , | | K | a | m | a | l | \0 |
| **3** | S | i | n | g | h | , | | K | r | i | s | h | n | a | \0 |
| **4** | A | l | i | , | | M | i | c | h | a | e | l | \0 | | |
| **5** | S | a | w | h | , | | A | n | i | s | a | \0 | | | |
| **6** | K | h | a | n | , | | C | a | r | o | l | \0 | | | |
| **7** | O | w | e | n | , | | D | a | v | i | d | \0 | | | |

To do so will require a declaration such as:

```
char list[8][15];
```

To cater for longer names, we can increase 15 and to cater for more names, we can increase 8.

The *process* of sorting **list** is essentially the same as sorting an array of integers. The major difference is that whereas we use **<** to compare two numbers, we must use **strcmp** to compare two names. In the function **insertionSort** on the previous page, the **while** condition changes from

```
while (k >= lo && key < list[k])
```

to

```
while (k >= lo && strcmp(key, list[k]) < 0)
```

where **key** is now declared as **char key[15]**.

Also, we must now use **strcpy** (since we can't use = for strings) to assign a name to another location. Here is the complete function:

```
void insertionSort(char list[][15], int lo, int hi) {
//sort list[lo] to list[hi] in alphabetical order
  int j, k; char key[15];
  for (j = lo + 1; j <= hi; j++) {
    strcpy(key, list[j]);
    k = j - 1; //start comparing with previous item
    while (k >= lo && strcmp(key, list[k]) < 0) {
      strcpy(list[k + 1], list[k]);
      --k;
    }
    strcpy(list[k + 1], key);
  } //end for
} end insertionSort
```

Recall that when a two-dimensional array is used as a parameter, the *second* dimension must be specified using a constant (or a **#defined** constant identifier). The first dimension can be left unspecified, similar to when a one-dimensional array is used as a parameter.

We write a simple **main** routine to test this version of **insertionSort**. Here it is:

**Program P1.2**

```
#include <stdio.h>
#include <string.h>
main() {
  void insertionSort(char [][], int, int);
  int n, j;
  char name[8][15] = {"Taylor, Victor", "Duncan, Denise",
      "Ramdhan, Kamal", "Singh, Krishna", "Ali, Michael",
      "Sawh, Anisa", "Khan, Carol", "Owen, David" };
  n = 8;
  insertionSort(name, 0, n-1);
  printf("\nThe sorted names are\n\n");
  for (j = 0; j < n; j++) printf("%s\n", name[j]);
} //end main
```

The declaration of **name** initializes it with the eight names as shown on page 8. When run, the program produces the following output:

```
The sorted names are

Ali, Michael
Duncan, Denise
Khan, Carol
Owen, David
Ramdhan, Kamal
Sawh, Anisa
Singh, Krishna
Taylor, Victor
```

## 1.4 Sorting parallel arrays

It is quite common to have related information in different arrays. For example, suppose, in addition to **name**, we have an integer array **id** such that **id[j]** is an identification number associated with **name[j]**, as shown on the next page.

Consider the problem of sorting the names in alphabetical order. At the end, we would want each name to have its correct id number. So, for example, **name[0]** should contain “Ali, Michael” and **id[0]** should contain 6669.

| | name | id |
|---|---|---|
| 0 | Taylor, Victor | 3050 |
| 1 | Duncan, Denise | 2795 |
| 2 | Ramdhan, Kamal | 4455 |
| 3 | Singh, Krishna | 7824 |
| 4 | Ali, Michael | 6669 |
| 5 | Sawh, Anisa | 5000 |
| 6 | Khan, Carol | 5464 |
| 7 | Owen, David | 6050 |

To achieve this, each time a name is moved during the sorting process, the corresponding id number must also be moved. Since the name and id number must be moved "in parallel", we say we are doing a "parallel sort" or we are sorting "parallel arrays". We re-write **insertionSort** to illustrate how to sort parallel arrays. We call it **parallelSort**:

```
void parallelSort(char list[][15], int id[], int lo, int hi) {
//sort list[lo] to list[hi] in alphabetical order, ensuring that
//each name remains with its original id number
  int j, k, m;
  char key[15];
  for (j = lo + 1; j <= hi; j++) {
    strcpy(key, list[j]);
    m = id[j]; // extract the id number
    k = j - 1; //start comparing with previous item
    while (k >= lo && strcmp(key, list[k]) < 0) {
      strcpy(list[k + 1], list[k]);
      id[j + 1] = id[j]; // move up id number when we move a name
      --k;
    }
    strcpy(list[k + 1], key);
    id[k + 1] = m; // store the id number in the same position as the name
  } //end for
} //end parallelSort
```

## 1.5 Binary search

*Binary search* is a very fast method for searching a list of items for a given one, *providing the list is sorted* (either ascending or descending). To illustrate the method, consider a list of 13 numbers, sorted in ascending order.

**num**

| 17 | 24 | 31 | 39 | 44 | 49 | 56 | 66 | 72 | 78 | 83 | 89 | 96 |
|---|---|---|---|---|---|---|---|---|---|---|---|---|
| 0 | 1 | 2 | 3 | 4 | 5 | 6 | 7 | 8 | 9 | 10 | 11 | 12 |

Suppose we wish to search for 66. The search proceeds as follows:

- First, we find the middle item in the list. This is 56 in position 6. We compare 66 with 56. Since 66 is bigger, we know that if 66 is in the list at all, it *must* be *after* position 6, since the numbers are in ascending order. In our next step, we confine our search to locations 7 to 12.
- Next, we find the middle item from locations 7 to 12. In this case, we can choose either item 9 or item 10. The algorithm we will write will choose item 9, that is, 78.

  We compare 66 with 78. Since 66 is smaller, we know that if 66 is in the list at all, it *must* be *before* position 9, since the numbers are in ascending order. In our next step, we confine our search to locations 7 to 8.
- Next, we find the middle item from locations 7 to 8. In this case, we can choose either item 7 or item 8. The algorithm we will write will choose item 7, that is, 66.

  We compare 66 with 66. Since they are the same, our search ends successfully, finding the required item in position 7.

Suppose we were searching for 70. The search will proceed as above until we compare 70 with 66 (in location 7).

- Since 70 is bigger, we know that if 70 is in the list at all, it *must* be *after* position 7, since the numbers are in ascending order. In our next step, we confine our search to locations 8 to 8. This is just one location.
- We compare 70 with item 8, that is, 72. Since 70 is smaller, we know that if 70 is in the list at all, it *must* be *before* position 8. Since it can't be after position 7 *and* before position 8, we conclude that it is not in the list.

At each stage of the search, we confine our search to some portion of the list. Let us use the variables **lo** and **hi** as the subscripts which define this portion. In other words, our search will be confined to **num[lo]** to **num[hi]**.

Initially, we want to search the entire list so that we will set **lo** to 0 and **hi** to 12, in this example.

How do we find the subscript of the middle item? We will use the calculation

```
mid = (lo + hi) / 2;
```

Since integer division will be performed, the fraction, if any, is discarded. For example when **lo** is 0 and **hi** is 12, **mid** becomes 6; when **lo** is 7 and **hi** is 12, **mid** becomes 9; and when **lo** is 7 and **hi** is 8, **mid** becomes 7.

As long as **lo** is less than or equal to **hi**, they define a non-empty portion of the list to be searched. When **lo** is equal to **hi**, they define a single item to be searched. If **lo** ever gets bigger than **hi**, it means we have searched the entire list and the item was not found.

Based on these ideas, we can now write a function **binarySearch**. To be more general, we will write it so that the calling routine can specify which portion of the array it wants the search to look for the item.

Thus, the function must be given the item to be searched for (**key**), the array (**list**), the start position of the search (**lo**) and the end position of the search (**hi**). For example, to search for the number 66 in the array **num**, above, we can issue the call **binarySearch(66, num, 0, 12)**.

The function must tell us the result of the search. If the item is found, the function will return its location. If not found, it will return -1.

```
int binarySearch(int key, int list[], int lo, int hi) {
//search for key from list[lo] to list[hi]
//if found, return its location; otherwise, return -1
  int mid;
  while (lo <= hi) {
    mid = (lo + hi) / 2;
    if (key == list[mid]) return mid; // found
    if (key < list[mid]) hi = mid - 1;
    else lo = mid + 1;
  }
  return -1; //lo and hi have crossed; key not found
} //end binarySearch
```

If **item** contains a number to be searched for, we can write code as follows:

```
int ans = binarySearch(item, num, 0, 12);
if (ans == -1) printf("%d not found\n", item);
else printf("%d found in location %d\n", item, ans);
```

If we wish to search for **item** from locations **i** to **j**, we can write

```
int ans = binarySearch(item, num, i, j);
```

## 1.6 Searching an array of strings

We can search a sorted array of strings (names in alphabetical order, say) using the same technique we used for searching an integer array. The major differences are in the declaration of the array and the use of **strcmp**, rather than **==** or **<**, to compare two strings. Here is the string version of **binarySearch** (next page):

As usual, 15 could be replaced by a **#defined** constant identifier to make the function more flexible.

```
int binarySearch(char key[15], char list[][15], int lo, int hi) {
//search for key from list[lo] to list[hi]
//if found, return its location; otherwise, return -1
  int mid, cmp;
  while (lo <= hi) {
    mid = (lo + hi) / 2;
    cmp = strcmp(key, list[mid]);
    if (cmp == 0) return mid; // found
    if (cmp < 0) hi = mid - 1;
    else lo = mid + 1;
  }
  return -1; //lo and hi have crossed; key not found
} //end binarySearch
```

The function can be tested with **main** shown here:

**Program P1.3**

```
#include <stdio.h>
#include <string.h>
main() {
  int binarySearch(char [], char [][15], int, int);
  int n, j;
  char name[8][15] = {"Ali, Michael","Duncan, Denise",
      "Khan, Carol","Owen, David", "Ramdhan, Kamal",
      "Sawh, Anisa", "Singh, Krishna", "Taylor, Victor"};
  n = binarySearch("Ali, Michael", name, 0, 7);
  printf("%d\n", n);  //will print 0, location of Ali, Michael
  n = binarySearch("Taylor, Victor", name, 0, 7);
  printf("%d\n", n); //will print 7, location of Taylor, Victor
  n = binarySearch("Owen, David", name, 0, 7);
  printf("%d\n", n); //will print 3, location of Owen, David
  n = binarySearch("Sandy, Cindy", name, 0, 7);
  printf("%d\n", n); //will print -1 since Sandy, Cindy is not in the list
} //end main
```

This sets up the array **name** with the names in alphabetical order. It then calls **binarySearch** with various names and prints the result of each search.

## 1.7 Example - word frequency count

Let us write a program to read an English passage and count the number of times each word appears. Output consists of an alphabetical listing of the words and their frequencies.

We can use the following outline to develop our program:

```
while there is input
  get a word
  search for word
  if word is in the table
    add 1 to its count
  else
    add word to the table
    set its count to 1
  endif
endwhile
print table
```

This is a typical "search and insert" situation. We search for the next word among the words stored so far. If the search succeeds, we need only increment its count. If the search fails, the word is put in the table and its count set to 1.

A major design decision here is how to search the table which, in turn, will depend on where and how a new word is inserted in the table. The following are two possibilities:

(1) A new word is inserted in the next free position in the table. This implies that a sequential search must be used to look for an incoming word since the words would not be in any particular order. This method has the advantages of simplicity and easy insertion, but searching takes longer as more words are put in the table.

(2) A new word is inserted in the table in such a way that the words are always in alphabetical order. This may entail moving words which have already been stored so that the new word may be slotted in the right place. However, since the table is in order, a binary search can be used to search for an incoming word.

For this method, searching is faster but insertion is slower than in (1). Since, in general, searching is done more frequently than inserting, (2) might be preferable.

Another advantage of (2) is that, at the end, the words will already be in alphabetical order and no sorting will be required. If (1) is used, the words will need to be sorted to obtain the alphabetical order.

We will write our program using the approach in (2). The complete program is shown as Program P1.4.

**Program P1.4**

```
#include <stdio.h>
#include <string.h>
#include <ctype.h>
#include <stdlib.h>
#define MaxWords 50
#define MaxLength 10
main() {
  int getWord(FILE *, char[]);
  int search(char [], char[][MaxLength+1], int);
  void addToList(char[], char [][MaxLength+1], int[], int, int);
  void printResults(FILE *, char [][MaxLength+1], int[], int);
  char wordList[MaxWords+1][MaxLength+1], word[MaxLength+1];
  int frequency[MaxWords+1], numWords = 0, j, loc;
  FILE * in = fopen("passage.txt", "r");
  if (in == NULL){
    printf("Cannot find file\n");
   exit(1);
  }
  FILE * out = fopen("output.txt", "w");
  if (out == NULL){
    printf("Cannot create output file\n");
   exit(2);
  }
  for (j = 1; j <= MaxWords; j++) frequency[j] = 0;
  while (getWord(in, word) != 0) {
    loc = binarySearch(word, wordList, 1, numWords);
    if (loc > 0) ++frequency[loc];
    else //this is a new word
      if (numWords < MaxWords) { //if table is not full
        addToList(word, wordList, frequency, -loc, numWords);
        ++numWords;
      }
      else fprintf(out, "'%s' not added to table\n", word);
  }
  printResults(out, wordList, frequency, numWords);
} // end main

int getWord(FILE * in, char str[]) {
// stores the next word, if any, in str; word is converted to lowercase
// returns 1 if a word is found; 0, otherwise
```

```
  char ch;
  int n = 0;
  // read over white space
  while (!isalpha(ch = getc(in)) && ch != EOF) ; //empty while body
  if (ch == EOF) return 0;
  str[n++] = tolower(ch);
  while (isalpha(ch = getc(in)) && ch != EOF)
    if (n < MaxLength) str[n++] = tolower(ch);
  str[n] = '\0';
  return 1;
} // end getWord

int binarySearch(char item[], char list[][MaxLength+1], int lo, int hi) {
//searches list[lo..hi] for item; if found, return its location
//if not found, return the negative of the location in which to insert
  while (lo <= hi) {
    int mid = (lo + hi)/2;
    int result = strcmp(item, list[mid]);
    if (result == 0) return mid;
    if (result < 0) hi = mid - 1;
    else lo = mid + 1;
  }
  return -lo; //not found; should be inserted in location lo
} //end binarySearch

void addToList(char item[], char list[][MaxLength+1], int freq[], int p,
               int n) {
//adds item in position list[p]; sets freq[p] to 1
//shifts list[n] down to list[p] to the right
  int j;
  for (j = n; j >= p; j--) {
    strcpy(list[j+1], list[j]);
    freq[j+1] = freq[j];
  }
  strcpy(list[p], item);
  freq[p] = 1;
} //end addToList

void printResults(FILE *out, char list[][MaxLength+1], int freq[], int n) {
  int j;
  fprintf(out, "\nWords       Frequency\n\n");
  for (j = 1; j <= n; j++)
    fprintf(out, "%-15s %2d\n", list[j], freq[j]);
} //end printResults
```

When Program P1.4 was run with the following data:

```
The quick brown fox jumps over the lazy dog.
Congratulations!
If the quick brown fox jumped over the lazy dog then
Why did the quick brown fox jump over the lazy dog?
To recuperate!
```

it produced the following output:

```
Words          Frequency

brown               3
congratula          1
did                 1
dog                 3
fox                 3
if                  1
jump                1
jumped              1
jumps               1
lazy                3
over                3
quick               3
recuperate          1
the                 6
then                1
to                  1
why                 1
```

### Comments on Program P1.4

- For our purposes, we assume that a word begins with a letter and consists of letters only. If you wish to include other characters (like a hyphen or apostrophe), you need only change the **getWord** function.
- **MaxWords** denotes the maximum number of distinct words catered for. For testing the program, we have used 50 for this value. The arrays are declared using **MaxWords + 1**. We will store words from **wordList[1]** to **wordList[MaxWords]**. We will not use **wordList[0]**. This will make it slightly more convenient to write a flexible **binarySearch** routine (see below).

  If the number of distinct words in the passage exceeds **MaxWords** (50, say), any words after the 50th will be read but not stored and a message to that effect will be printed. However, the count for a word already stored will be incremented if it is encountered again.
- **MaxLength** (we use 10 for testing) denotes the maximum length of a word. Strings are declared using **MaxLength + 1** to cater for **\0** which must be added at the end of each string.
- **main** checks that the input file exists and that the output file can be created. Next, it initializes the frequency counts to 0. It then processes the words in the passage based on the outline on page 14.

- **getWord** reads the input file and stores the next word found in its string argument. It returns 1 if a word is found and 0, otherwise. If a word is longer than **MaxLength**, only the first **MaxLength** letters are stored; the rest are read and discarded. For example, **congratulations** is truncated to **congratula** using a word size of 10.

  All words are converted to lowercase so that, for instance, **The** and **the** are counted as the same word.
- **binarySearch** is written so that if the word is found, its location is returned. If the word is not found, and **n** is the location in which it *should* be inserted, **-n** is returned. It is for this reason that we do not use **wordList[0]**. If we did, we would not be able to easily distinguish between a word *found* in location 0 and a word that *needs to be inserted* in location 0 (since 0 = -0).
- **addToList** is given the location in which to insert a new word. Words to the right of, and including, this location, are shifted one position to make room for the new word.
- Whereas the latest C standard allows a variable to be declared in a **for** statement, as in

  ```
  for (int j = 1; j <= n; j++)
  ```

  some (older) compilers will not allow it. If you use one of these compilers, just declare the variable at the head of the function, as illustrated in **addToList** and **printResults**.
- In declaring a *function prototype*, some compilers allow a two-dimensional array parameter to be declared as in **char [][]**, with no size specified for either dimension. Others require that the size of the second dimension *must* be specified. Specifying the size of the second dimension should work on all compilers.

## 1.8 Merging ordered lists

Merging is the process by which two or more ordered lists are combined into one ordered list. For example, given two lists of numbers, **A** and **B**, as follows:

```
A: 21 28 35 40 61 75
B: 16 25 47 54
```

they can be combined into one ordered list, C:

```
C: 16 21 25 28 35 40 47 54 61 75
```

The list **C** contains all the numbers from lists **A** and **B**. How can the merge be performed?

One way to think about it is to imagine that the numbers in the given lists are stored on cards, one per card, and the cards are placed face up on a table, with the smallest at the top. We can imagine the lists **A** and **B** as follows:

```
21    16
28    25
35    47
40    54
61
75
```

We look at the top two cards, 21 and 16. The smaller, 16, is removed and placed in **C**. This exposes the number 25.

The top two cards are now 21 and 25. The smaller, 21, is removed and added to **C** which now contains 16 21. This exposes the number 28.

The top two cards are now 28 and 25. The smaller, 25, is removed and added to **C** which now contains 16 21 25. This exposes the number 47.

The top two cards are now 28 and 47. The smaller, 28, is removed and added to **C** which now contains 16 21 25 28. This exposes the number 35.

The top two cards are now 35 and 47. The smaller, 35, is removed and added to **C** which now contains 16 21 25 28 35. This exposes the number 40.

The top two cards are now 40 and 47. The smaller, 40, is removed and added to **C** which now contains 16 21 25 28 35 40. This exposes the number 61.

The top two cards are now 61 and 47. The smaller, 47, is removed and added to **C** which now contains 16 21 25 28 35 40 47. This exposes the number 54.

The top two cards are now 61 and 54. The smaller, 54, is removed and added to **C** which now contains 16 21 25 28 35 40 47 54. The list **B** has no more numbers.

We copy the remaining elements (61 75) of **A** to **C**, which now contains:

```
16 21 25 28 35 40 47 54 61 75
```

and the merge is completed.

At each step of the merge, we compare the smallest remaining number of **A** with the smallest remaining number of **B**. The smaller of these is added to **C**. If the smaller comes from **A**, we move on to the next number in **A**; if the smaller comes from **B**, we move on to the next number in **B**.

This is repeated until all the numbers in either **A** or **B** have been used. If all the numbers in **A** have been used, we add the remaining numbers from **B** to **C**. If all the numbers in **B** have been used, we add the remaining numbers from **A** to **C**.

We can express the logic of the merge as follows:

```
while (at least one number remains in both A and B) {
  if (smallest in A < smallest in B)
    add smallest in A to C
    move on to next number in A
  else
    add smallest in B to C
    move on to next number in B
  endif
}
if (A has ended) add remaining numbers in B to C
else add remaining numbers in A to C
```

### *Implementing the merge*

Assume that an array **A** contains *m* numbers stored in **A[0]** to **A[m-1]** and an array **B** contains *n* numbers stored in **B[0]** to **B[n-1]**. Assume that the numbers are stored in ascending order. We wish to merge the numbers in **A** and **B** into another array **C** such that **C[0]** to **C[m+n-1]** contains all the numbers in **A** and **B** sorted in ascending order.

We will use integer variables **i**, **j** and **k** to subscript the arrays **A**, **B** and **C**, respectively. "Moving on to the next position" in an array can be done by adding 1 to the subscript variable. We can implement the merge with the following code:

```
i = 0; //i points to the first (smallest) number in A
j = 0; //j points to the first (smallest) number in B
k = -1; //k will be incremented before storing a number in C[k]
while (i < m && j < n) {
  if (A[i] < B[j]) C[++k] = A[i++];
  else C[++k] = B[j++];
}
if (i == m) //copy B[j] to B[n-1] to C
  for ( ; j < n; j++) C[++k] = B[j];
else // j == n, copy A[i] to A[m-1] to C
  for ( ; i < m; i++) C[++k] = A[i];
```

Program P1.5 (next page) shows a simple **main** function which tests the above logic. We write the merge as a function which, given the arguments **A**, **m**, **B**, **n** and **C**, performs the merge and returns the number of elements, **m + n**, in **C**. When run, the program prints the contents of **C**, thus:

```
16 21 25 28 35 40 47 54 61 75
```

**Program P1.5**

```
#include <stdio.h>
main() {
  int merge(int[], int, int[], int, int[]);
  int A[] = {21, 28, 35, 40, 61, 75};
  int B[] = {16, 25, 47, 54};
  int j, C[20];
  int n = merge(A, 6, B, 4, C);
  for (j = 0; j < n; j++) printf("%d ", C[j]);
  printf("\n\n");
} //end main

int merge(int A[], int m, int B[], int n, int C[]) {
  int i = 0; //i points to the first (smallest) number in A
  int j = 0; //j points to the first (smallest) number in B
  int k = -1; //k will be incremented before storing a number in C[k]
  while (i < m && j < n) {
    if (A[i] < B[j]) C[++k] = A[i++];
    else C[++k] = B[j++];
  }
  if (i == m) ///copy B[j] to B[n-1] to C
    for ( ; j < n; j++) C[++k] = B[j];
  else // j == n, copy A[i] to A[m-1] to C
    for ( ; i < m; i++) C[++k] = A[i];
  return m + n;
} //end merge
```

As a matter of interest, we can also implement **merge** as follows:

```
int merge(int A[], int m, int B[], int n, int C[]) {
  int i = 0; //i points to the first (smallest) number in A
  int j = 0; //j points to the first (smallest) number in B
  int k = -1; //k will be incremented before storing a number in C[k]
  while (i < m || j < n) {
    if (i == m) C[++k] = B[j++];
    else if (j == n) C[++k] = A[i++];
    else if (A[i] < B[j]) C[++k] = A[i++];
    else C[++k] = B[j++];
  }
  return m + n;
} //end merge
```

The **while** loop expresses the following logic: as long as there is at least one element to process in either **A** *or* **B**, we enter the loop. If we are finished with **A** (**i == m**), copy an element from **B** to **C**. If we are finished with **B** (**j == n**), copy an element from **A** to **C**. Otherwise, copy the smaller of **A[i]** and **B[j]** to **C**. Each time we copy an element from an array, we add 1 to the subscript for that array.

While the previous version implements the merge in a straightforward way, it seems reasonable to say that this version is a bit neater.

## Exercises 1

1. A survey of 10 pop artists is made. Each person votes for an artist by specifying the number of the artist (a value from 1 to 10). Each voter is allowed one vote for the artist of his/her choice. The vote is recorded as a number from 1 to 10. The number of voters is unknown beforehand but the votes are terminated by a vote of 0. Any vote which is not a number from 1 to 10 is a spoilt vote. A file, **votes.txt**, contains the names of the candidates. The first name is considered as candidate 1, the second as candidate 2, and so on. The names are followed by the votes. Write a program to read the data and evaluate the results of the survey.

   Print the results in alphabetical order by artist name and in order by votes received (most votes first). Print all output to the file, **results.txt**.
2. Write a program to read names and phone numbers into two arrays. Request a name and print the person's phone number. Use binary search to look up the name.
3. Write a program to read English words and their equivalent Spanish words into two arrays. Request the user to type several English words. For each, print the equivalent Spanish word. Choose a suitable end-of-data marker. Search for the typed words using binary search. Modify the program so that the user types Spanish words instead.
4. The *median* of a set of $n$ numbers (not necessarily distinct) is obtained by arranging the numbers in order and taking the number in the middle. If $n$ is odd, there is a unique middle number. If $n$ is even, then the average of the two middle values is the median. Write a program to read a set of $n$ positive integers (assume $n < 100$) and print their median; $n$ is not given but 0 indicates the end of the data.
5. The *mode* of a set of $n$ numbers is the number which appears most frequently. For example, the mode of 7 3 8 5 7 3 1 3 4 8 9 is 3. Write a program to read a set of $n$ positive integers (assume $n < 100$) and print their mode; $n$ is not given but 0 indicates the end of the data.
6. An array **chosen** contains **n** distinct integers arranged in no particular order. Another array **winners** contains **m** distinct integers arranged in *ascending* order. Write code to determine how many of the numbers in **chosen** appear in **winners**.
7. A multiple-choice examination consists of twenty questions. Each question has five choices, labelled **A**, **B**, **C**, **D** and **E**. The first line of data contains the correct answers to the twenty questions in the first 20 *consecutive* character positions, for example:

   ```
   BECDCBAADEBACBAEDDBE
   ```

Each subsequent line contains the answers for a candidate. Data on a line consists of a candidate number (an integer), followed by one or more spaces, followed by the twenty answers given by the candidate in the next twenty *consecutive* character positions. An **X** is used if a candidate did not answer a particular question. You may assume all data are valid and stored in a file **exam.dat**. A sample line is:

```
4325    BECDCBAXDEBACCAEDXBE
```

There are at most 100 candidates. A line containing a "candidate number" 0 only indicates the end of the data.

Points for a question are awarded as follows—correct answer: 4 points; wrong answer: -1 point; no answer: 0 points

Write a program to process the data and print a report consisting of candidate number and the total points obtained by the candidate, *in ascending order by candidate number*. At the end, print the average number of points gained by the candidates.

8. **A** is an array sorted in descending order. **B** is an array sorted in descending order. Merge **A** and **B** into **C** so that **C** is in *descending* order.
9. **A** is an array sorted in descending order. **B** is an array sorted in descending order. Merge **A** and **B** into **C** so that **C** is in *ascending* order.
10. **A** is an array sorted in ascending order. **B** is an array sorted in descending order. Merge **A** and **B** into **C** so that **C** is in *ascending* order.
11. An array **A** contains integers that first increase in value and then decrease in value, for example,

| 17 | 24 | 31 | 39 | 44 | 49 | 36 | 29 | 20 | 18 | 13 |
|---|---|---|---|---|---|---|---|---|---|---|
| 0 | 1 | 2 | 3 | 4 | 5 | 6 | 7 | 8 | 9 | 75 |

It is unknown at which point the numbers start to decrease. Write efficient code to code to copy the numbers in **A** to another array **B** so that **B** is sorted in ascending order. Your code must take advantage of the way the numbers are arranged in **A**.

12. Two words are anagrams if one word can be formed by rearranging all the letters of the other word, for example: section, notices. Write a program to read two words and determine if they are anagrams.

    Write another program to read a list of words and find all sets of words such that words within a set are anagrams of each other.

# 2 Structures

**In this chapter, we will explain:**

- what is a structure and how to declare one
- how to use **typedef** to work with structures more conveniently
- how to work with an array of structures
- how to search an array of structures
- how to sort an array of structures
- how to declare *nested* structures
- how to use structures to manipulate fractions
- how structures can be passed to a function
- how to use structures to solve a 'voting' problem

In C, a structure is a collection of one or more variables, possibly of different types, grouped together under a single name for convenient handling.

There are many situations in which we wish to process data about a certain entity or object but the data itself consists of items of various types. For example, the data for a student (the *student record*) may consist of several *fields* such as a name, address and telephone number (all of type string), number of courses taken (integer), fees payable (floating-point), names of courses (string), grade obtained (character), etc.

The data for a car may consist of manufacturer, model and registration number (string), seating capacity and fuel capacity (integer), mileage and price (floating-point). For a book, we may wish to store author and title (string), price (floating-point), number of pages (integer), type of binding—hardcover, paperback, spiral (string)—and number of copies in stock (integer).

Suppose we wish to store data for 100 students in a program. One approach is to have a separate array for each field and use subscripts to link the fields together. Thus **name[j]**, **address[j]**, **fees[j]**, etc. refer to the data for the *j*th student.

The problem with this approach is that if there are many fields, the handling of several parallel arrays becomes clumsy and unwieldy. For example, suppose we want to pass a student's data to a function via the parameter list. This will involve the passing of several arrays. Also, if we are sorting the students by name, say, each time two names are interchanged, we have to write statements to interchange the data in the other arrays as well. In such situations, C structures are convenient to use.

## 2.1 How to declare a structure

Consider the problem of storing a date in a program. A date consists of three parts—the day, the month and the year. Each of these parts can be represented by an integer. For example, the date "September 14, 2006" can be represented by the day, 14, the month, 9, and the year 2006. We say that a date consists of three *fields*, each of which is an integer.

If we wish, we could also represent a date by using the *name* of the month, rather than its number. In this case, a date consists of three fields, one of which is a string and the other two are integers.

In C, we can declare a *date type* as a *structure* using the keyword **struct**. Consider the declaration:

```
struct date {int day, month, year;};
```

It consists of the word **struct** followed by some name we choose to give to the structure (**date**, in the example); this is followed by the declarations of the fields enclosed in left and right braces. Note the semicolon at the end of the declaration just before the right brace—this is the usual case of a semicolon ending a declaration. The right brace is followed by a semicolon, ending the **struct** declaration.

We could also have written the declaration as:

```
struct date {
  int day;
  int month;
  int year;
};
```

where each field is declared individually. This could be written as

```
struct date {int day; int month; int year;};
```

but the former style is preferred for its readability.

Given the **struct** declaration, we can declare variables of type **struct date**, as in:

```
struct date dob; //to hold a "date of birth"
```

This declares **dob** as a "structure variable" of type **date**. It has three fields called **day**, **month** and **year**. This can be pictured as:

| | day | month | year |
|---|---|---|---|
| dob | | | |

We refer to the day field as **dob.day**, the month field as **dob.month** and the year field as **dob.year**. In C, the period (.), as used here, is referred to as the "structure member operator".

In general, *a field is specified by the structure name, followed by a period, followed by the field name.*

We could declare more than one variable at a time, as in:

```
struct date borrowed, returned; //for a book in a library, say
```

Each of these variables has 3 fields—**day**, **month** and **year**. The fields of **borrowed** are referred to by **borrowed.day**, **borrowed.month** and **borrowed.year**. The fields of **returned** are referred to by **returned.day**, **returned.month** and **returned.year**.

In this example, each field is an **int** and can be used in any context in which an **int** variable can be used. For example, to assign the date "November 14, 2006" to **dob**, we can use:

```
dob.day = 14;
dob.month = 11;
dob.year = 2006;
```

This can be pictured as:

| | day | month | year |
|---|---|---|---|
| dob | 14 | 11 | 2006 |

We can also read values for **day**, **month** and **year** with

```
scanf("%d %d %d", &dob.day, &dob.month, &dob.year);
```

If **today** was a **struct date** variable holding a date, we could assign all the fields of **today** to **dob**, say, with:

```
dob = today;
```

This one statement is equivalent to

```
dob.day = today.day;
dob.month = today.month;
dob.year = today.year;
```

We can print the "value" of **dob** with

```
printf("The party is on %d/%d/%d\n", dob.day, dob.month, dob.year);
```

For this example, this will print

```
The party is on 14/11/2006
```

Note that each field has to be printed individually. We could also write a function **printDate**, say, which prints a date given as an argument. For example,

```
void printDate(struct date d) {
  printf("%d/%d/%d \n", d.day, d.month, d.year);
}
```

The call

```
printDate(dob);
```

will print

```
14/11/2006
```

The construct **struct date** is a bit cumbersome to use, compared to single word types such **int** or **double**. Fortunately, C provides us with **typedef** to make working with structures a little more convenient.

### *2.1.1 typedef*

We can use **typedef** to give a name to some existing type, and this name can then be used to declare variables of that type. We can also use **typedef** to construct shorter or more meaningful names for predefined C types or for user-declared types, such as structures. For example, the statement

```
typedef int Whole;
```

declares a new type-name **Whole** which is synonymous with the predefined type **int**. Note that **Whole** appears in the same position as a variable would, not right after the word **typedef**. We can then declare variables of type **Whole**, as in

```
Whole amount, numCopies;
```

This is exactly equivalent to

```
int amount, numCopies;
```

For those accustomed to the term **real** of languages like Pascal or FORTRAN, the statement:

```
typedef float Real;
```

allows them to declare variables of type **Real**. In this book, we use at least one uppercase letter to distinguish type names declared using **typedef**.

We could give a short, meaningful name, **Date**, to the date structure above with the declaration:

```
typedef struct date {
  int day;
  int month;
  int year;
} Date;
```

Recall that C distinguishes between uppercase and lowercase letters so that **date** is different from **Date**. We could, if we wished, have used any other identifier, such as **DateType**, instead of **Date**.

We could now declare "structure variables" of type **Date**, such as:

```
Date dob, borrowed, returned;
```

Notice how much shorter and neater this is compared to

```
struct date dob, borrowed, returned;
```

Since there is hardly any reason to use this second form, we could omit **date** from the above declaration and write

```
typedef struct {
  int day;
  int month;
  int year;
} Date;
```

Thereafter, we can use **Date** whenever the **struct** is required. For example, we can rewrite **printDate** as:

```
void printDate(Date d) {
  printf("%d/%d/%d \n", d.day, d.month, d.year);
}
```

---

To pursue the date example, suppose we wish to store the "short" name—the first 3 letters, e.g. Aug—of the month. We will need to use a declaration such as:

```
typedef struct {
  int day;
  char month[4]; //one position for \0 to end string
  int year;
} Date;
```

We can represent the date "November 14, 2006" in a **Date** variable **dob** with:

```
dob.day = 14;
strcpy(dob.month, "Nov");
dob.year = 2006;
```

and we can write **printDate** as follows:

```
void printDate(Date d) {
  printf("%s %d, %d \n", d.month, d.day, d.year);
}
```

The call

```
printDate(dob);
```

will print

```
Nov 14, 2006
```

Suppose we wish to store information about students. For each student, we want to store their name, age and gender (male or female). Assuming that a name is no longer than 30 characters, we could use the declaration

```
typedef struct {
  char name[31];
  int age;
  char gender;
} Student;
```

We can now declare variables of type **Student**, as in

```
Student stud1, stud2;
```

Each of **stud1** and **stud2** will have its own fields—**name**, **age** and **gender**. We can refer to these fields with

```
stud1.name  stud1.age  stud1.gender
stud2.name  stud2.age  stud2.gender
```

As usual, we can assign values to these fields or read values into them. And, if we wish, we can assign all the fields of **stud1** to **stud2** with the statement

```
stud2 = stud1;
```

## 2.2 Working with an array of structures

Suppose we want to store data on 100 students. We will need an array of size 100 and each element of the array will hold the data for one student. Thus each element will have to be a structure—we need an "array of structures".

We can declare the array with

```
Student pupil[100];
```

similar to how we say "**int pupil[100]**" to declare an integer array of size 100.

This allocates storage for **pupil[0]**, **pupil[1]**, **pupil[2]**,..., up to **pupil[99]**. Each element **pupil[j]** consists of 3 fields which can be referred to by

```
pupil[j].name  pupil[j].age  pupil[j].gender
```

Firstly, we will need to store some data in the array. Assume we have data in the following format (name, age, gender):

```
"Jones, John" 24 M
"Mohammed, Lisa" 33 F
"Singh, Sandy" 29 F
"Layne, Dennis" 49 M
"END"
```

Suppose the data are stored in a file **input.txt** and **in** is declared as

```
FILE * in = fopen("input.txt", "r");
```

If **str** is a character array, assume we can call the function **getString(in, str)** to store the next data string in quotes in **str** without the quotes. Also assume that **readChar(in)** will read the data and return the next non-whitespace character.

**Exercise**: write the functions **getString** and **readChar**.

We can read the data into the array **pupil** with the following code:

```
int n = 0;
char temp[31];
getString(in, temp);
while (strcmp(temp, "END") != 0) {
  strcpy(pupil[n].name, temp);
  fscanf(in, "%d", &pupil[n].age);
  pupil[n].gender = readChar(in);
  n++;
  getString(in, temp);
}
```

At the end, **n** contains the number of students stored and **pupil[0]** to **pupil[n-1]** contain the data for those students.

To ensure that we do not attempt to store more data than we have room for in the array, we should check that **n** is within the bounds of the array. Assuming that **MaxItems** has the value 100, this can be done by changing the **while** condition to

```
while (n < MaxItems && strcmp(temp, "END") != 0)
```

or by inserting

```
if (n == MaxItems) break;
```

just after the statement **n++;** inside the loop.

## 2.3 Searching an array of structures

With the data stored in the array, we can manipulate it in various ways. For instance, we can write a function to search for a given name. Assuming the data are stored in no particular order, we can use a sequential search as follows:

```
int search(char key[], Student list[], int n) {
//search for key in list[0] to list[n-1]
//if found, return the location; if not found, return -1
  int j;
  for (j = 0; j < n; j++)
    if (strcmp(key, list[j].name) == 0) return j;
  return -1;
} //end search
```

Given the above data, the call

```
search("Singh, Sandy", pupil, 4)
```

will return 2 and the call

```
search("Layne, Sandy", pupil, 4)
```

will return -1.

## 2.4 Sorting an array of structures

Suppose we want the list of students in alphabetical order by name. It will be required to sort the array **pupil**. The following function uses an insertion sort to do the job. The *process* is identical to sorting an **int** array, say, except that the **name** field is used to govern the sorting.

```
void sort(Student list[], int n) {
//sort list[0] to list[n-1] by name using an insertion sort
  Student temp;
  int j, k;
  for (j = 1; j < n; j++) {
    temp = list[j];
    k = j - 1;
    while (k >= 0 && strcmp(temp.name, list[k].name) < 0) {
      list[k + 1] = list[k];
      k = k - 1;
    }
  }
  list[k + 1] = temp;
} //end sort
```

Observe the statement

```
list[k + 1] = list[k];
```

This assigns *all* the fields of **list[k]** to **list[k + 1]**.

If we want to sort the students in order by age, all we need to change is the **while** condition. To sort in *ascending* order, we write

```
while (k >= 0 && temp.age < list[k].age) //move smaller numbers to the left
```

and to sort in *descending* order, we write

```
while (k >= 0 && temp.age > list[k].age) //move bigger numbers to the left
```

We could even separate the list into male and female students by sorting on the **gender** field. Since 'F' comes before 'M' in alphabetical order, we can put the females first by writing

```
while (k >= 0 && temp.gender < list[k].gender) //move Fs to the left
```

and we can put the males first by writing

```
while (k >= 0 && temp.gender > list[k].gender ) //move Ms to the left
```

## 2.5 Putting it all together

We illustrate the ideas discussed above in Program P2.1. The program

- reads data for students from a file, **input.txt**, and stores them in an array of structures
- prints the data in the order stored in the array
- tests **search** by reading several names and looking for them in the array
- sorts the data in alphabetical order by **name**
- prints the sorted data

The program also illustrates how the functions **getString** and **readChar** may be written. **getString** lets us read a string enclosed within *any* 'delimiter' characters. For example, we could specify a string as **$John Smith$** or **"John Smith"**. This is a very flexible way of specifying a string. *Each* string can be specified with its own delimiters which could be different for the next string. It is particularly useful for specifying strings which may include special characters such as the double quotes without having to use an escape sequence like \".

**Program P2.1**

```
#include <stdio.h>
#include <stdlib.h>
#include <string.h>
#include <ctype.h>
typedef struct {
  char name[31];
  int age;
  char gender;
} Student;

main() {
  Student pupil[100];
  char aName[31];
  int j;
  void getString(FILE *, char[]);
  int getData(FILE *, Student[]);
  int search(char[], Student[], int);
  void sort(Student[], int);
  void printStudent(Student);
  void getString(FILE *, char[]);
```

```
  FILE * in = fopen("input.txt", "r");
  if (in == NULL) {
    printf("input file not found");
    exit(1);
  }
  int numStudents = getData(in, pupil);
  if (numStudents == 0) {
    printf("No data supplied for students");
    exit(1);
  }
  printf("\n");
  for (j = 0; j < numStudents; j++) printStudent(pupil[j]);
  printf("\n");

  getString(in, aName);
  while (strcmp(aName, "END") != 0) {
    int ans = search(aName, pupil, numStudents);
    if (ans == -1) printf("%s not found\n", aName);
    else printf("%s found at location %d\n", aName, ans);
    getString(in, aName);
  }

  sort(pupil, numStudents);
  printf("\n");
  for (j = 0; j < numStudents; j++) printStudent(pupil[j]);
} //end main

void printStudent(Student t) {
  printf("Name: %s Age: %d Gender: %c\n", t.name, t.age, t.gender);
} //end printStudent

int getData(FILE *in, Student list[]) {
  int n = 0;
  char temp[31];
  void getString(FILE *, char[]);
  char readChar(FILE *);

  getString(in, temp);
  while (strcmp(temp, "END") != 0) {
    strcpy(list[n].name, temp);
    fscanf(in, "%d", &list[n].age);
    list[n].gender = readChar(in);
    n++;
    getString(in, temp);
  }
  return n;
} //end getData
```

```
int search(char key[], Student list[], int n) {
//search for key in list[0] to list[n-1]
//if found, return the location; if not found, return -1
  int j;
  for (j = 0; j < n; j++)
    if (strcmp(key, list[j].name) == 0) return j;
  return -1;
} //end search

void sort(Student list[], int n) {
//sort list[0] to list[n-1] by name using an insertion sort
  Student temp;
  int j, k;
  for (j = 1; j < n; j++) {
    temp = list[j];
    k = j - 1;
    while (k >= 0 && strcmp(temp.name, list[k].name) < 0) {
      list[k + 1] = list[k];
      k = k - 1;
    }
   list[k + 1] = temp;
  } //end for
} end sort

void getString(FILE * in, char str[]) {
//stores, in str, the next string within delimiters
// the first non-whitespace character is the delimiter
// the string is read from the file 'in'

  char ch, delim;
  int n = 0;
  str[0] = '\0';
  // read over white space
  while (isspace(ch = getc(in))) ; //empty while body
  if (ch == EOF) return;

  delim = ch;
  while (((ch = getc(in)) != delim) && (ch != EOF))
    str[n++] = ch;
  str[n] = '\0';
} // end getString

char readChar(FILE * in) {
  char ch;
  while (isspace(ch = getc(in))) ; //empty while body
  return ch;
} //end readChar
```

If the file **input.txt** contains the following data:

```
"Jones, John" 24 M
"Mohammed, Lisa" 33 F
"Singh, Sandy" 29 F
"Layne, Dennis" 49 M
"Singh, Cindy" 16 F
"Ali, Imran" 39 M
"Kelly, Trudy" 30 F
"Cox, Kerry" 25 M
"END"

"Kelly, Trudy"
"Layne, Dennis"
"Layne, Cindy"
"END"
```

the program prints

```
Name: Jones, John Age: 24 Gender: M
Name: Mohammed, Lisa Age: 33 Gender: F
Name: Singh, Sandy Age: 29 Gender: F
Name: Layne, Dennis Age: 49 Gender: M
Name: Singh, Cindy Age: 16 Gender: F
Name: Ali, Imran Age: 39 Gender: M
Name: Kelly, Trudy Age: 30 Gender: F
Name: Cox, Kerry Age: 25 Gender: M

Kelly, Trudy found at location 6
Layne, Dennis found at location 3
Layne, Cindy not found

Name: Ali, Imran Age: 39 Gender: M
Name: Cox, Kerry Age: 25 Gender: M
Name: Jones, John Age: 24 Gender: M
Name: Kelly, Trudy Age: 30 Gender: F
Name: Layne, Dennis Age: 49 Gender: M
Name: Mohammed, Lisa Age: 33 Gender: F
Name: Singh, Cindy Age: 16 Gender: F
Name: Singh, Sandy Age: 29 Gender: F
```

## 2.6 Nested structures

C allows us to use a structure as part of the definition of another structure—a structure within a structure, called a *nested* structure. Consider the student structure. Suppose that, instead of age, we wish to store the student's date-of-birth. This might be a better choice since a student's date-of-birth is fixed whereas his age changes and the field will have to be updated every year.

We could use the declaration

```
typedef struct {
  char name[31];
  Date dob;
  char gender;
} Student;
```

If **mary** is a variable of type **Student**, then **mary.dob** refers to her date-of-birth. But **mary.dob** is *itself* a **Date** structure. If necessary, we can refer to *its* fields with **mary.dob.day**, **mary.dob.month** and **mary.dob.year**.

If we want to store a name in a more flexible way, for example, first name, middle initial and last name, we could use a structure like

```
typedef struct {
  char first[21];
  char middle;
  char last[21];
} Name;
```

The **Student** structure now becomes

```
typedef struct {
  Name name;
  Date dob;
  char gender;
} Student;
```

which contains two structures, **Name** and **Date**.

If **st** is a variable of type **Student**,

> **st.name** refers to a structure of the type **Name**;
> **st.name.first** refers to the student's first name and
> **st.name.last[0]** refers to the first letter of her last name.

Now, if we want to sort the array **pupil** by last name, the **while** condition becomes

```
while (k >= 0 && strcmp(temp.name.last, pupil[k].name.last) < 0)
```

A structure may be nested as deeply as you wish. The dot (.) operator associates from left to right. So that if **a**, **b** and **c** are structures,

```
a.b.c.d
```

is interpreted as

```
((a.b).c).d
```

## 2.7 Fractions

Consider the problem of working with fractions, where a fraction is represented by two integer values: one for the numerator and the other for the denominator. For example, $\frac{5}{9}$ is represented by the two numbers 5 and 9.

We will use the following structure to represent a fraction:

```
typedef struct {
  int num;
  int den;
} Fraction;
```

If **a** is variable of type **Fraction**, we can store $\frac{5}{9}$ in **a** with

```
a.num = 5;
a.den = 9;
```

This can be pictured as

| | num | den |
|---|---|---|
| a | 5 | 9 |

We can also read two values representing a fraction and store them in **a** with a statement such as

```
scanf("%d %d", &a.num, &a.den);
```

We can write a function to print a fraction. For example,

```
void printFraction(Fraction f) {
  printf("%d/%d", f.num, f.den);
}
```

will print 5/9 when called with **printFraction(a)**.

### 2.7.1 Manipulating fractions

We can write functions to perform various operations on fractions. For instance, since

$$\frac{a}{b} + \frac{c}{d} = \frac{ad + bc}{bd}$$

we can write a function to add two fractions as follows:

```
Fraction addFraction(Fraction a, Fraction b) {
  Fraction c;
  c.num = a.num * b.den + a.den * b.num;
  c.den = a.den * b.den;
  return c;
}
```

Similarly, we can write functions to subtract, multiply and divide fractions.

```
Fraction subFraction(Fraction a, Fraction b) {
  Fraction c;
  c.num = a.num * b.den - a.den * b.num;
  c.den = a.den * b.den;
  return c;
}

Fraction mulFraction(Fraction a, Fraction b) {
  Fraction c;
  c.num = a.num * b.num;
  c.den = a.den * b.den;
  return c;
}

Fraction divFraction(Fraction a, Fraction b) {
  Fraction c;
  c.num = a.num * b.den;
  c.den = a.den * b.num;
  return c;
}
```

To illustrate their use, suppose we want to find

$$\frac{2}{5} \text{ of } \left\{\frac{3}{7} + \frac{5}{8}\right\}$$

We can do this with the following statements:

```
Fraction a, b, c, sum, ans;
a.num = 2; a.den = 5;
b.num = 3; b.den = 7;
c.num = 5; c.den = 8;
sum = addFraction(b, c);
ans = mulFraction(a, sum);
printFraction(ans);
```

Strictly speaking, the variables **sum** and **ans** are not necessary. We could get the same result with

```
printFraction(mulFraction(a, addFraction(b, c)));
```

When run, this code will print

```
118/280
```

which is the correct answer.

However, if you wish, you can write a function to reduce a fraction to its lowest terms. This can be done by finding the HCF (highest common factor) of the numerator and denominator. You then divide the numerator and denominator by their HCF. For example, the HCF of 118 and 280 is 2 so 118/280 reduces to 59/140. Writing this function is left as an exercise.

## 2.8 A voting problem

This example will be used to illustrate several points concerning the passing of arguments to functions. It further highlights the differences between array arguments and simple variable arguments. We will show how a function can return more than one value to a calling function by using a structure.

**Problem**: In an election, there are seven candidates. Each voter is allowed one vote for the candidate of his/her choice. The vote is recorded as a number from 1 to 7. The number of voters is unknown beforehand but the votes are terminated by a vote of 0. Any vote which is not a number from 1 to 7 is an invalid (spoilt) vote.

A file, **votes.txt**, contains the names of the candidates. The first name is considered as candidate 1, the second as candidate 2, and so on. The names are followed by the votes. Write a program to read the data and evaluate the results of the election. Print all output to the file, **results.txt**.

Your output should specify the total number of votes, the number of valid votes and the number of spoilt votes. This is followed by the votes obtained by each candidate and the winner(s) of the election.

Given the following data:

```
Victor Taylor
Denise Duncan
Kamal Ramdhan
Michael Ali
Anisa Sawh
Carol Khan
Gary Owen

3 1 2 5 4 3 5 3 5 3 2 8 1 6 7 7 3 5
6 9 3 4 7 1 2 4 5 5 1 4 0
```

your program should send the output shown on the next page to **results.txt**.

We now explain how we can solve this problem using C structures. Consider the declarations

```
typedef struct {
  char name[31];
  int numVotes;
} PersonData;
PersonData candidate[8];
```

```
Invalid vote: 8
Invalid vote: 9

Number of voters: 30
Number of valid votes: 28
Number of spoilt votes: 2

Candidate       Score

Victor Taylor     4
Denise Duncan     3
Kamal Ramdhan     6
Michael Ali       4
Anisa Sawh        6
Carol Khan        2
Gary Owen         3

The winner(s):
Kamal Ramdhan
Anisa Sawh
```

Here, **candidate** is an array of structures. We will use **candidate[1]** to **candidate[7]** for the 7 candidates; we will not use **candidate[0]**. An element **candidate[j]** is not just a single data item but a structure consisting of two fields. These fields can be referred to as

**candidate[j].name** and **candidate[j].numVotes**

To make the program flexible, we will define symbolic constants with:

```
#define MaxCandidates 7
#define MaxNameLength 30
```

and change the above declarations to

```
typedef struct {
  char name[MaxNameLength + 1];
  int numVotes;
} PersonData;
PersonData candidate[MaxCandidates + 1];
```

The solution is based on the following outline:

```
initialize
process the votes
print the results
```

The function **initialize** will read the names from the file **in** and set the vote counts to 0. The file is passed as an argument to the function. We will read a candidate's name in two parts (first name and last name) and then join them together to create a single name which we will store in **person[j].name**. Data will be read for **max** persons. Here is the function:

```
void initialize(PersonData person[], int max, FILE *in) {
  char lastName[MaxNameLength];
  int j;
  for (j = 1; j <= max; j++) {
    fscanf(in, "%s %s", person[j].name, lastName);
    strcat(person[j].name, " ");
    strcat(person[j].name, lastName);
    person[j].numVotes = 0;
  }
} //end initialize
```

Processing the votes will be based on the following outline:

```
get a vote
while the vote is not 0
  if the vote is valid
    add 1 to validVotes
    add 1 to the score of the appropriate candidate
  else
    print invalid vote
    add 1 to spoiltVotes
  endif
  get a vote
endwhile
```

After all the votes are processed, this function will need to return the number of valid and spoilt votes. But how can a function return more than one value? It can, if the values are stored in a structure and the structure returned as the "value" of the function.

We will use the declaration

```
typedef struct {
  int valid, spoilt;
} VoteCount;
```

and write **processVotes** as shown on the next page.

Next, we write **main** (shown on page 43), preceded by the compiler directives and the structrue declarations.

The declarations of **PersonData** and **VoteCount** come before **main**. This is done so that other functions can refer to them, without having to repeat the entire declarations. If they were declared in **main**, then the names **PersonData** and **VoteCount** would be known only in **main** and other functions would have no access to them.

```
VoteCount processVotes(PersonData person[], int max,
                              FILE *in, FILE *out) {
  int v;
  VoteCount temp;
  temp.valid = temp.spoilt = 0;
  fscanf(in, "%d", &v);
  while (v != 0) {
    if (v < 1 || v > max) {
      fprintf(out, "Invalid vote: %d\n", v);
      ++temp.spoilt;
    }
    else {
      ++person[v].numVotes;
      ++temp.valid;
    }
    fscanf(in, "%d", &v);
  } //end while
  return temp;
} //end processVotes
```

Now that we know how to read and process the votes, it remains only to determine the winner(s) and print the results. We will delegate this task to the function **printResults**.

Using the sample data, the array **candidate** will contain the following values after all the votes have been tallied (remember we are not using **candidate[0]**).

| | name | numVotes |
|---|---|---|
| 1 | Victor Taylor | 4 |
| 2 | Denise Duncan | 3 |
| 3 | Kamal Ramdhan | 6 |
| 4 | Michael Ali | 4 |
| 5 | Anisa Sawh | 6 |
| 6 | Carol Khan | 2 |
| 7 | Gary Owen | 3 |

To find the winner, we must first find the largest value in the array. To do this, we will call a function **getLargest** with

```
int win = getLargest(candidate, 1, MaxCandidates);
```

which will set **win** to the *subscript* of the largest value in the **numVotes** field from **candidate[1]** to **candidate[7]** (since **MaxCandidates** is 7). In our example, **win** will be set to 3 since the largest value, 6, is in position 3. (6 is also in position 5 but we just need the largest value which we can get from either position).

```
#include <stdio.h>
#include <string.h>
#define MaxCandidates 7
#define MaxNameLength 30

typedef struct {
  char name[MaxNameLength + 1];
  int numVotes;
} PersonData;

typedef struct {
  int valid, spoilt;
} VoteCount;

main() {
  void initialize(PersonData [], int, FILE *);
  VoteCount processVotes(PersonData [], int, FILE *, FILE *);
  void printResults(PersonData [], int, VoteCount, FILE *);

  PersonData candidate[MaxCandidates + 1];
  VoteCount count;
  FILE *in = fopen("votes.txt", "r");
  FILE *out = fopen("results.txt", "w");

  initialize(candidate, MaxCandidates, in);
  count = processVotes(candidate, MaxCandidates, in, out);
  printResults(candidate, MaxCandidates, count, out);

  fclose(in);
  fclose(out);
} //end main
```

Here is **getLargest**:

```
int getLargest(PersonData person[], int lo, int hi) {
//returns the index of the highest vote from person[lo] to person[hi]
  int j, big = lo;
  for (j = lo + 1; j <= hi; j++)
    if (person[j].numVotes > person[big].numVotes) big = j;
  return big;
} //end getLargest
```

Now that we know the largest value is in **candidate[win].numVotes**, we can 'step through' the array, looking for those candidates with that value. This way, we will find all the candidates, if there is more than one, with the highest vote and declare them as winners.

An outline of **printResults** is as follows:

```
printResults
  print the number of voters, valid votes and spoilt votes
  print the score of each candidate
  determine and print the winner(s)
```

The details are given in the function **printResults**:

```
void printResults(PersonData person[], int max, VoteCount c, FILE *out) {
  int j, getLargest(PersonData [], int, int);
  fprintf(out, "\nNumber of voters: %d\n", c.valid + c.spoilt);
  fprintf(out, "Number of valid votes: %d\n", c.valid);
  fprintf(out, "Number of spoilt votes: %d\n", c.spoilt);
  fprintf(out, "\nCandidate      Score\n\n");

  for (j = 1; j <= max; j++)
    fprintf(out, "%-15s %3d\n", person[j].name, person[j].numVotes);

  fprintf(out, "\nThe winner(s)\n");
  int win = getLargest(person, 1, max);
  int winningVote = person[win].numVotes;
  for (j = 1; j <= max; j++)
    if (person[j].numVotes == winningVote)
        fprintf(out, "%s\n", person[j].name);
} //end printResults
```

Suppose it were required to print the names of the candidates in *descending* order by **numVotes**. To do this, the structure array **candidate** must be sorted in descending order using the **numVotes** field to control the sorting. This could be done by the function call

```
sortByVote(candidate, 1, MaxCandidates);
```

where **sortByVote** (shown on the next page) uses an insertion sort and is written using the formal parameter **person** (any name will do).

Observe that the structure of the function is pretty much the same as if we were sorting a simple integer array. The major difference is in the **while** condition where we must specify which field is used to determine the sorting order. (In this example, we also use **>**, rather than **<**, since we are sorting in descending order rather than ascending order.) When we are about to process **person[j]**, we copy it to the temporary structure, **insertItem**. This frees **person[j]** so that **person[j-1]** may be shifted into position **j**, if necessary. To shift an array element to the right, we use the simple assignment

```
person[k + 1] = person[k];
```

to move the entire structure (two fields, in this example).

```
void sortByVote(PersonData person[], int lo, int hi) {
//sort person[lo..hi] in descending order by numVotes
  int j, k;
  PersonData insertItem;
  for (j = lo + 1; j <= hi; j++) { // process person[lo+1] to person[hi]
    // insert person j in its proper position
    insertItem = person[j];
    k = j -1;
    while (k >= lo && insertItem.numVotes > person[k].numVotes) {
        person[k + 1] = person[k];
        --k;
    }
    person[k + 1] = insertItem;
  }
} //end sortByVote
```

If we need to sort the candidates in alphabetical order, we could use the function **sortByName**:

```
void sortByName(PersonData person[], int lo, int hi) {
//sort person[lo..hi] in alphabetical order by name
  int j, k;
  PersonData insertItem;
  for (j = lo + 1; j <= hi; j++) { // process person[lo+1] to person[hi]
    // insert person j in its proper position
    insertItem = person[j];
    k = j -1;
    while (k > 0 && strcmp(insertItem.name, person[k].name) < 0) {
        person[k + 1] = person[k];
        --k;
    }
    person[k + 1] = insertItem;
  }
} //end sortByName
```

The function **sortByName** is identical with **sortByVote** except for the **while** condition which specifies which field is used in comparisons and the use of **<** for sorting in ascending order. Note the use of the standard string function, **strcmp**, for comparing two names. If **strcmp(s1, s2)** is negative, it means that the string **s1** comes before the string **s2** in alphabetical order.

As an exercise, re-write the program for solving the voting problem so that it prints the results in descending order by votes and in alphabetical order.

## 2.9 Passing structures to functions

In the voting problem, we saw examples where **candidate**, an array of structures, was passed to various functions. We now discuss some other issues that arise in passing a structure to a function.

Consider a structure for a 'book type' with the following fields:

```
typedef struct {
  char author[31];
  char title[51];
  char binding;        //paperback, hardcover, spiral, etc.
  double price;
  int quantity;        //quantity in stock
} Book;
Book text;
```

This declares a new type called **Book** and **text** is declared as a variable of type **Book**.

We could pass individual fields to functions in the usual way; for a simple variable, its value is passed but, for an array variable, its address is passed. Thus,

```
fun1(text.quantity);   // value of text.quantity is passed
fun2(text.binding);    // value of text.binding is passed
fun3(text.price);      // value of text.price is passed
```

but,

```
fun4(text.title);      // address of array text.title is passed
```

We could even pass the first letter of the title, as in:

```
fun5(text.title[0]);   // value of first letter of title is passed
```

To pass the entire structure, we use:

```
fun6(text);
```

Of course, the header for each of these functions must be written with the appropriate parameter type.

In the last example, the fields of **text** are copied to a temporary place (called the *run-time heap*) and the copy is passed to **fun6**, that is, the structure is passed "by value". If a structure is complicated or contains arrays, the copying operation could be time-consuming. In addition, when the function returns, the values of the structure elements must be removed from the heap; this adds to the overhead—the extra processing required to perform a function call.

To avoid this overhead, the *address* of the structure could be passed. We will show how to do this when we discuss pointers in the next chapter.

## Exercises 2

1. Do Exercise 1 on page 22 using structures.
2. Write a program to read names and phone numbers into a structure array. Request a name and print the person's phone number. Use binary search to look up the name.
3. Do Exercise 3 on page 22 using a structure array to hold the words.
4. Do Exercise 6 on page 23 using a structure to hold a candidate's data.
5. Write a function which, given two date structures, **d1** and **d2**, returns `-1` if **d1** comes before **d2**, `0` if **d1** is the same as **d2** and `1` if **d1** comes after **d2**.
6. Write a function which, given two date structures, **d1** and **d2**, returns the number of days that **d2** is ahead of **d1**. If **d2** comes before **d1**, return a negative value.
7. A time in 24-hour clock format is represented by two numbers: e.g. `16 45` means the time `16:45`, that is 4:45 p.m. Using a structure to represent a time, write a function which given two time structures, **t1** and **t2**, returns the number of minutes from **t1** to **t2**. For example, if the two given times are `16 45` and `23 25` your function should return `400`.

   Modify the function so that it works as follows: if **t2** is less than **t1**, take it to mean a time for the *next* day. For example, given the times `20:30` and `6:15`, take this to mean 8.30 p.m. to 6.15 a.m. of the next day. Your function should return `585`.
8. A length, specified in metres and centimetres, is represented by two integers. For example, the length 3m 75cm is represented by `3 75`. Using a structure to represent a length, write functions to compare, add and subtract two lengths.
9. A file contains the names and distances jumped by athletes in a long jump competition. Using a structure to hold a name and distance (which is itself a structure as in 8, above), write a program to read the data and print a list of names and distance jumped in order of merit (best jumper first).
10. At a school's bazaar, activities were divided into 'stalls'. At the close of the bazaar, the manager of each stall submitted information to the Principal consisting of the name of the stall, the income earned and its expenses. Some sample data were:

    ```
    Games 2300.00 1000.00
    Sweets 900.00 1000.00
    ```

    Using a structure to hold a stall's data, write a program to read the data and print a report consisting of stall name and net income (income - expenses), *in order of decreasing net income* (that is, with the most profitable stall first and the least profitable stall last). In addition, print the number of stalls, the total profit or loss of the bazaar and the stall(s) which made the most profit. Assume that a line containing **xxxxxx** only ends the data.
11. A data file contains registration information for six courses—CS20A, CS21A, CS29A, CS30A, CS35A and CS36A. Each line of data consists of a 7-digit student registration number followed by six (ordered) values, each of which is `0` or `1`. A value of `1` indicates that the student is registered for the corresponding course; `0` means he is not. Thus `1 0 1 0 1 1` means that the student is registered for CS20A, CS29A, CS35A and CS36A, but not for CS21A and CS30A. You may assume that there are no more than 100 students and a registration number `0` ends the data. Write a program to read the data and produce a class list for each course. Each list consists of the registration numbers of those students taking the course.

# 3 Pointers

## In this chapter, we will explain:

- what is a *pointer*
- how to declare pointer variables
- how to *de-reference* a pointer
- how a function can change the value of a variable in a 'calling' function
- some issues involved in passing an array as an argument to a function
- how to work with *character* pointers
- the meaning of pointer arithmetic
- how to use pointers to structures
- how to use *pointers to functions* to write general-purpose routines
- what are *void* pointers and how to use them

In C, arguments to functions are passed "by value". Suppose the function **test** is called with the variable **num** as argument, thus:

```
test(num);
```

The *value* of **num** is copied to a temporary location and *this* location is passed to **test**. In this scenario, **test** has no access whatsoever to the original argument **num** and, hence, cannot change it in any way.

Does this mean that a function can *never* change the value of a variable in another function? It can, but in order to do so, it must have access to the *address* of the variable—the location in memory where the variable is stored.

If a computer has 1 million bytes of memory, its memory locations range from 0 to 999,999. Among other things, memory locations are used for storing the values of variables. Suppose a variable **num** has the value 36 and this value is stored at memory location 5000. We say the *storage address* (or, simply, the *address*) of **num** is 5000.

The operator **&**, when applied to a variable, returns the address of the variable. For example, suppose **num** is stored in location 5000. Then the value of **&num** is 5000.

The term *pointer* is used to refer to an address in memory. A *pointer variable* is one which can hold the address of a memory location.

If **ptr** is a pointer variable, we can assign a value to it, thus:

```
ptr = &num;
```

This statement stores the *address of* **num** (whatever it may be) in **ptr**. We say that **ptr** 'points to' **num**.

But how do we declare **ptr** to be a pointer variable? First, we observe that, in C, a given pointer variable can 'point to' values of *one type* only (but see **void** pointers on page 63). The declaration of the pointer variable specifies the type. For example, the declaration

```
int *ptr;
```

is read as '**int** pointer **ptr**' and declares **ptr** to be a *pointer* variable which can 'point to' (hold the address of) **int** values only. (Of course, since **ptr** can assume only one value at a time, it can point to only one integer at any given time.) The declaration could also have been written as:

```
int* ptr;
```

or

```
int * ptr;
```

Suppose the *address* of **num** is 5000 and the *value* of **num** is 17. The statement

```
ptr = &num;
```

assigns the value 5000 to **ptr**. Assuming **ptr** is stored at location 800, this can be pictured as

| ptr | 800 | | num | 5000 |
|---|---|---|---|---|
| 5000 | | | 17 | |

We use ***ptr** to refer to 'the value pointed at by **ptr**'[1] (in effect, the value of **num**), and can be used in any context that an integer can. For example, if **m** is **int**, then

```
m = *ptr + 7;
```

assigns the value 24 (17 + 7) to **m**.

It is sometimes helpful to think of * and **&** as cancelling out each other. For instance, if **ptr = &num**, then

```
*ptr ≡ *(&num) ≡ num;
```

An interesting assignment is

```
num = *ptr + 1;
```

This is exactly equivalent to

```
num = num + 1;
```

It could even be written as

```
(*ptr)++;
```

[1] Getting the value pointed to is called *de-referencing* the pointer.

This says increment whatever **ptr** is pointing at. The brackets around ***ptr** are necessary. Without the brackets, ***ptr++** would mean 'take the value pointed to by **ptr**, then increment the value of **ptr**'—see the section on pointer arithmetic, page 55, for what it means to increment a pointer. To increment **num** by a value other than 1 (5, say), one could write

```
(*ptr) += 5;
```

In many respects, **ptr** is just like any other variable and we can change its value if necessary. For example,

```
ptr = &m;
```

assigns the *address* of **m** to **ptr**. The old value of **ptr** is lost. Now **ptr** points to the value of **m** rather than **num**.

## 3.1 Passing pointers as arguments

Consider the problem of getting a function to change the value of a variable in the 'calling' function. Specifically, let us attempt to write a function to add 6 to its integer argument. A naive attempt might be Program 3.1. The 'comments' are for reference only.

**Program P3.1**

```
#include <stdio.h>
main() {
  void test(int);
  int n = 14;
  printf("%d\n", n);  // printf1
  test(n);
  printf("%d\n", n);  // printf2
} //end main

void test(int a) {
  a = a + 6;
  printf("%d\n", a);  // printf3
} //end test
```

When run, this program will print

```
14    (printf1)
20    (printf3)
14    (printf2)
```

At the end, the value of **n** is still 14. Clearly, **test** was unable to change the value of **n**.

As written, there is no way for **test** to change the value of **n** (declared in **main**) since it has no access to **n**. The only way **test** can change the value of **n** is if the *address of* **n** is passed to **test**. This can be achieved by calling **test** with

```
test(&n);
```

But now, since the actual argument is a pointer, we must change the definition of the formal parameter in **test** so that it is also a pointer. Program P3.2 incorporates the changes:

**Program P3.2**

```
#include <stdio.h>
main() {
  void test(int *);
  int n = 14;
  printf("%d\n", n);   // printf1
  test(&n);
  printf("%d\n", n);   // printf2
} //end main

void test(int *a) {
  *a = *a + 6;
  printf("%d\n", *a); // printf3
} //end test
```

The function prototype

```
void test(int *);
```

indicates that the argument to **test** is an 'integer pointer'. The formal parameter **a** is declared accordingly. The integer value 'pointed at' by **a** is denoted by ***a**. When **test** is called with

```
test(&n);
```

the *address* of **n** (5000, say) is passed to it; **test**, therefore, has access to whatever value is stored at this address, and may change it if desired. In this case, it adds 6 to the value at location 5000, effectively adding 6 to the value of **n**. When run, Program P3.2 will print:

```
14    (printf1)
20    (printf3)
20    (printf2)
```

At the end, the value of **n** in **main** has been changed to 20 by the function **test**.

It should now be clear why it is necessary to put the ampersand (&) in front of variables when we use the standard input function **scanf(...)** to read data. The only way **scanf(...)** can put a value into an actual argument is if its *address* is passed to it. For example, in the statement

```
scanf("%d", &n);
```

the *address* of **n** is passed to **scanf**; this enables **scanf** to store the value read in the location occupied by **n**.

*For the cognoscenti*: even with pointers, it is still true that, in C, arguments are passed by value and a function *cannot* change the value of an original argument passed to it. Suppose **ptr = &n** and consider the call

```
test(ptr);
```

The value of the argument, **ptr**, is determined. Suppose it is 5000. This value is copied to a temporary location and *this* location is passed to **test** where it is known as **a**. Thus the *value* of **a** is 5000.

When interpreted as an address, this is the address of the variable **n**, in **main**. Thus the function has access to **n** and can change it, if desired. But note that **test** cannot change the value of the *original* argument **ptr** since only a *copy* of **ptr** was passed. However, as we have seen, it can change the value *pointed to* by **ptr**.

## 3.2 More on passing an array as an argument

We have learnt that when an *array name* is used as an actual argument, the address of its first element is passed to the function. Consider Program P3.3:

**Program P3.3**

```
#include <stdio.h>
main() {
  void test(int val[], int max);
  int j, list[5];

  for (j = 0; j < 5; j++) list[j] = j;
  test(list, 5);
  for (j = 0; j < 5; j++) printf("%d ", list[j]);
  printf("\n");
} //end main

void test(int val[], int max) {
// add 25 to each of val[0] to val[max - 1]
  int j;
  for (j = 0; j < max; j++) val[j] += 25;
} //end test
```

When run, this program prints

```
25 26 27 28 29
```

In **main**, the elements **list[0]** to **list[4]** are set to 0, 1, 2, 3 and 4, respectively.

When the call

```
test(list, 5);
```

is made, the address of **list[0]** is passed to **test** where it becomes known as **val[0]**. The function adds 25 to each of **val[0]** to **val[4]**. But since **val[0]** to **val[4]** occupy the same storage as **list[0]** to **list[4]**, the function effectively adds 25 to **list[0]**, **list[1]**, **list[2]**, **list[3]** and **list[4]**.

The call

```
test(list, 5);
```

could be replaced by

```
test(&list[0], 5);
```

since, in both cases, the address of the first element of **list** is passed to the function. In other words, an array name *is* a pointer—the *address of the first element* of the array.

An interesting variation is the call

```
test(&list[2], 3);
```

Here, the address of element **list[2]** is passed to **test**. In the function, *this* address is matched with **val[0]**. The net effect is that

**val[0]** matches with **list[2]**;
**val[1]** matches with **list[3]**;
**val[2]** matches with **list[4]**;

These elements are incremented by 25 so that the program prints

```
0  1  27  28  29
```

In case you are wondering, it would be invalid to attempt something like

```
test(&list[2], 5);
```

since this implies that, starting at **list[2]**, there are at least five elements in the array, and, in our case, there are only three. What would happen is that, in the function, **val[3]** and **val[4]** would be associated with the locations in memory immediately following **list[4]**. The contents of these locations would be altered with unpredictable consequences.

## 3.3 Character pointers

Suppose **word** is declared as an array of characters:

```
char word[20];
```

We have emphasized that the array name **word** is a synonym for the address of its first element, **word[0]**. Thus

```
word ≡ &word[0]
```

In effect, **word** 'points to' the first character of the array and is, in fact, a pointer—a *character* pointer, to be more precise. However, **word** is not a pointer *variable* but, rather, a pointer *constant*—we can't change its value, which is the address of **word[0]**.

Whenever a string constant appears in a program, the characters without the quotes are stored somewhere in memory; **\0** is added at the end and the address of the first character is used in place of the string. For example, in

```
printf("Enter a number:");
```

what is actually passed to **printf** is a character pointer whose value is the address of the first character of the string

```
Enter a number:
```

stored somewhere in memory and terminated by **\0**.

Consider the declaration:

```
char *errorMessage;
```

It is permitted to write

```
errorMessage = "Cannot divide by 0\n";
```

The effect is that the characters of the string (properly terminated by **\0**) are stored somewhere in memory (starting at address 800, say) and the address of the first character (800) is assigned to **errorMessage**. This can be used as in:

```
printf("%s", errorMessage);
```

or, simply,

```
printf(errorMessage);
```

Note that **errorMessage** is a pointer *variable* whose value can be changed, if desired. For example,

```
errorMessage = "Negative argument to square root\n";
```

sets **errorMessage** to point to the new string. Of course, the string previously pointed at by **errorMessage** now becomes inaccessible. If we wanted to save the old value of **errorMessage**, we could have done something like

```
oldMessage = errorMessage;
```

assuming that **oldMessage** is also a character pointer. It is important to observe that this assignment simply stores the (pointer) value of **errorMessage** in **oldMessage**. No characters are copied. For example, suppose

```
"Cannot divide by 0\n"
```

was stored starting at address 500. After the assignment (above), the value of **oldMessage** is 500 and, hence, points to the string. There is nothing wrong or invalid in having several variables 'point to' the same location. It is exactly the same as, for instance, several integer variables having the same value.

## 3.4 Pointer arithmetic

We saw above that a pointer variable could be assigned to another pointer variable. C also permits us to increment and decrement pointer variables but these operations have special meanings when applied to pointers.

Consider

```
char *verse = "The day is done";
```

The string **"The day is done"** is stored somewhere in memory and **verse** is assigned the address of the first character, **T**. In addition,

```
verse + 1   is the address of 'h';
verse + 2   is the address of 'e';
verse + 3   is the address of ' ';
    etc.
```

If required, we could change the value of **verse** with constructions such as

```
verse++;
verse += j;
```

As an example, the following will print the characters of the string pointed at by **verse**, one per line:

```
while (*verse != '\0')
  printf("%c\n", *verse++);
```

***verse** refers to the character currently pointed at by **verse**. After this character has been printed, **verse** is incremented to point to the next character.

The above discussion relates to character pointers. But suppose **ptr** is a pointer to integers, say. What is the meaning of

```
ptr + 1 or ptr + k?
```

To illustrate the ideas involved, consider an integer array **num** declared as

```
int num[5];
```

We know by now that the name **num** refers to the address of **num[0]**. What is new is that

**num + 1** is the address of **num[1]**;
**num + 2** is the address of **num[2]**;
**num + 3** is the address of **num[3]**;
**num + 4** is the address of **num[4]**;

This holds regardless of how many storage locations are occupied by an integer. For example, suppose an integer occupies 4 bytes and the address of **num[0]** is 800.

The value of the array name **num** is 800, and the value of, say, **num + 1** (pointer arithmetic) is the address of **num[1]**, that is, 800 + 4 = 804. Similarly,

the value of **num + 2** is 808;
the value of **num + 3** is 812;
the value of **num + 4** is 816;

In general, suppose a pointer, **p**, is declared to point at a type of value which occupies **k** locations of storage. Incrementing **p** by 1 has the effect of adding **k** to the current value of **p** so that **p** now points to the *next* item of the type that **p** is declared to point at.

Thus, using pointer arithmetic, 'adding 1' means getting the address of the next item (no matter how many locations away) and 'adding **j**' means getting the address of the **j**th item beyond the current one. Thus **p + j** is the address of the **j**th element beyond the one pointed to by **p**.

Since, for example,

**num + 2** is the address of **num[2]**, i.e., **&num[2]**,

it follows that

***(num + 2)** is equivalent to ***(&num[2])**, that is, **num[2]**.

(Think of * and **&** as cancelling each other.)

---

The following prints the values in the array **num**, one per line:

```
for (j = 0 ; j < 5; j++)
  printf("%d\n", *(num + j));
```

***(num + j)** could be replaced by **num[j]** and the effect would be exactly the same.

One might wonder, in this example, about the meaning of **num + 5**, say. Theoretically, this is the address of element **num[5]**, but this element does not exist. However, it is not invalid to attempt to use **num + 5**. But if, for instance, we attempt to print ***(num + 5)**, we will print whatever happens to be stored in memory at the address designated by **num + 5**, or worse, get a memory access or address error. In either case, the moral is that you must not attempt to refer to array elements you have not declared.

We will illustrate the intimate relationship between arrays and pointers by writing two versions of a function, **length**, which finds the length of a string.

Suppose **word** is declared as

```
char word[MaxLength]; // MaxLength is a symbolic constant
```

then in order to find the length of a string stored in **word**, one can call the function

```
length(word);
```

**length** assumes that **word** consists of characters terminated by **\0**. The value returned is the number of characters excluding **\0**. Since what is passed to the function is the address of the first character (i.e., **&word[0]**), the function can be written with the formal parameter declared either as an array or as a pointer. Which version is used has no effect on how the function is called. First we write the array version.

```
int length(char string[]) {
  int n = 0;
  while (string[n] != '\0') n++;
  return n;
}
```

Now we write the pointer version:

```
int length(char *strPtr) { // string pointer
  int n = 0;
  while (*strPtr != '\0') {
    n++;
    strPtr++;
  }
  return n;
}
```

We could even increment **strPtr** as part of the **while** test, giving:

```
int length(char *strPtr) {
  int n = 0;
  while (*strPtr++ != '\0') n++;
  return n;
}
```

Which version is better? It depends on your point of view. Whereas the array version is more readable, the pointer version is more efficient. In the array version, it is clear that at each step we are looking at the **n**th element of the string. This is not so obvious in the pointer version. However, evaluating **string[n]** requires evaluation of the subscript **n** which is then converted into the address of element **n**. The pointer version deals with the address directly.

We have mentioned before that an array name is a constant and, hence, it's value can't be changed. There may appear to be a conflict in that the function, when passed the array name, increments it (**strPtr++**) to move on to the next character.

But remember that the formal parameter in the function definition *is* a variable. When the function is called with **length(word)**, say, the value of **word** (the address of the first character) is copied to a temporary location and this location is passed to the function, where it is known as **strPtr**. The effect is that **strPtr** is simply initialized to the value of **word**. Incrementing **strPtr** in the function has no effect on the value of **word** in the calling function.

## 3.5 Pointers to structures

Just as it is possible to take the address of an **int** or **double** variable, so too can one take the address of a structure variable. On page 46, we mentioned that when we make the call

```
fun6(text);
```

where **text** is a structure variable of type **Book**, the fields of **text** are copied to the run-time heap and the copy is passed to **fun6**, that is, the structure is passed "by value". If a structure is complicated or contains arrays, the copying operation could be time-consuming. In addition, when the function returns, the values of the structure elements must be removed from the heap; this adds to the overhead—the extra processing required to perform a function call.

To avoid this overhead, the *address* of the structure could be passed, as in:

```
fun7(&text);
```

Of course, in **fun7**, the corresponding formal parameter must be declared appropriately, such as:

```
void fun7(Book *bp)
```

Now, only a single value (the address) has to be copied to (and later removed from) the heap. And given the address, the function has access to the original argument **text** and can change it, if desired.

It is also possible to pass the address of an individual field to a function. For array fields, this happens automatically, as in:

```
fun4(text.title);        // address of text.title is passed
```

For simple variables, the structure name (*not* the field name) must be preceded by **&**, as in:

```
fun3(&text.price);       // address of text.price is passed
```

For example, we could read values for **price** and **quantity** with:

```
scanf("%lf %d", &text.price, &text.quantity); //"lf" since price is double
```

---

Using the declaration

```
typedef struct {
  char name[31];
  int age;
  char gender;
} Student;
```

consider

```
Student child, *sp;
```

This declares **child** to be a structure variable of type **Student**. It also declares **sp** to be a *pointer to* a structure of the type **Student**. In other words, the values which **sp** can assume are addresses of variables of type **Student**. For example, the statement

```
sp = &child;
```

is valid and assigns the *address* of the structure variable **child** to **sp**. If the fields of **child** are stored starting at memory location 6000, then the value 6000 is assigned to **sp**.

As with pointers to other types, ***sp** refers to the structure that **sp** is pointing at. In this example, ***sp** is a synonym for **child**. We can refer to the fields of the structure that **sp** is pointing at by using the dot operator (.) as in

(*sp).name, (*sp).age and (*sp).gender

The brackets around ***sp** are required since **.** has higher precedence than *. Without them, ***sp.age**, for instance, would be interpreted as ***(sp.age)**. This implies that **sp.age** is a pointer; since it is not, it will produce an error.

Pointers to structures occur so frequently in C that a special alternative notation is provided. If **sp** is pointing to a structure of type **Student**, then

| | |
|---|---|
| **sp -> name** | refers to the 'name' field, |
| **sp -> age** | refers to the 'age' field, and |
| **sp -> gender** | refers to the 'gender' field, |

**->** is a 'minus' sign followed by a 'greater than' sign.

We will see many examples of the use of pointers to structures in the next chapter.

The following gives a summary of valid operations on structures:

- A field can be accessed using the 'structure member' (.) operator, as in **text.author**.
- A structure variable can be assigned the value of another structure variable of the same type.
- The address-of operator **&** can be applied to a structure name to give the address of the structure, e.g. **&text**. **&** can also be applied to an element of a structure. However, **&** must precede the structure name, not the field name. For example, **&text.price** is valid but **text.&price** and **&price** are not.
- If **p** is a pointer to a structure, then ***p** refers to the structure. For example, if **p** contains the address of the structure **text**, then

```
(*p).title   //brackets required since . has higher precedence than *
```

refers to the **title** field. However, the *structure pointer* (arrow) operator **->** (a minus sign immediately followed by **>**) is more commonly used to refer to a field, as in:

```
p -> title
```

## 3.6 Pointers to functions

In the same way that an array name is the address of its first element, so too a function name is the address of the function. To put it another way, a function name is a *pointer* to the function in much the same way that an array name is a pointer to the array. In C, a pointer to a function can be manipulated in much the same way as other pointers; in particular, it can be passed to functions. This is especially handy for writing general-purpose routines.

As an example, consider the problem of producing two-column tables such as tables of squares, reciprocals, square roots, weight conversions, temperature conversions, etc. In each table, the first column consists of an ascending sequence of integers and the second has the associated values.

We could write separate functions for each type of table we want to produce. But we could also write *one* function (called **makeTable**, say) which produces the various tables. Which specific table is produced depends on which function is passed to **makeTable**.

How do we specify a function as a parameter? Consider the function definition:

```
void makeTable(int first, int last, double (*fp) (int)) {
  for (int j = first; j <= last; j++)
    printf("%2d  %0.3f\n", j, (*fp)(j));
}
```

The heading says that **makeTable** takes three arguments—the first two are integers and the third, **fp**, is a pointer to a function which takes an **int** argument and returns a **double** value. The brackets around ***fp** in

```
double (*fp) (int)
```

are necessary. If they are omitted,

```
double *fp (int)
```

would mean that **fp** is a function returning a pointer to a **double**, which is quite different from what is intended.

In the **printf** statement, the function call **(*fp) (j)** is interpreted as follows:

- **fp** is a pointer to a function; ***fp** *is* the function;
- **j** is the actual argument to the function call; the brackets around **j** are the usual brackets around a function's argument(s);
- the value returned by the call should be a **double** which would match the **%f** specification;
- the brackets around ***fp** are necessary since **()** has higher precedence than *. Without them, ***fp(j)** would be equivalent to ***(fp(j))** which is meaningless in this context.

But how do we use **makeTable** to produce a table of reciprocals, say? Suppose we want to produce the table from 1 to 10. We would like to use a statement such as:

```
makeTable(1, 10, reciprocal);
```

to get the required table, where **reciprocal** is a function which takes an **int** value and returns a **double** value—the reciprocal of the integer. It could be written as:

```
double reciprocal(int x) {
  return 1.0 / x;
}
```

Note that in the call

```
makeTable(1, 10, reciprocal);
```

the function name **reciprocal** is a pointer to a function, so it matches the third parameter of **makeTable**. Program P3.4 (next page) shows all the pieces put together in one complete program.

If we now wish to create a table of squares, all we need are

the function prototype:

```
double square(int);
```

the function call:

```
makeTable(1, 10, square);
```

**Program P3.4**

```
#include <stdio.h>
main() {
  void makeTable(int, int, double (*fp) (int));
  double reciprocal(int);
  makeTable(1, 10, reciprocal);
} //end main

void makeTable(int first, int last, double (*fp) (int)) {
  for (int j = first; j <= last; j++)
    printf("%2d   %0.3f\n", j, (*fp)(j));
} //end makeTable

double reciprocal(int x) {
  return 1.0 / x;
} //end reciprocal
```

and the function definition:

```
double square(int x) {
  return x * x;
}
```

---

As another example, consider the problem of evaluating the definite integral

$$\int_a^b f(x)dx$$

using the Trapezoidal Rule with $n$ strips. The rule states that an approximation to the above integral is given by

$$h\{(f(a) + f(b))/2 + f(a + h) + f(a + 2h) + \ldots + f(a + (n-1)h)\}$$

where $h = (b - a)/n$.

We would like to write a general function **integral** which, given **a**, **b**, **n** and a function, **f**, returns the value of the integral. To evaluate the integrals of different functions, we would need only to pass the appropriate function to **integral**. Consider the following version of **integral**:

```
double integral(double a, double b, int n, double (*fp) (double)) {
  double h, sum;
  h = (b - a) / n;
  sum = ((*fp)(a) + (*fp)(b)) / 2.0;
  for (int j = 1; j < n ; j++)
    sum += (*fp)(a + j * h);
  return h * sum;
} //end integral
```

The declaration

```
double (*fp) (double)
```

says that **fp** is a pointer to a function which takes a **double** argument and returns a **double** value. ***fp** denotes the function and **(*fp)(a)** is a call to the function with argument **a**.

To show how **integral** can be used, suppose we want to find an approximation to

$$\int_0^2 (x^2 + 5x + 3)dx$$

using 20 strips.

We would need to write a function such as **quadratic**, thus:

```
double quadratic(double x) {
  return x * x + 5.0 * x + 3.0;
}
```

and the call

```
integral(0, 2, 20, quadratic)
```

would return the value of the integral.

## 3.7 Void pointers

As we have emphasized, a pointer variable in C can point to one type of value only. However, C allows the declaration and use of *void* (also called *generic*) pointers—pointers which may point to any type of object. For example,

```
void *pv;
```

declares **pv** as a **void** pointer, and

```
void *getNode(int size);
```

declares **getNode** as a function which returns a **void** pointer.

Any valid address can be assigned to a **void** pointer. In particular, a pointer to **int** (or **double** or **float**, etc) can be assigned to a **void** pointer variable. Given

```
double d, *dp;
```

it is permitted to write

```
dp = &d; //assign the address of d to dp
pv = dp; //assign a double pointer to a void pointer variable
```

But even though **pv** and **dp** have the same pointer value after the above assignment, it is invalid to think of ***pv** as a **double**. In other words, we should not attempt to de-reference a **void** pointer. However, if we *know* that **pv** contains a double pointer, we can 'tell' this to C using a cast, and de-reference it, thus:

```
* (double *) pv
```

Void pointers are useful for writing general-purpose functions where you do not want to restrict a function to returning a specific type of pointer. Also, declaring a function parameter as a **void** pointer allows the *actual* argument to be any type of pointer.

For example, suppose we want to write a function to accept an address and print the value stored at that address. If we *know* that the address will be a **double** pointer, say, we can write the function like this:

```
void dprint(double *p) {
  printf("%0.3lf\n", *p); //print to 3 decimal places
}
```

But what if we want the function to work no matter what type of pointer is passed? We can try and specify the parameter as a **void** pointer, thus:

```
void vprint(void *p) {      //this won't work
  printf("%0.3lf\n", *p);
}
```

but this won't work. Remember that an address is just a positive integer (8000, say). When this number is sent to the function, **print** will not know what type of value is stored at that address, so it will not know how to interpret ***p** in **printf**. (In **dprint**, above, it *knows* that ***p** is a **double** value).

So, in addition to the pointer, we need to tell the function what type of value is stored so the pointer can be de-referenced correctly. We can do this via another argument (**t**, say). To illustrate, we write the function assuming **t** = 1 means an **int** pointer is passed and **t** = 2 means a **double** pointer is passed.

```
void print(void *p, int t){
  if (t == 1) printf("%d\n", *(int *) p);
   else if (t == 2) printf("%0.3lf\n", *(double *) p);
   else printf("error: unknown type\n");
} //end print
```

Consider the following code:

```
int n = 375;
double d = 2.71865;
print(&n, 1); //int pointer passed
print(&d, 2); //double pointer passed
```

When executed, this will print

```
375
2.719
```

The function **print** can be easily extended to handle other types.

---

C permits a **void** pointer to be assigned to any other type of pointer as in:

```
float *fp = pv;
```

However, it is up to you to ensure that the assignment makes sense. For instance, if **pv** contains an **int** pointer, it makes no sense to assign it to a **float** pointer variable. On the other hand, if you *know* that **pv** contains a **float** pointer, then the assignment is meaningful.

*Programming note*: if you use a C++ compiler to compile your C programs, you will get an error if you try to assign a **void** pointer to another pointer type. You will need to cast the **void** pointer to the appropriate type before assigning, as in

```
fp = (float *) pv;
```

Even though assigning a **void** pointer without casting is permitted in C, good programming practice dictates that you should use a cast anyway.

---

## Exercises 3

1. What is meant by 'an argument is passed by value'?
2. Which type of argument in C is not passed by value? How is it passed?
3. How is it possible for a function to change the value of an actual argument?
4. In **main**, there are two **int** variables, **a** and **b**. Write a function which, when called, interchanges the values of **a** and **b** so that the change is known in **main**.
5. In **main**, there are three **int** variables, **a**, **b** and **c**. Write a function which, when called, stores the sum of **a** and **b** in **c** so that **c** is changed in **main**.
6. Explain the differences between a character pointer and a character array.
7. The character pointer **msgPtr** is pointing to a string of characters. What happens when **msgPtr** is assigned to another character pointer **oldPtr**?
8. How is a pointer similar to an integer?
9. How does pointer arithmetic differ from ordinary integer arithmetic?

10. What is the difference between **num[j]** and ***(num + j)**?

11. If **ps** is a pointer to a structure which contains an **int** field **score**, what is the difference between **(*ps).score** and **ps -> score**?

12. If a function $f$ is continuous in the interval $[a, b]$ and $f(a)f(b) < 0$ then, since $f$ changes sign, there must exist some $c$ in $[a, b]$ for which $f(c) = 0$. Assume there is one such $c$. It can be found as follows:

    - bisect the interval $[a, b]$;
    - determine in which half $f$ changes sign;

    This is repeated giving a sequence of intervals, each smaller than the last and each containing $c$. The procedure can be terminated when the interval is arbitrarily small or $f$ is 0 at one of the endpoints.

    Write a function which, given $f$, $a$ and $b$, returns an approximation to $c$. Test your function using the function $5x^2 + 3x - 14$ with a solution in the interval [2, 3].

13. Write a function to calculate the value of the definite integral

    $$\int_a^b f(x)dx$$

    using Simpson's rule (below) with $n$ strips; $n$ must be even. An approximation to the integral is given by

    $$\frac{h}{3}\{ (f(a) + 4f(a + h) + 2f(a + 2h) + ...+ 2f(a + (n-2)h) + 4f(a+ (n-1)h) + f(b) \}$$

    where $h = (b - a)/n$.

    Test your function on some simple integrals.

    What happens if the number of strips is increased?

14. What is a **void** pointer? How are **void** pointers useful?

15. An **int** pointer is assigned to a void pointer variable, **vp**. How can we print the value pointed to by **vp**?

16. It is permitted to assign a **void** pointer to another type of pointer variable. What should you be mindful of in making such an assignment?

17. Apart from **void** pointers, where else can you use the word **void** in C?

# 4 Linked lists

**In this chapter, we will explain:**

- the notion of a linked list
- how to write declarations for working with a linked list
- how to count the nodes in a linked list
- how to search for an item in a linked list
- how to find the last node in a linked list
- the difference between static storage and dynamic storage allocation
- how to allocate and free storage in C using **malloc**, **calloc**, **sizeof** and **free**
- how to build a linked list by adding a new item at the end of the list
- how to build a linked list by adding a new item at the head of the list
- how to build a linked list by adding a new item in such a way that the list is always sorted
- how to delete items from a linked list
- how to use linked lists to determine if a phrase is a palindrome
- how to merge two sorted linked lists

---

When values are stored in a one-dimensional array ($x$[0] to $x$[n]), say), they can be thought of as being organized as a 'linear list'. Consider each item in the array as a *node*. A linear list means that the nodes are arranged in a linear order such that

> $x$[0] is the first node
> $x$[n] is the last node
> if $0 < k <= n$, then $x[k]$ is preceded by $x[k - 1]$
> if $0 <= k < n$ then $x[k\ ]$ is followed by $x[k + 1]$

Thus, given a node, the 'next' node is assumed to be in the next location, if any, in the array. The order of the nodes is the order in which they appear in the array, starting from the first. Consider the problem of inserting a new node between two existing nodes $x[k]$ and $x[k + 1]$.

This can be done only if $x[k + 1]$ and the nodes after it are moved to make room for the new node. Similarly, the deletion of $x[k]$ involves the movement of the nodes $x[k +1]$, $x[k + 2]$, etc. Accessing any given node is easy; all we have to do is provide the appropriate subscript.

In many situations, we use an array for representing a linear list. But we can also represent such a list by using an organization in which each node in the list points *explicitly* to the next node. This new organization is referred to as a *linked list*.

In a (singly) linked list, each node contains a pointer which points to the next node in the list. We can think of each node as a cell with two components:

where **data** can actually be one or more fields (depending on what needs to be stored in a node), and **next** 'points to' the next node of the list. (You can use any names you want, instead of **data** and **next**).

Since the **next** field of the *last* node does not point to anything, we must set it to a special value called the "null pointer". In C, the "null pointer" value is denoted by the standard identifier **NULL**, defined in **<stdlib.h>** and **<stdio.h>**.

In addition to the cells of the list, we need a pointer variable (**top**, say) which points to the first item in the list. If the list is empty, the value of **top** is **NULL**.

Pictorially, we represent a linked list as follows:

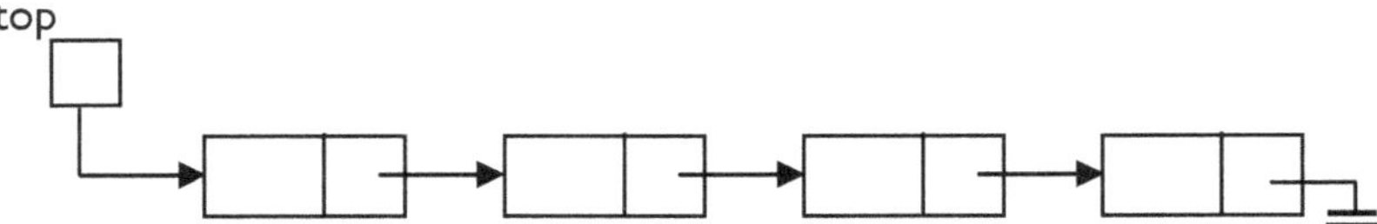


The electrical earth symbol ⏚ is used to represent the null pointer.

Traversing a linked list is like going on a treasure hunt. You are told where the first item is. This is what **top** does. When you get to the first item, *it* directs you to where the second item is (this is the purpose of **next**). When you get to the second item, *it* tells you where the third item is (via **next**), and so on. When you get to the last item, its "null pointer" tells you that that is the end of the hunt (the end of the list).

How can we represent a linked list in a C program? Since each node consists of at least two fields, we will need to use a **struct** to define the format of a node. The **data** component can consist of one or more fields (possibly including structures). The type of these fields will depend on what kind of data needs to be stored.

But what is the type of the **next** field? We know it's a pointer, but a pointer to what? It's a pointer to a structure which is just like the one being defined![2] As an example, suppose the data at each node is a positive integer. We can define the node as follows (using **num** instead of **data**):

---

[2] This is usually called a self-referencing structure.

```
struct node {
  int num;
  struct node *next;
};
```

or using **typedef**:

```
typedef struct node {
  int num;
  struct node *next;
} Node, *NodePtr; // we also declare a name for "struct node *"
```

The variable **top** can now be defined as a pointer to a **node**, thus:

```
Node *top;
```

or

```
NodePtr top;
```

As explained before, the **struct** declaration of **node**, as we have written it, does not allocate any storage for any variables. It simply specifies the form that such variables will take. However, the declaration of **top** does allocate storage, but only for a *pointer* to a **node**. The *value* of **top** can be the address of a node but, so far, there are no nodes in the list. How can storage be allocated to nodes of the list? We will see how to do this in Section 4.2 but, first, we look at some basic operations which may be performed on a linked list.

## 4.1 Basic operations on a linked list

For illustrative purposes, we assume that we have a linked list of integers. We ignore, for the moment, *how* the list might be built.

### *4.1.1 Counting the nodes in a linked list*

Perhaps the simplest operation is to count the number of nodes in a list. To illustrate, we write a function which, given a pointer to a linked list, returns the number of nodes in the list.

Before we write the function, let us see how we can traverse the items in the list, starting from the first one. Suppose **top** points to the head of the list. Consider the code

```
curr = top;
while (curr != NULL) curr = curr -> next;
```

Initially, **curr** points to the first item, if any, in the list. If it is not **NULL**, the statement

```
curr = curr -> next;
```

is executed. This sets **curr** to point to 'whatever the current node is pointing to'; in effect, the next node. For example, given the list:

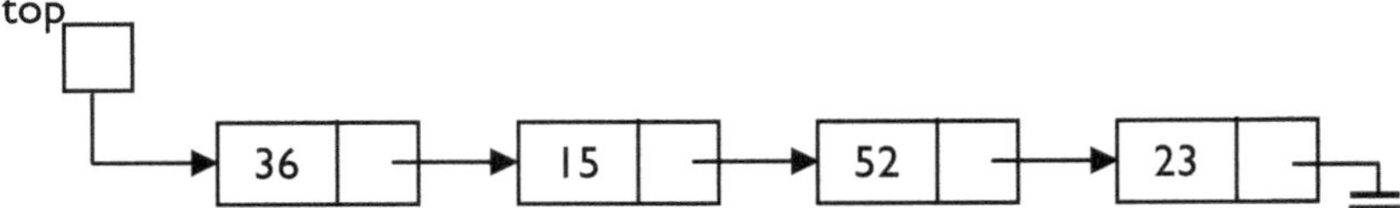


Initially, **curr** points to (the node containing) 36. Since **curr** is not **NULL**, it is set to point to whatever 36 is pointing to, that is, (the node containing) 15.

The **while** condition is tested again. Since **curr** is not **NULL**, **curr = cur -> next** is executed, setting **curr** to point to whatever 15 is pointing to, that is, 52.

The **while** condition is tested again. Since **curr** is not **NULL**, **curr = cur -> next** is executed, setting **curr** to point to whatever 52 is pointing to, that is, 23.

The **while** condition is tested again. Since **curr** is not **NULL**, **curr = cur -> next** is executed, setting **curr** to point to whatever 23 is pointing to, that is, **NULL**.

The **while** condition is tested again. Since **curr** *is* **NULL**, the while loop is no longer executed.

Note that each time **curr** is not **NULL**, we enter the **while** loop. But the number of times that **curr** is *not* **NULL** is exactly the same as the number of items in the list. So in order to count the number of items in the list, we just have count how many times the **while** body is executed.

To do this, we use a counter initialized to 0 and increment it by 1 inside the **while** loop. We can now write the function as follows (we call it **length**):

```
int length(NodePtr top) {
  int n = 0;
  NodePtr curr = top;
  while (curr != NULL) {
    n++;
    curr = curr -> next;
  }
  return n;
} //end length
```

Note that if the list is empty, **curr** will be **NULL** the first time and the **while** loop will not be executed. The function will return 0, the correct result.

Strictly speaking, the variable **curr** is not necessary. The function will work fine if we omit **curr** and replace **curr** by **top** in the function. At the end of the execution of the function, **top** will be **NULL**.

You may be worried that you have lost access to the list. But do not be. Remember that **top** in **length** is a *copy* of whatever variable (**head**, say) is pointing to the list in the calling function. Changing **top** has no effect whatsoever on **head**. When **length** returns, **head** is still pointing to the first item in the list.

### 4.1.2 Searching a linked list

Another common operation is to search a linked list for a given item. For example, given the list

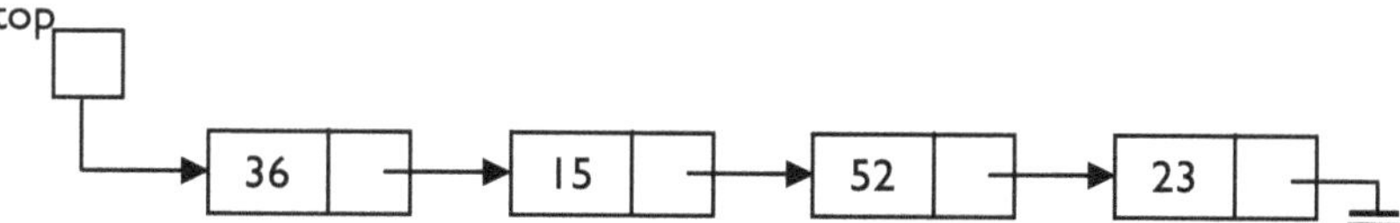


we may wish to search for the number 52. Our search should be able to tell us that 52 is in the list. On the other hand, if we searched for 25, our search should report that 25 is not in the list.

Suppose the number we are searching for is stored in the variable, **key**. The search proceeds by comparing **key** with each number in the list, starting from the first one. If **key** matches with any item, we have found it. If we get to the end of the list and **key** did not match any item, we can conclude that **key** is not in the list.

We must write the logic so that the search ends if we find a match *or* we reach the end of the list. Put another way, the search continues if we have not reached the end of the list *and* we do not have a match. If **curr** points to some item in the list, we can express this logic as:

```
while (curr != NULL && key != curr -> num) curr = curr -> next;
```

The condition **curr != NULL** must be written first. If **curr** *is* **NULL**, the **&&** is false and the second condition **key != curr -> num** is not evaluated.

If we wrote

```
while (key != curr -> num && curr != NULL) curr = curr -> next; //wrong
```

and **curr** happens to be **NULL**, our program will crash when it tries to retrieve **curr -> num**; in effect, this asks for the number pointed to by **curr** but if **curr** is **NULL**, it does not point to anything. We say we are trying to "de-reference a **NULL** pointer", and that is an error.

Let us write the search as a function which, given a pointer to the list and **key**, returns the node containing **key** if it is found. If not found, the function returns **NULL**.

We assume the node declaration from the previous section. Our function will return a value of type **NodePtr**. Here it is:

```
NodePtr search(NodePtr top, int key) {
  while (top != NULL && key != top -> num)
    top = top -> next;
  return top;
} //end search
```

If **key** is not in the list, **top** will become **NULL** and **NULL** will be returned. If **key** is in the list, the **while** loop is exited when **key = top -> num**; at this stage, **top** is pointing to the node containing **key** and *this* value of **top** is returned.

### 4.1.3 Finding the last node in a linked list

Sometimes, we need to find the pointer to the last node in a list. Recall that the last node in the list is distinguished by *its* **next** pointer being **NULL**. Here is a function which returns a pointer to the last node in a given list. If the list is empty, the function returns **NULL**.

```
NodePtr getLast(NodePtr top) {
  if (top == NULL) return NULL;
  while (top -> next != NULL)
    top = top -> next;
  return top;
} //end getLast
```

We get to the **while** statement if **top** is not **NULL**. It therefore makes sense to ask about **top -> next**. If *this* is not **NULL**, the loop is entered and **top** is set to this non-**NULL** value. This ensures that the **while** condition is defined the next time it is executed. When **top -> next** *is* **NULL**, **top** is pointing at the last node and *this* value of **top** is returned.

## 4.2 Dynamic storage allocation – malloc, calloc, sizeof, free

Consider the problem of reading positive integers (terminated by 0) and building a linked list which contains the numbers in the order in which they were read. For example, given the data

```
36 15 52 23 0
```

we want to build the following linked list:

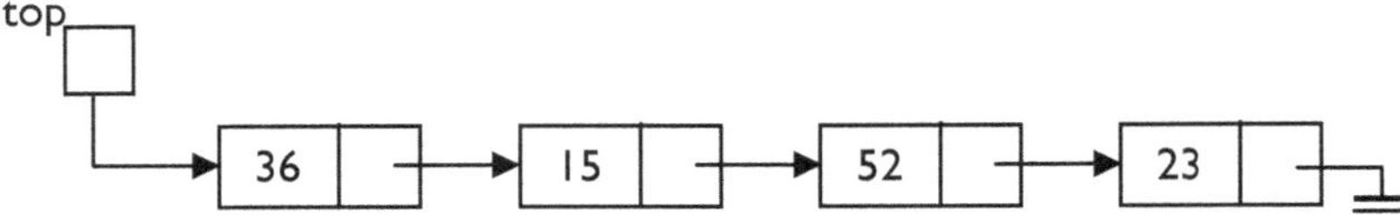

One question which arises is how many nodes will there be in the list? This, of course, depends on how many numbers are supplied. One disadvantage of using an array for storing a linear list is that the size of the array must be specified beforehand. If, when the program is run, it finds that it needs to store more items than this size allows, it may have to be aborted.

With the linked list approach, whenever a new node must be added to the list, storage is allocated for the node and the appropriate pointers are set. Thus we allocate just the right amount of storage for the list—no more, no less.

We do use extra storage for the pointers, but this is more than compensated for by more efficient use of storage as well as easy insertions and deletions. Allocating storage 'as needed' is usually referred to as *dynamic storage allocation*. (On the other hand, array storage is referred to as *static* storage).

In C, storage can be allocated dynamically by using the standard functions **malloc** and **calloc**. In order to use these functions (and **free**, later), your program must be preceded by the header line

```
#include <stdlib.h>
```

This is also needed to use **NULL**, the null pointer definition in C.

---

## *malloc*

The prototype for **malloc** is

```
void *malloc(size_t size);
```

where **size_t** is an implementation-defined unsigned integer type defined in the standard header **<stddef.h>**. Typically, **size_t** is the same as **unsigned int** or **unsigned long int**. To all intents and purposes, we can think of **size** as a positive integer.

**malloc** allocates **size** bytes of memory and returns a pointer to the first byte. The storage is *not* initialized. If **malloc** is unable to find the requested amount of storage, it returns **NULL**.

When your program calls **malloc**, it is important to verify that the requested storage has been successfully allocated. In order to use the storage allocated, the pointer returned must be assigned to a pointer variable of the appropriate type. For example, assuming that **cp** is a character pointer, the statement:

```
cp = malloc(20);
```

allocates 20 bytes of storage and stores the address of the first byte in **cp**. To be safe, your program should check that **cp** is not **NULL** before continuing.

**Note**: In general, a pointer to one type may not be *directly* assigned to a pointer of another type; however, assignment is possible if an explicit cast is used. For example, given the declarations

```
int *ip;
double *dp;
```

the assignment

```
ip = dp;        // wrong
```

is invalid. However, it is valid to use

```
ip = (int *) dp;        // right
```

On the other hand, values of type **void** * may be assigned to pointers of other types without using a cast. In the example above, no cast is required to assign the **void** * returned by **malloc** to the character pointer **cp**. However, even though assigning a **void** pointer without casting is permitted in C, good programming practice dictates that you should use a cast anyway. In the above example, it is better to use

```
cp = (char *) malloc(20);
```

---

## *calloc*

The prototype for **calloc** is

```
void *calloc(size_t num, size_t size);
```

**calloc** allocates **num** * **size** bytes of memory and returns a pointer to the first byte. (Another way of looking at it is that **calloc** allocates enough memory for an array of **num** objects each of size **size**). All bytes returned are initialized to 0. If **calloc** is unable to find the requested amount of storage, it returns **NULL**.

When your program calls **calloc**, it is important to verify that the requested storage has been successfully allocated. In order to use the storage allocated, the pointer returned must be assigned to a pointer variable of the appropriate type. As an example, assuming that **cp** is a character pointer, the statement:

```
cp = calloc(10, 20);
```

allocates $10 \times 20 = 200$ bytes of storage and stores the address of the first byte in **cp**. To be safe, the program should check that **cp** is not **NULL** before continuing. As mentioned before, it is good programming practice to use

```
cp = (char *) calloc(10, 20);
```

**calloc** is useful for allocating storage for arrays. For example, if we know that a **double** variable occupies 8 bytes and we want to allocate space for 25 elements, we could use

```
double *dp = (double *) calloc(25, 8);
```

When executed, **dp** will point to the first element of the array, **dp + 1** will point to the second and, in general, **dp + j - 1** will point to the jth element.

If we do not know the size of a type, and even if we do, we should use **sizeof** (see next).

## *sizeof*

**sizeof** is a standard unary operator that returns the number of bytes needed for storing its argument. For example,

```
sizeof (int)
```

returns the number of bytes needed for storing an **int** variable.

The argument to **sizeof** is either a type or a variable. If it is a type (like **int** or **float** or **double**), it must be enclosed in parentheses. If it is a variable or a type defined using **typedef**, the parentheses are optional. For example, if **root** is a variable of type **double**, then both

```
sizeof root
```

and

```
sizeof (root)
```

are valid and return the number of bytes needed for storing **root**. Similarly,

```
sizeof Book
```

and

```
sizeof (Book)
```

are both valid and return the number of bytes needed for storing a **Book** structure (see page 46).

**sizeof** is used mainly for writing portable code, where the code depends on the number of bytes needed for storing various data types. For example, an integer may occupy 2 bytes on one machine but 4 bytes on another. Using **sizeof (int)** (instead of 2 or 4) in your program ensures that the program will work on either machine.

**sizeof** is used quite often with the functions **malloc** and **calloc**. For example, the statement:

```
double *dp = malloc(sizeof (double));
```

allocates enough storage for storing a **double** variable and assigns the address of the first byte to **dp**.

Another example is

```
float *fp = calloc(10, sizeof (float));
```

Here, storage is allocated for **10 float**s and the address of the first is stored in **fp**.

One can also use type names defined with **typedef** as the argument to **sizeof**. Using the declarations above,

```
np = malloc(sizeof (Node));
```

allocates enough storage for one Node structure, and assigns the address of the first byte to **np**.

---

### *free*

The function **free** is related to **malloc** and **calloc**. It is used to free storage acquired by calls to **malloc** and **calloc**. Its prototype is

```
void free(void *ptr);
```

and it releases the storage pointed to by **ptr**. For example, to free the storage pointed to by **np**, above, one could use:

```
free(np);
```

Observe that even though **free** expects a **void** pointer, it is not *necessary* to explicitly cast **np** (a **Node** pointer) into a **void** pointer. Of course, it is perfectly acceptable, but a bit cumbersome, to use

```
free((void *) np);
```

It is a **fatal error** to attempt to free storage not obtained by a call to **malloc** or **calloc**.

---

## 4.3 Building a linked list – adding new item at the tail

Consider again the problem of building a linked list of positive integers in the order in which they are given. If the incoming numbers are (0 terminates the data)

```
36 15 52 23 0
```

we want to build the following linked list:

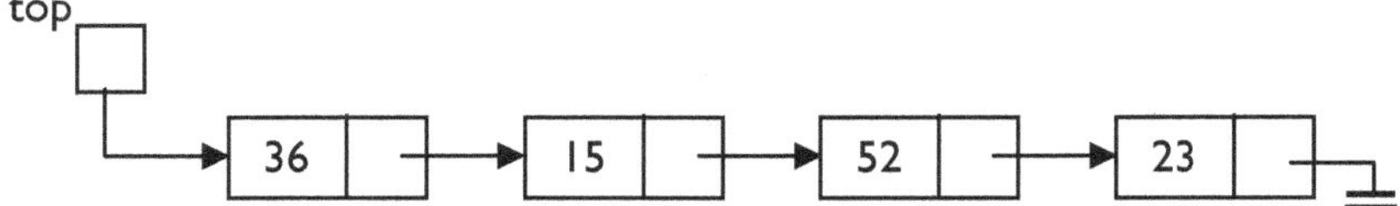


In our solution, we start with an empty list. Our program will reflect this with the statement

```
top = NULL;
```

The symbolic constant **NULL**, denoting the "null pointer" value, is defined in **<stdio.h>** and **<stdlib.h>**.

When we read a new number, we must

- allocate storage for a node;
- put the number in the new node;
- make the new node the last one in the list.

We assume the following declaration for defining a node:

```
typedef struct node {
  int num;
  struct node *next;
} Node, *NodePtr;
```

Let us write a function, **makeNode**, which, given an integer argument, allocates storage for the node, stores the integer in it and returns a pointer to the new node. It will also set the **next** field to **NULL**. Here is **makeNode**:

```
NodePtr makeNode(int n) {
  NodePtr np = (NodePtr) malloc(sizeof (Node));
  np -> num = n;
  np -> next = NULL;
  return np;
}
```

Consider the call

```
makeNode(36);
```

First, storage for a new node is allocated. Assuming an **int** occupies 4 bytes and a pointer occupies 4 bytes, the size of **Node** is 8 bytes. So 8 bytes are allocated starting at address 4000, say. This is illustrated by:

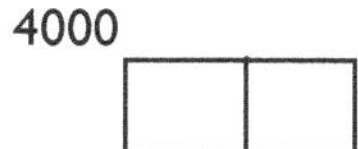


**makeNode** then stores 36 in the **num** field and **NULL** in the **next** field, giving:

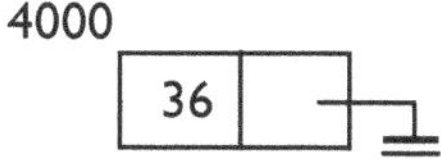


The value 4000 is then returned by **makeNode**.

When we read the first number, we must create a node for it and set **top** to point to the new node. In our example, when we read 36, we must create the following:

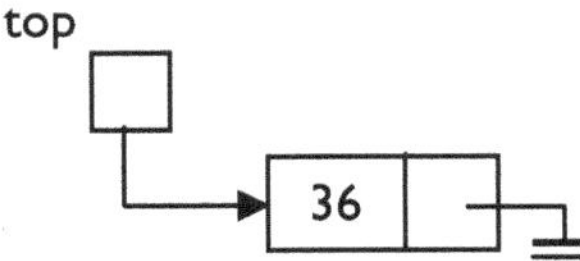


If **n** contains the new number, this can be accomplished with a statement such as

```
if (top == NULL) top = makeNode(n);
```

From the example above, **makeNode** returns 4000 which is stored in **top**. Effectively, **top** now 'points to' the node containing 36. There are no arrows inside the computer but the effect is achieved with the following:

For each subsequent number, we must set the **next** field of the current last node to point to the new node. The new node becomes the last node. Suppose the new number is 15. We must create:

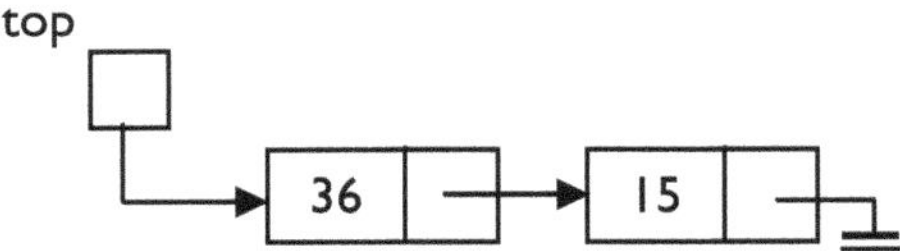


But how do we find the last node of the existing list? One method is to start at the top of the list and follow the **next** pointers until we encounter **NULL**. This is time-consuming if we have to do it for each new number. A better approach is to keep a pointer (**last**, say) to the last node of the list. This pointer is updated as new nodes are added. The code for this could be written like this:

```
np = makeNode(n);    //create a new node
if (top == NULL) top = np;    //set top if first node
else last -> next = np;//set last -> next for other nodes
last = np;      //update last to  new node
```

Suppose there is just one node in the list; this is also the last node. In our example, the value of **last** will be 4000. Suppose the node containing 15 is stored at location 2000. We have the following situation:

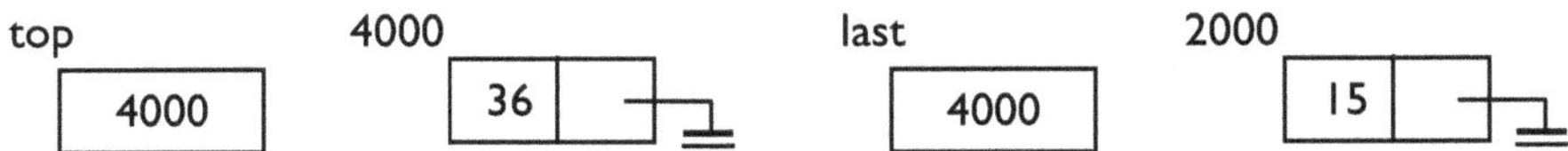


The above code will set the **next** field at location 4000 to 2000 and set **last** to 2000. The following is the result:

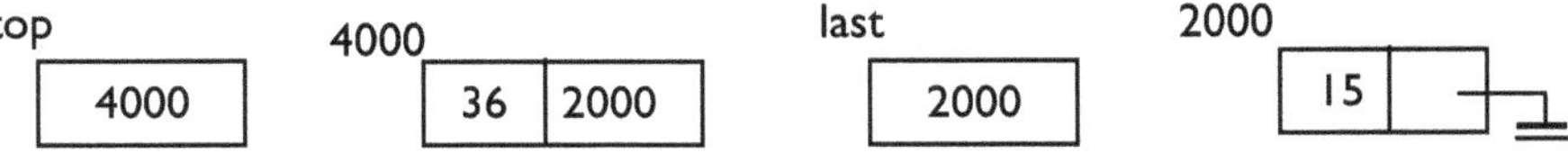

Now **top** (4000) points to the node containing 36; this node's **next** field is 2000 and, hence, points to the node containing 15. This node's **next** field is **NULL**, indicating the end of the list. The value of **last** is 2000, the address of the last node in the list.

Program P4.1 (shown on the next page) reads the numbers and creates the linked list as discussed. In order to verify that the list has been built correctly, we should print its contents. The function **printList** traverses the list from the first node to the last, printing the number at each node.

**Point to note:**

The statement

```
if (scanf("%d", &n) != 1) n = 0;
```

deserves some mention. Normally, we would simply have written

```
scanf("%d", &n);
```

But, here, we take advantage of the value returned by **scanf** to do some error checking.

When **scanf** is called, it stores data in the requested variable(s) and returns the number of values successfully stored. So if we ask it to read one value, it should return 1 unless some error occurred (like end-of-file being reached or non-numeric data found when a number was expected). If we ask it to read 2 values and only one is assigned, it will return 1.

In this program, if a value was not successfully read into **n**, **scanf** will return 0. In this case, **n** is set to 0, forcing an exit from the **while** loop.

## 4.4 Insertion into a linked list

A list with one pointer in each node is called a *one-way linked list*. One important characteristic of such a list is that access to the nodes is via the 'top of list' pointer and the pointer field in each node. (However, other explicit pointers may point to specific nodes in the list, for example, the pointer **last**, above, which pointed to the last node in the list). This means that access is restricted to being sequential. The only way to get to node 4, say, is via nodes 1, 2 and 3. Since we can't access the *k*th node directly, we will not be able, for instance, to perform a binary search on a linked list. The great advantage of a linked list is that it allows for easy insertions and deletions anywhere in the list.

Suppose we want to insert a new node between the second and third nodes. We can view this simply as insertion after the second node. For example, suppose **prev** points to the second node and **np** points to the new node:

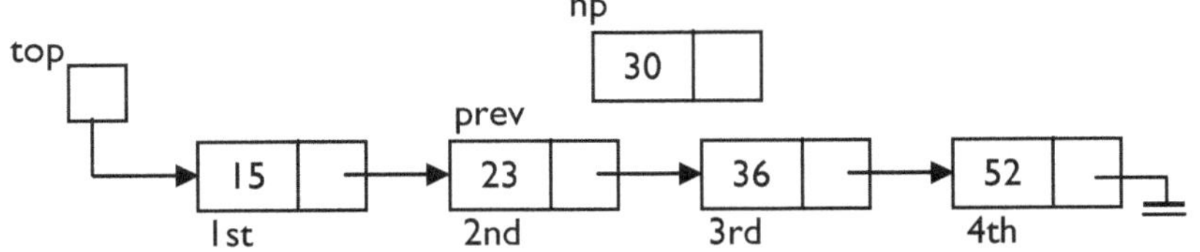


**Program P4.1**

```
#include <stdio.h>
#include <stdlib.h>
typedef struct node {
  int num;
  struct node *next;
} Node, *NodePtr;

main() {
  void printList(NodePtr);
  NodePtr makeNode(int);
  int n;
  NodePtr top, np, last;

  top = NULL;
  if (scanf("%d", &n) != 1) n = 0;
  while (n != 0) {
    np = makeNode(n);          //create a new node containing n
    if (top == NULL) top = np; //set top if first node
    else last -> next = np;    //set last -> next for other nodes
    last = np;                 //update last to  new node
    if (scanf("%d", &n) != 1) n = 0;
  }
  printList(top);
} //end main

NodePtr makeNode(int n) {
  NodePtr np = (NodePtr) malloc(sizeof (Node));
  np -> num = n;
  np -> next = NULL;
  return np;
} //end makeNode

void printList(NodePtr np) {
  while (np != NULL) {  // as long as there's a node
    printf("%d\n", np -> num);
    np = np -> next;  // go on to the next node
  }
} //end printList
```

We can insert the new node by setting its **next** field to point to the third node and the **next** field of the second node to point to the new node. Note that the second node is all we need to do the insertion; *its* **next** field will give us the third node. The insertion can be done with:

```
np -> next = prev -> next;
prev -> next = np;
```

The first statement says 'let the new node point to whatever the second node is pointing at, i.e., the third node'. The second statement says 'let the second node point to the new node'. The net effect is that the new node is inserted between the second and the third. The new node becomes the third node and the original third node becomes the fourth node. This changes the above list into:

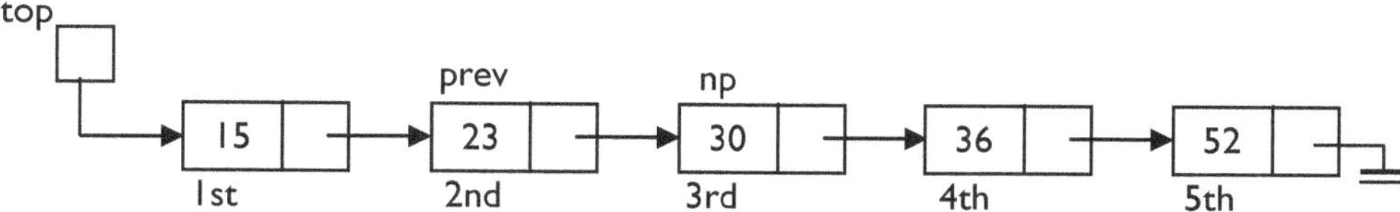


Does this code work if **prev** were pointing at the last node so that we are, in fact, inserting after the last node? Yes. If **prev** is the last node then **prev -> next** is **NULL**. Therefore, the statement

```
np -> next = prev -> next;
```

sets **np -> next** to **NULL** so that the new node becomes the last node. As before, **prev -> next** is set to point to the new node. This is illustrated by changing

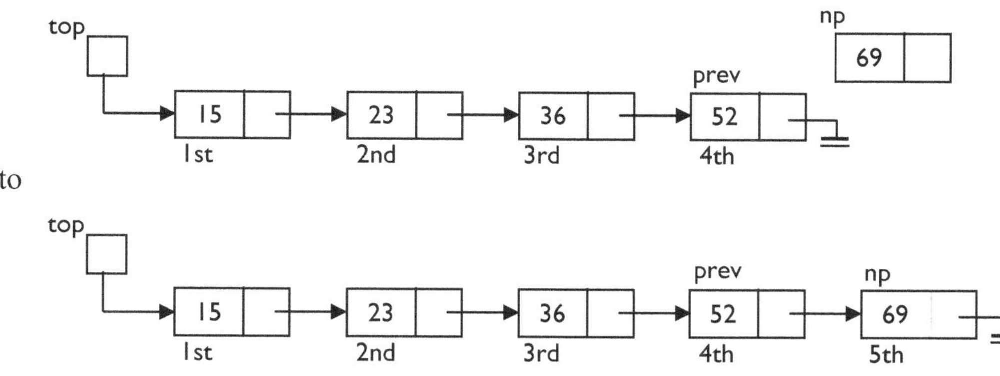


In many situations, it is required to insert a new node at the head of the list. That is, we want to make the new node the first node. Assuming that **np** points to the new node, we want to convert

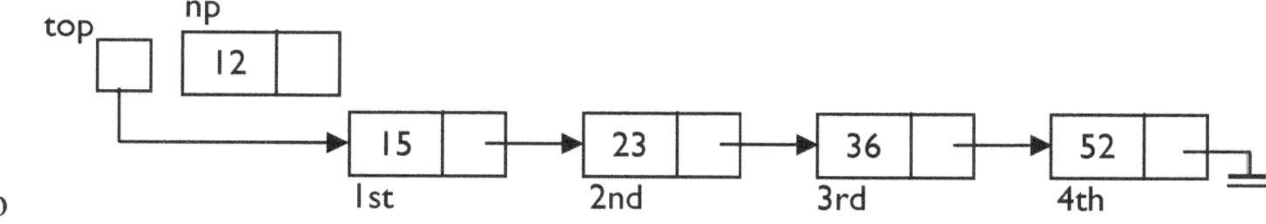


to

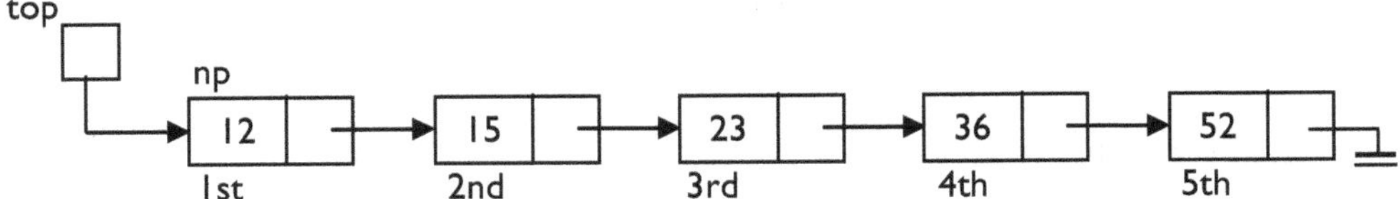


This can be done with the code:

```
np -> next = top;
top = np;
```

The first statement sets the new node to point to whatever **top** is pointing at (that is, the first node), and the second statement updates **top** to point to the new node.

You should observe that the code works even if the list is initially empty (that is, if **top** is **NULL**). In this case, it converts

into

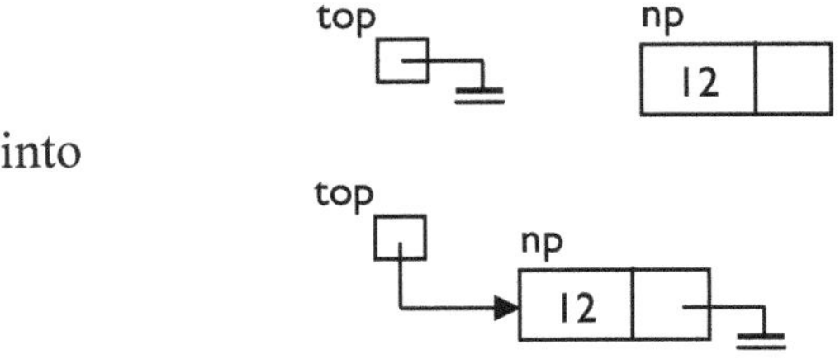


## 4.5 Building a linked list – adding new item at the head

Consider again the problem of building a linked list of positive integers but, this time, we insert each new number at the head of the list rather than at the end. The resulting list will have the numbers in reverse order to how they are given. If the incoming numbers are (0 terminates the data)

```
36 15 52 23 0
```

we want to build the following linked list:

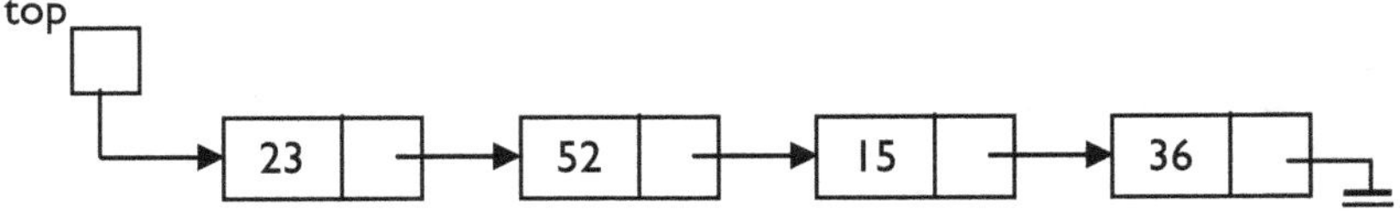


The program to build the list in reverse order is actually simpler than the previous one. We show only the **main** function of Program P4.2 (next page). The rest of the program is identical to Program P4.1.

The only changes are in the **while** loop. As each new number is read, we set its link to point to the first node, and we set **top** to point to the new node, making it the (new) first node.

**Program P4.2**

```
//add new numbers at the head of the list
main() {
  void printList(NodePtr);
  NodePtr makeNode(int);
  int n;
  NodePtr top, np;
  top = NULL;
  if (scanf("%d", &n) != 1) n = 0;
  while (n != 0) {
    np = makeNode(n);          //create a new node containing n
    np -> next = top;          //set link of new node to first node
    top = np;                  //set top to point to new node
    if (scanf("%d", &n) != 1) n = 0;
  }
  printList(top);
} //end main
```

Program P4.1 inserts incoming numbers at the tail of the list. This is an example of adding an item to a *queue*. A queue is a linear list in which insertions occur at one end and deletions (see next) occur at the other end.

Program P4.2 inserts incoming numbers at the head of the list. This is an example of adding an item to a *stack*. A stack is a linear list in which insertions and deletions occur *at the same end*. In stack terminology, when we add an item, we say the item is *pushed* onto the stack. Deleting an item from a stack is referred to as *popping* the stack.

## 4.6 Deletion from a linked list

Deleting a node from the top of a linked list is accomplished by

```
top = top -> next;
```

This says let **top** point to whatever the first node was pointing at (that is, the second node, if any). Since **top** is now pointing at the second node, effectively, the first node has been deleted from the list. This statement changes

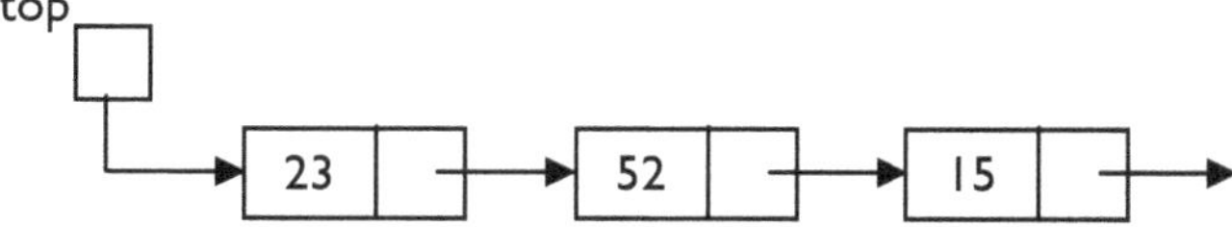


to

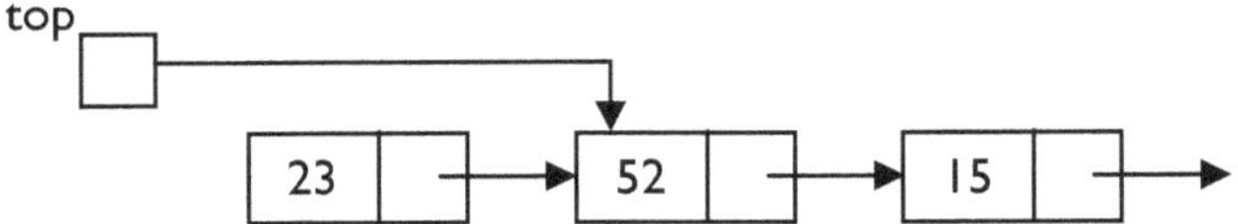


Of course, before we delete, we should check that there *is* something to delete, that **top** is not **NULL**.

If there is only one node in the list, deleting it will result in the empty list; **top** will become **NULL**.

To delete an arbitrary node from a linked list requires more information. Suppose **curr** (for 'current') points to the node to be deleted. Deleting this node requires that we change the **next** field of the *previous* node. This means we must know the pointer to the previous node; suppose it is **prev** (for 'previous'). Then deletion of node **curr** can be accomplished by

```
prev -> next = curr -> next;
```

This changes

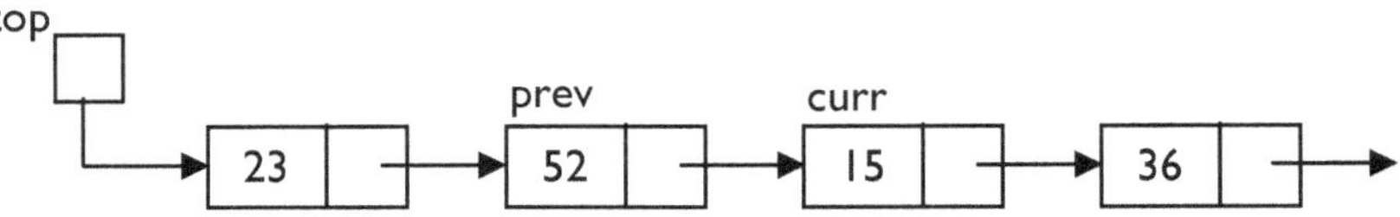


to

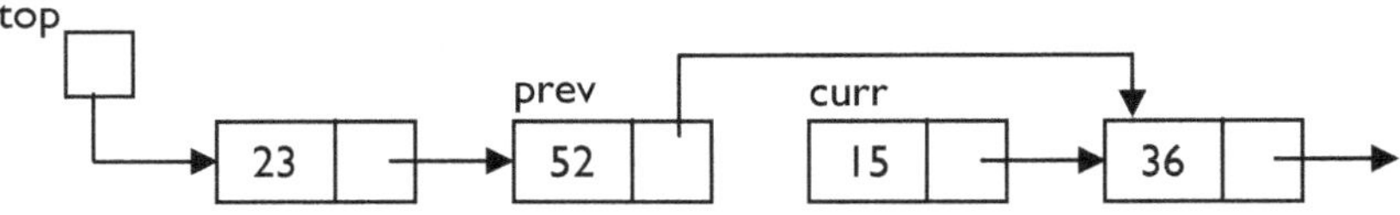


Effectively, the node pointed to by **curr** is no longer in the list—it has been deleted.

One may wonder what happens to nodes which have been deleted. In our discussion above, 'deletion' meant 'logical deletion', that is, as far as processing the list is concerned, the deleted nodes are not present. But the nodes are still in memory, occupying storage, even though we may have lost the pointers to them.

If we have a large list in which many deletions have occurred, then there will be a lot of 'deleted' nodes scattered all over memory. These nodes occupy storage even though they will never, and cannot, be processed. We may need to delete them physically from memory.

C provides us with a function, **free**, to free the storage space occupied by nodes which we need to delete. The space to be freed should have been obtained by a call to **malloc** or **calloc**. The function call **free(p)** frees the space pointed to by **p**.

To illustrate its use, deleting the first node of the list can be accomplished by

```
old = top;             // save the pointer to the node to be deleted
top = top -> next;     // set top to point to the 2nd node, if any
free(old);             // free the space occupied by the first node
```

where **old** is the same kind of pointer as **top**.

To delete a node from elsewhere in the list where **curr** points to the node to be deleted and **prev** points to the previous node, we can use:

```
prev -> next = curr -> next;   // logical deletion
free(curr);                    // free the space occupied by the deleted node
```

The **free** statement will change

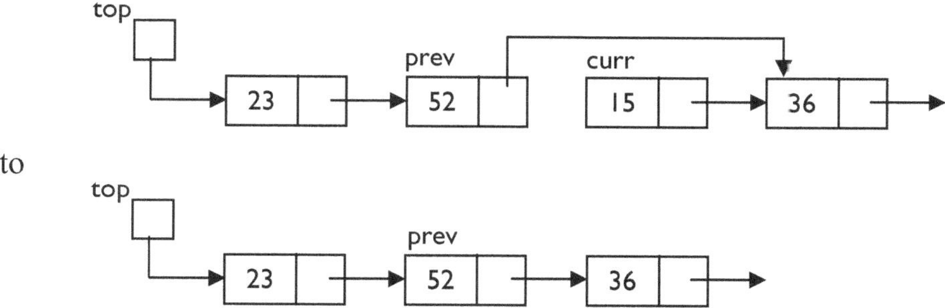


The storage occupied by **curr** no longer exists as far as our program is concerned.

## 4.7 Building a sorted linked list

As a third possibility, suppose we want to build the list of numbers so that it is always sorted in ascending order. If the incoming numbers are (0 terminates the data)

```
36 15 52 23 0
```

we want to build the following list:

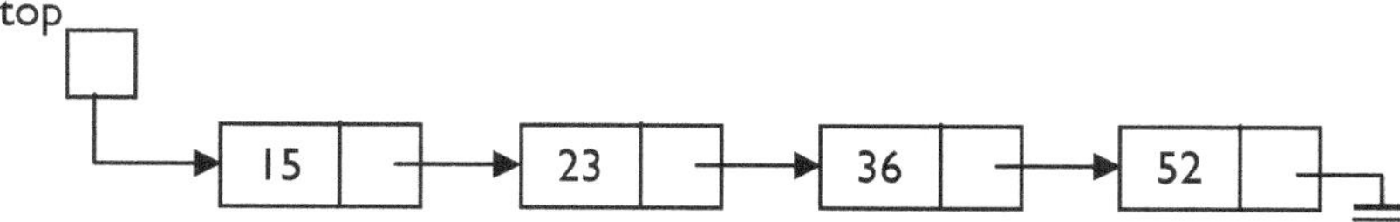


When a new number is read, it is inserted in the existing list (which is initially empty) in its proper place. The first number is simply added to the empty list.

Each subsequent number is compared with the numbers in the existing list. As long as the new number is greater than a number in the list, we move down the list until the new number is smaller than, or equal to, an existing number or we come to the end of the list.

To facilitate the insertion of the new number, before we leave a node and move on to the next one, we must save the pointer to it in case the new number must be inserted after this node. However, we can only know this when we compare the new number with the number in the next node.

To illustrate these ideas, consider the sorted list

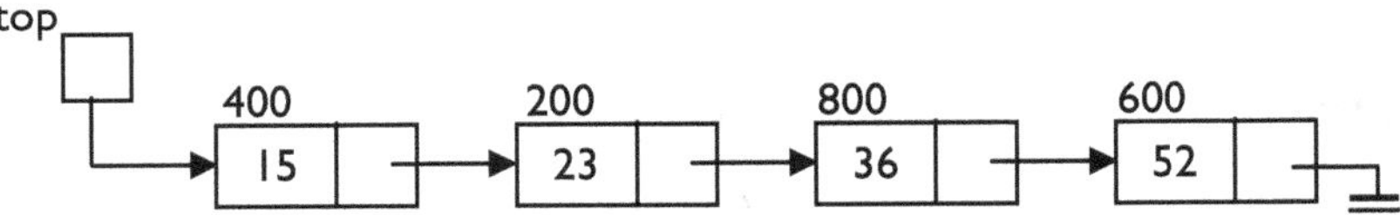


and suppose we want to add a new number (30, say) to the list so that it remains sorted. Assume the number above a node is the address of the node. Thus the value of **top** is 400.

First, we compare 30 with 15. It is bigger, so we move on to the next number, 23, saving the address (400) of 15.

Next, we compare 30 with 23. It is bigger, so we move on to the next number, 36, saving the address (200) of 23. We no longer need the address (400) of 15.

Next, we compare 30 with 36. It is smaller, so we have found the number *before* which we must insert 30. This is the same as inserting 30 *after* 23. Since we had saved the address of 23, we can now perform the insertion.

We will use the following code to process the new number, **n**:

```
prev = NULL;
curr = top;
while (curr != NULL && n > curr -> num) {
  prev = curr;
  curr = curr -> next;
}
```

Initially, **prev** is **NULL** and **curr** is 400. The insertion of 30 proceeds as follows:

- 30 is compared with **curr -> num**, 15. It is bigger so we set **prev** to **curr** (400) and set **curr** to **curr -> next**, 200; **curr** is not **NULL**.
- 30 is compared with **curr -> num**, 23. It is bigger so we set **prev** to **curr** (200) and set **curr** to **curr -> next**, 800; **curr** is not **NULL**.
- 30 is compared with **curr -> num**, 36. It is smaller so we exit the **while** loop with **prev** being 200 and **curr** being 800.

We have the following situation:

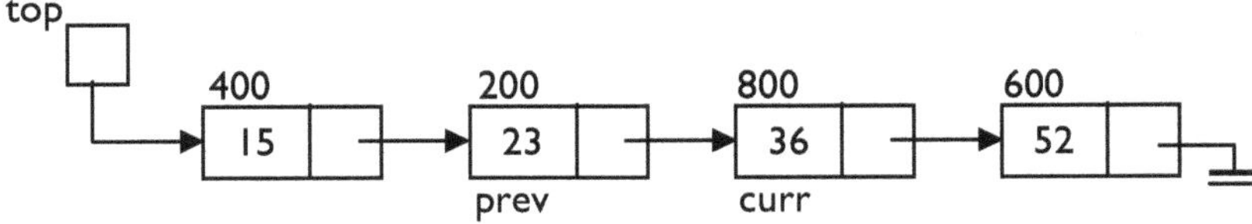

If the new number is stored in a node pointed to by **np**, we can now add it to the list with the following code:

```
np -> next = curr;  //we could also use prev -> next for curr
prev -> next = np;
```

This will change

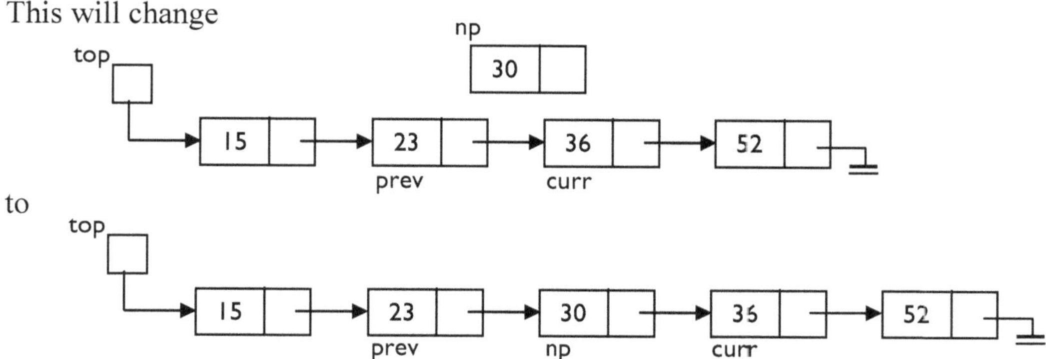


to

top

| 15 | 23 | 30 | 36 | 52 |
|---|---|---|---|---|
| | prev | np | curr | |

As an exercise, verify that this code will work if the number to be added is bigger than all the numbers in the list. Hint: when will the **while** loop exit?

If the number to be added is *smaller* than all the numbers in the list, it must be added at the head of the list and becomes the new first node in the list. This means that the value of **top** has to be changed to the new node.

The **while** loop above will work in this case as well. The **while** condition will be false on the very first test (since **n** will be smaller than **curr -> num**). On exit, we simply test if **prev** is *still* **NULL**; if it is, the new node must be inserted at the top of the list.

If the list were initially empty, the **while** loop will exit immediately (since **curr** will be **NULL**). In this case also, the new node must be inserted at the top of the list, becoming the only node in the list.

Program P4.3 contains all the details. The insertion of a new node in its proper position in the list is delegated to the function **addInPlace.** This function returns a pointer to the top of the modified list.

**Program P4.3**

```
#include <stdio.h>
#include <stdlib.h>

typedef struct node {
   int num;
   struct node *next;
} Node, *NodePtr;

main() {
   void printList(NodePtr);
```

```
  NodePtr addInPlace(NodePtr, int);
  int n;
  NodePtr top = NULL;
  if (scanf("%d", &n) != 1) n = 0;
  while (n != 0) {
    top = addInPlace(top, n);
    if (scanf("%d", &n) != 1) n = 0;
  }
  printList(top);
} //end main

NodePtr addInPlace(NodePtr top, int n) {
// This functions inserts n in its ordered position in a (possibly empty)
// list pointed to by top, and returns a pointer to the new list
  NodePtr np, curr, prev, makeNode(int);

  np = makeNode(n);
  prev = NULL;
  curr = top;
  while (curr != NULL && n > curr -> num) {
    prev = curr;
    curr = curr -> next;
  }
  if (prev == NULL) { //new number must be added at the top
    np -> next = top;
    return np; //the top of the list has changed to the new node
  }
  np -> next = curr;
  prev -> next = np;
  return top; //the top of the list has not changed
} //end addInPlace

NodePtr makeNode(int n) {
  NodePtr np = (NodePtr) malloc(sizeof (Node));
  np -> num = n;
  np -> next = NULL;
  return np;
} // end makeNode

void printList(NodePtr np) {
  while (np != NULL) {  // as long as there's a node
    printf("%d\n", np -> num);
    np = np -> next;  // go on to the next node
  }
} //end printList
```

## 4.8 Example - palindrome

Consider the problem of determining if a given string is a *palindrome* (the same when spelt forwards or backwards). Examples of palindromes (ignoring case, punctuation and spaces) are:

```
civic
Racecar
Madam, I'm Adam.
A man, a plan, a canal, Panama.
```

If all the letters were of the same case (upper or lower) and the string (**word**, say) contained no spaces or punctuation marks, we *could* solve the problem as follows:

```
compare the first and last letters
if they are different, the string is not a palindrome
if they are the same, compare the second and second to last letters
if they are different, the string is not a palindrome
if they are the same, compare the third and third to last letters
```

and so on; we continue until we find a non-matching pair (and it's not a palindrome) or there are no more pairs to compare (and it is a palindrome).

This method is efficient but it requires us to be able to access any letter in the word directly. This is possible if the word is stored in an array and we use a subscript to access any letter. However, if the letters of the word are stored in a linked list, we cannot use this method since we can only access the letters sequentially.

In order to illustrate how linked lists may be manipulated, we will use linked lists to solve the problem using the following idea:

```
(1) store the original phrase in a linked list, one character per node
(2) create another list containing the letters only of the phrase, all
    converted to lowercase and stored in reverse order, call this list1
(3) reverse list1 to get list2
(4) compare list1 with list2, letter by letter, until we get a mismatch
    (phrase is not a palindrome) or we come to the end of the lists
    (phrase is a palindrome)
```

Consider the phrase **Damn Mad!**; this will be stored as:

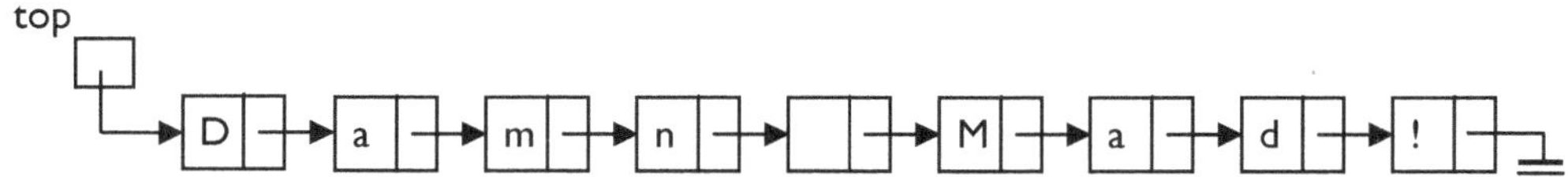


Step (2), above, will convert this to

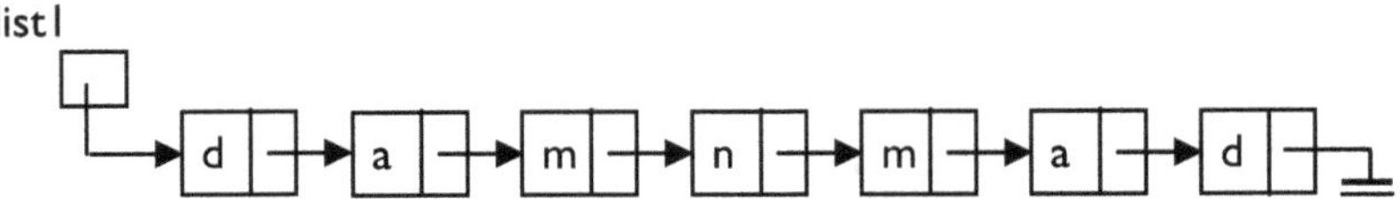


Step (3), above, will reverse this list to get

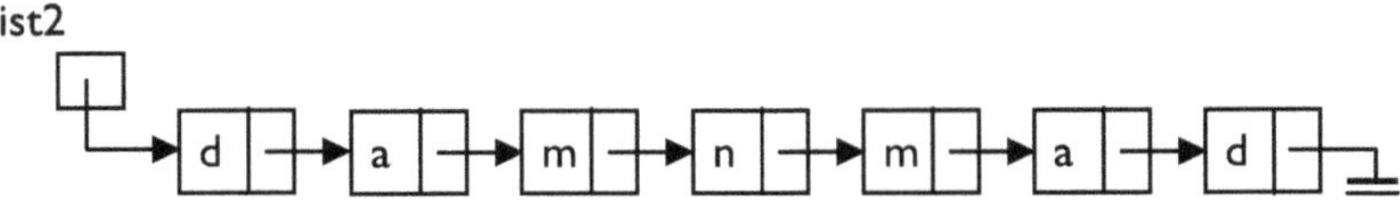


Comparing **list1** and **list2** will reveal that **Damn Mad!** is a palindrome.

We will write a program which prompts the user to type a phrase and tells her if it is a palindrome or not. It then prompts for another phrase. To stop, the user must press "Enter" only.

We will write a function, **getPhrase**, which will read the data and store the characters of the phrase in a linked list, one character per node. The function will return a pointer to the list. This function must build the linked list in the order in which the characters are read—each new character is added at the end of the list.

We will write another function, **reverseLetters**, which, given a pointer to a list of characters, creates another list containing the letters only, all converted to lowercase and stored in reverse order. As each letter is encountered, it is converted to lowercase and added to the *front* of the new list.

To complete the job, we will write a function, **compare**, which implements step (4), above.

These functions are shown in Program P4.4 (next page) which solves the palindrome problem. The following is a sample run of the program:

```
Type a phrase. (To stop, press "Enter" only): Damn Mad!
is a palindrome
Type a phrase. (To stop, press "Enter" only): So Many Dynamos!
is a palindrome
Type a phrase. (To stop, press "Enter" only): Rise to vote, sir.
is a palindrome
Type a phrase. (To stop, press "Enter" only): Thermostat
is not a palindrome
Type a phrase. (To stop, press "Enter" only): A Toyota's a Toyota.
is a palindrome
Type a phrase. (To stop, press "Enter" only):
```

**Program P4.4**

```
#include <stdio.h>
#include <stdlib.h>
#include <ctype.h>

typedef struct node {
  char ch;
  struct node * next;
} Node, *NodePtr;

main() {
  NodePtr getPhrase();
  NodePtr reverseLetters(NodePtr);
  int compare(NodePtr, NodePtr);
  NodePtr phrase, s1, s2;

  printf("Type a phrase. (To stop, press 'Enter' only): ");
  phrase = getPhrase();
  while (phrase != NULL) {
    s1 = reverseLetters(phrase);
    s2 = reverseLetters(s1);
    if (compare(s1, s2) == 0) printf("is a palindrome\n");
    else printf("is not a palindrome\n");
    printf("Type a word. (To stop, press 'Enter' only): ");
    phrase = getPhrase();
  }
} //end main

NodePtr getPhrase() {
  NodePtr top = NULL, last, np;
  char c = getchar();
  while (c != '\n') {
    np = (NodePtr) malloc(sizeof(Node));
    np -> ch = c;
    np -> next = NULL;
    if (top == NULL) top = np;
    else last -> next = np;
    last = np;
    c = getchar();
  }
  return top;
} //end getPhrase
```

```
NodePtr reverseLetters(NodePtr top) {
  NodePtr rev = NULL, np;
  char c;
  while (top != NULL) {
    c = top -> ch;
    if (isalpha(c)) { // add to new list
      np = (NodePtr) malloc(sizeof(Node));
      np -> ch = tolower(c);
      np -> next = rev;
      rev = np;
    }
    top = top -> next; //go to next character of phrase
  }
  return rev;
} //end reverseLetter

int compare(NodePtr s1, NodePtr s2) {
//return -1 if s1 < s2, +1 if s1 > s2 and 0 if s1 = s2
  while (s1 != NULL) {
    if (s1 -> ch < s2 -> ch) return -1;
    else if (s1 -> ch > s2 -> ch) return 1;
    s1 = s1 -> next;
    s2 = s2 -> next;
  }
  return 0;
}
```

## 4.9 Merging two sorted linked lists

In Section 1.8, we considered the problem of merging two ordered lists. There, we showed how to solve the problem when the lists were stored in arrays. We now show how to solve the same problem when the lists are stored as linked lists.

Suppose the given lists are:

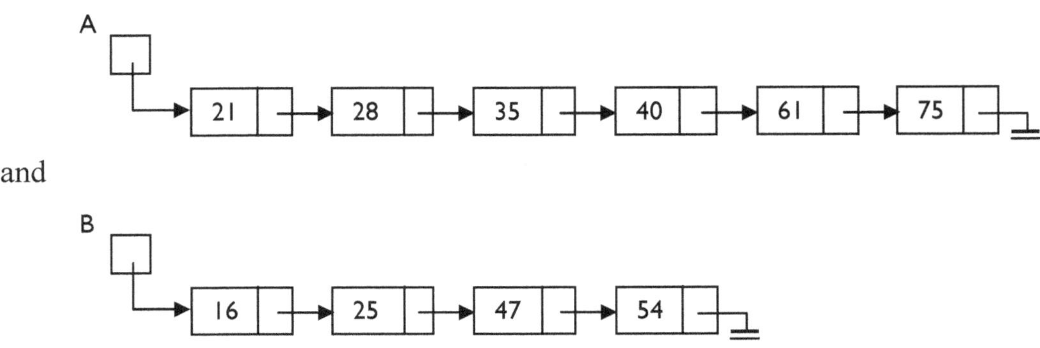

We wish to create one linked list with all the numbers in ascending order, thus:

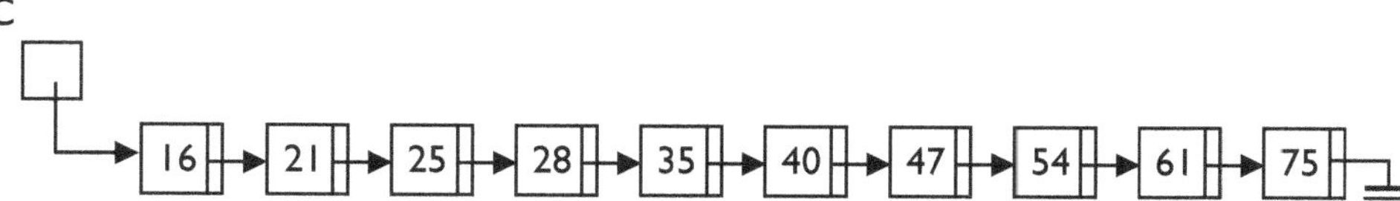


We *could* create the merged list by creating a new node for each number that we add to the list **C**. In other words, we leave the lists **A** and **B** untouched. However, we will perform the merge by *not* creating any new nodes. All numbers will remain in their original nodes. We will simply adjust pointers to create the merged list. At the end, the lists **A** and **B** will no longer exist.

We will use the same algorithm that we used on page 20. Here it is for easy reference:

```
while (at least one number remains in A and B) {
  if (smallest in A < smallest in B)
    add smallest in A to C
    move on to next number in A
  else
    add smallest in B to C
    move on to next number in B
  endif
}
if (A has ended) add remaining numbers in B to C
else add remaining numbers in A to C
```

We assume that the nodes of the lists are defined as:

```
typedef struct node {
  int num;
  struct node *next;
} Node, *NodePtr;
```

and **A**, **B** and **C** are declared as:

```
NodePtr A, B, C = NULL;
```

**A** and **B** point to the given lists and **C** will point to the merged list. Initially, **C** is **NULL**. Each new number must be added at the tail of C. To make this easy to do, we will keep a pointer to the current last node in **C** (we call it **last**).

The above algorithm translates into the code shown at the top of the next page.

Note the last **if** statement and how easy it is to "add the remaining elements" of a list to **C**. All we have to do is set the current last node of **C** to point to the list (**A** or **B**).

```
while (A != NULL && B != NULL) {
  if (A -> num < B -> num) {
    //add node pointed to by A to the tail of C;
    A = A -> next ;
  }
  else {
    //add node pointed to by B to the tail of C;
    B = B -> next ;
  }
}
if (A == NULL) last -> next = B;
else last -> next = A;
```

To complete the translation, we must show how to add a node (pointed to by **N**, say) to the tail of **C**. If **C** is empty, **N** becomes the only node in the list. If **C** is not empty, the current last node of **C** is set to point to **N**. In either case, **N** becomes the current last node of **C**. Thus,

```
//add node pointed to by A to the tail of C;
```

is translated into:

```
if (C == NULL) C = A; else last -> next = A;
last = A;
```

The case for adding the node pointed to by **B** is handled by replacing **A** with **B**.

In Program P4.5 (next page), we write a function, **merge**, which, given the sorted lists **A** and **B**, performs the merge and returns a pointer to the merged list. We test **merge** by using the code from Program P4.1 (page 80) to create two sorted lists, merge them and print the merged list.

Recall that Program P4.1 builds a list in the order in which the numbers are supplied. Thus, you must enter the numbers for a list in ascending order. As an exercise, you can use code from Program P4.3 to build the lists in ascending order regardless of the order in which the numbers are supplied.

A sample run of Program P4.5 is shown below:

```
Enter numbers for the first list (0 to end)
2 4 6 8 10 12 0
Enter numbers for the second list (0 to end)
1 3 5 7 0

The merged list is
1 2 3 4 5 6 7 8 10 12
```

**Program P4.5**

```
#include <stdio.h>
#include <stdlib.h>
typedef struct node {
  int num;
  struct node *next;
} Node, *NodePtr;

main() {
  void printList(NodePtr);
  NodePtr makeList(void);
  NodePtr merge(NodePtr, NodePtr);
  NodePtr A, B;

  printf("Enter numbers for the first list (0 to end)\n");
  A = makeList();
  printf("Enter numbers for the second list (0 to end)\n");
  B = makeList();
  printf("\nThe merged list is\n");
  printList(merge(A, B));
} //end main

NodePtr makeList() {
  NodePtr makeNode(int), np, top, last;
  int n;
  top = NULL;
  if (scanf("%d", &n) != 1) n = 0;
  while (n != 0) {
    np = makeNode(n);          //create a new node containing n
    if (top == NULL) top = np;          //set top if first node
    else last -> next = np;     //set last -> next for other nodes
    last = np; //update last to  new node
    if (scanf("%d", &n) != 1) n = 0;
  }
  return top;
} //end makeList

NodePtr makeNode(int n) {
  NodePtr np = (NodePtr) malloc(sizeof (Node));
  np -> num = n;
  np -> next = NULL;
  return np;
} //end makeNode
```

```
void printList(NodePtr np) {
  while (np != NULL) { // as long as there's a node
    printf("%d ", np -> num);
    np = np -> next; // go on to the next node
  }
  printf("\n\n");
} //end printList

NodePtr merge(NodePtr A, NodePtr B) {
  NodePtr C = NULL, last;
  while (A != NULL && B != NULL) {
    if (A -> num < B -> num) {
      if (C == NULL) C = A; else last -> next = A;
      last = A;
      A = A -> next ;
    }
    else {
      if (C == NULL) C = B; else last -> next = B;
      last = B;
      B = B -> next ;
    }
  } //end while
  if (A == NULL) last -> next = B;
  else last -> next = A;
  return C;
} //end merge
```

## Exercises 4

1. Write a function which, given a pointer to a linked list of integers, returns 1 if the list is sorted in ascending order and 0, otherwise.
2. Write code to reverse the nodes of a linked list by manipulating pointer fields only. No new nodes must be created.
3. Write a function to sort a linked list of integers as follows:
   (a) Find the largest value in the list.
   (b) Delete it from its position and insert it at the head of the list.
   (c) Starting from what is now the second element, repeat (a) and (b).
   (d) Starting from what is now the third element, repeat (a) and (b).

   Continue until the list is sorted.
4. Write a function to free all the nodes of a given linked list.
5. Write a function which takes 3 arguments—a pointer to a linked list of integers, and two integers **n** and **j**—and inserts **n** after the **j**th element of the list. If **j** is 0, **n** is inserted at the head of the list. If **j** is greater than the number of elements in the list, **n** is inserted after the last one.

6. The characters of a string are held on a linked list, one character per node.
   (a) Write a function which, given a pointer to a string and two characters, **c1** and **c2**, replaces all occurrences of **c1** with **c2**.
   (b) Write a function which, given a pointer to a string and a character, **c**, deletes all occurrences of **c** from the string. Return a pointer to the modified string.
   (c) Write a function which, given a pointer to a string, converts all lowercase letters to uppercase, leaving all the other characters unchanged.
   (d) Write a function which creates a new list consisting of the letters only in the given list, all converted to lowercase and stored in alphabetical order. Return a pointer to the new list.
   (e) Write a function which, given pointers to two strings, determines if the first is a substring of the other.
7. Write a function which, given an integer **n**, converts **n** to binary, and stores each bit in one node of a linked list with the *least* significant bit at the head of the list and the *most* significant bit at the tail. For example, given `13`, the bits are stored in the order `1 0 1 1`, from head to tail. Return a pointer to the head of the list.
8. Write a function which, given a pointer to a linked list of bits stored as in 7, *traverses the list once* and returns the decimal equivalent of the binary number.
9. You are given two pointers **b1** and **b2** each pointing to a binary number stored as in 7. You must return a pointer to a newly created linked list representing the binary sum of the given numbers with the *least* significant bit at the head of the list and the *most* significant bit at the tail of the list. Write functions to do this in two ways:
   (i) using the functions from 7 and 8
   (ii) performing a 'bit by bit' addition
10. Repeat exercises 7, 8 and 9 but, this time, store the bits with the *most* significant bit at the head of the list and the *least* significant bit at the tail.
11. Two words are anagrams if one word can be formed by rearranging all the letters of the other word, for example: treason, senator. A word is represented as a linked list with one letter per node of the list.

    Write a function which, given **w1** and **w2** each pointing to a word of lowercase letters, returns `1` if the words are anagrams and `0` if they are not. Base your algorithm on the following: for each letter in **w1**, search **w2** for it; if found, delete it and continue; otherwise, return `0`.
12. The children's game of 'count-out' is played as follows: $n$ children (numbered 1 to $n$) are arranged in a circle. A sentence consisting of $m$ words is used to eliminate one child at a time until one child is left.

    Starting at child 1, the children are counted from 1 to $m$ and the $m$th child is eliminated. Starting with the child after the one just eliminated, the children are again counted from 1 to $m$ and the $m$th child eliminated. This is repeated until one child is left. Counting is done circularly and eliminated children are not counted.

    Write a program to read values for $n$ and $m$ and print the number of the last remaining child. Use a linked list to hold the children.

    Hint: let the last node point to the first, creating a *circular* list.
13. The digits of an integer are held on a linked list in reverse order, one digit per node. Write a function which, given pointers to two integers, performs a digit by digit addition and returns a pointer to the digits of the sum stored in reverse order. Note: this idea can be used to add arbitrarily large integers.

# 5 Stacks and Queues

## In this chapter, we will explain:

- the notion of an abstract data type
- what is a stack
- how to implement a stack using an array
- how to implement a stack using a linked list
- how to implement a stack for a general data type
- how to create a header file for use by other programs
- how to convert an expression from infix to postfix
- how to evaluate an arithmetic expression
- what is a queue
- how to implement a queue using an array
- how to implement a queue using a linked list

## 5.1 Abstract data types

We are familiar with the notion of declaring variables of a given type (**double**, say) and then performing operations on those variables (e.g. add, multiply, assign) *without needing to know **how** those variables are stored inside the computer*. In this scenario, the compiler designer can change the way a **double** variable is stored and a programmer would *not* have to change his programs which use **double** variables. This is an example of an *abstract data type*.

An *abstract data type* is one which allows a user to manipulate the data type without any knowledge of *how* the data type is represented inside the computer. In other words, as far as the *user* is concerned, all he needs to know are the *operations* which can be performed on the data type. The person who is *implementing* the data type is free to change its implementation without affecting the users.

In this chapter, we will show how to implement stacks and queues as abstract data types.

## 5.2 Stacks

A *stack* as a linear list in which items are added at one end and deleted from the same end. The idea is illustrated by a "stack of plates" placed on a table, one on top the other. When a plate is needed, it is taken from the top of the stack. When a plate is washed, it is added at the top of the stack. Note that if a plate is now needed, this 'newest' plate is the one that is taken. A stack exhibits the "last in, first out" property.

To illustrate the stack ideas, we will use a stack of integers. Our goal is to define a *data type* called a *stack* so that a user can declare variables of this type and manipulate it in various ways. What are some of these ways?

As indicated above, we will need to add an item to the stack—the term commonly used is *push*. We will also need to take an item off the stack—the term commonly used is *pop*.

Before we attempt to take something off the stack, it is a good idea to ensure that the stack *has* something on it, that it is not empty. We will need an operation which tests if a stack is empty.

Given these three operations—*push*, *pop* and *empty*—let us illustrate how they can be used to read some numbers and print them in *reverse* order. For example, given the numbers

```
36 15 52 23
```

we wish to print

```
23 52 15 36
```

We can solve this problem by adding each new number to the top of a stack, `S`. After all the numbers have been placed on the stack, we can picture the stack as as follows:

```
23 (top of stack)
52
15
36 (bottom of stack)
```

Next, we remove the numbers, one at a time, printing each as it is removed.

We will need a way of telling when all the numbers have been read. We will use 0 to end the data. The logic for solving this problem can be expressed as:

```
create an empty stack, S
read(num)
while (num != 0) {
  push num onto S
  read(num)
}
while (S is not empty) {
  pop S into num //store the number at the top of S in num
  print num
}
```

We now show how we can implement a stack of integers and its operations.

### 5.2.1 *Implementing a stack using an array*

In the array implementation of a stack (of integers), we use an integer array (**ST**, say) for storing the numbers and an integer variable (**top**, say) which contains the subscript of the item at the top of the stack.

Since we are using an array, we will need to know its size in order to declare it. We will need to have some information about the problem to determine a reasonable size for the array. We will use the symbolic constant, **MaxStack**. If we attempt to push more than **MaxStack** elements onto the stack, a *stack overflow* error will be reported.

We can use the following to define the data type **Stack**:

```
typedef struct {
  int top;
  int ST[MaxStack];
} StackType, *Stack;
```

Valid values for **top** will range from 0 to **MaxStack - 1**. When we initialize a stack, we will set **top** to the "invalid subscript", -1.

We can now declare a "stack variable", **S**, with

```
Stack S;
```

Observe that **Stack** is declared as a *pointer* to the structure we call **StackType**. So, for instance, **S** is a pointer to a structure consisting of the variable **top** and the array **ST**. This is necessary since **top** and **ST** would need to be changed by the *push* and *pop* routines and the changes known to the calling function (**main**, say). This can be achieved by passing a *pointer* to them, in effect, the **Stack** variable.

In order to work with a stack, the first task is to create an empty stack. This is done by allocating storage for a **StackType**, assigning its address to a **Stack** variable and setting **top** to -1. We can use the following:

```
Stack initStack() {
  Stack sp = (Stack) malloc(sizeof(StackType));
  sp -> top = -1;
  return sp;
}
```

In **main**, say, we can declare and initialize a stack, **S**, with

```
Stack S = initStack();
```

When this statement is executed, the situation in memory can be represented by:

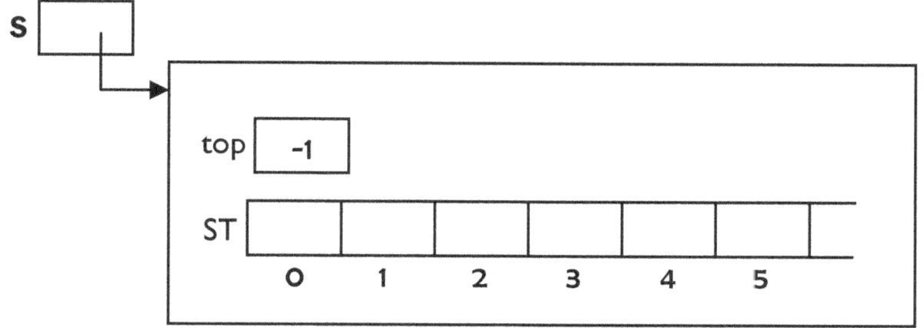


This represents the empty stack. In working with stacks, we will need a function which tells us whether a stack is empty or not. We can use the following:

```
int empty(Stack S) {
  return (S -> top == -1);
}
```

This simply checks whether **top** has the value `-1`.

The major operations on a stack are *push* and *pop*. To push an item, **n**, onto a stack, we must store it in **ST** and update **top** to point to it. The basic idea is:

```
add 1 to top
set ST[top] to n
```

However, we must guard against trying to add something to the stack when it is already full. The stack is full when **top** has the value **MaxStack - 1**, the subscript of the last element. In this case, we will report that the stack is full and halt the program. Here is **push**:

```
void push(Stack S, int n) {
  if (S -> top == MaxStack - 1) {
    printf("\nStack Overflow\n");
    exit(1);
  }
  ++(S -> top);
  S -> ST[S -> top] = n;
}
```

To illustrate, after the numbers 36, 15, 52 and 23 have been pushed onto **S**, our picture in memory looks like this:

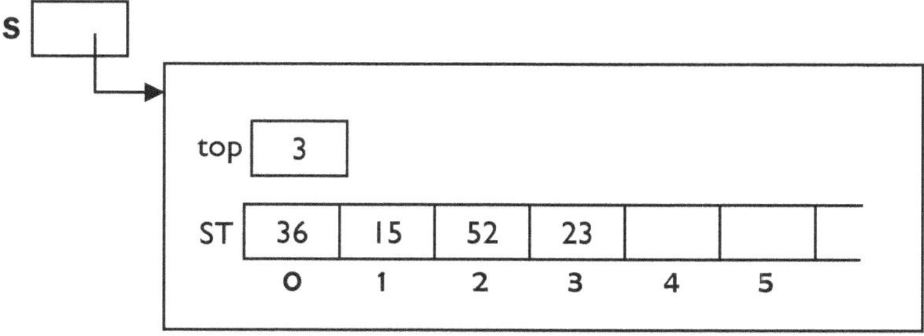

Finally, to pop an item off the stack, we return the value in location **top** and decrease **top** by 1. The basic idea is:

```
set hold to ST[top]
subtract 1 from top
return hold
```

Again, we must guard against trying to take something off an empty stack. What should we do if the stack is empty and **pop** is called? We could simply report an error and halt the program. However, it might be better to return some "rogue" value, indicating that the stack is empty. We take the latter approach in our function, **pop**:

```
int pop(Stack S) {
  if (empty(S)) return RogueValue; //a symbolic constant
  int hold = S -> ST[S -> top];
  --(S -> top);
  return hold;
}
```

Note that even though we have written **pop** to do something reasonable if it is called and the stack is empty, it is better if the programmer establishes that the stack is *not* empty (using the **empty** function) before calling **pop**.

We now write Program P5.1 (below) which reads some numbers, terminated by 0, and prints them in reverse order. The following shows a sample run of the program:

```
Enter some integers, ending with 0
1 2 3 4 5 6 7 8 9 0

Numbers in reverse order
9 8 7 6 5 4 3 2 1
```

It is important to observe that the code in **main** which uses the stack does so via the functions **initStack**, **push**, **pop** and **empty** and makes *no* assumption about *how* the stack elements are stored. This is the hallmark of an abstract data type—it can be used without the user needing to know how it is implemented.

Next, we will implement the stack using a linked list but **main** will remain exactly the same for solving the problem of printing the numbers in reverse order.

**Program P5.1**

```
#include <stdio.h>
#include <stdlib.h>
#define RogueValue -9999
#define MaxStack 10
```

```
typedef struct {
  int top;
  int ST[MaxStack];
} StackType, *Stack;

main() {
  Stack initStack();
  int empty(Stack);
  void push(Stack, int);
  int pop(Stack);
  int n;
  Stack S = initStack();
  scanf("%d", &n);
  while (n != 0) {
    push(S, n);
    scanf("%d", &n);
  }
  while (!empty(S))
    printf("%d ", pop(S));
  printf("\n");
} //end main

Stack initStack() {
  Stack sp = (Stack) malloc(sizeof(StackType));
  sp -> top = -1;
  return sp;
} //end initStack

int empty(Stack S) {
  return (S -> top == -1);
} //end empty

void push(Stack S, int n) {
  if (S -> top == MaxStack - 1) {
    printf("\nStack Overflow\n");
    exit(1);
  }
  ++(S -> top);
  S -> ST[S -> top]= n;
} //end push

int pop(Stack S) {
  if (empty(S)) return RogueValue;
  int hold = S -> ST[S -> top];
  --(S -> top);
  return hold;
} //end pop
```

### 5.2.2 *Implementing a stack using a linked list*

The array implementation of a stack has the advantages of simplicity and efficiency. However, one major disadvantage is the need to know what size to declare the array. Some reasonable guess has to be made but this may turn out to be too small (and the program has to halt) or too big (and storage is wasted).

To overcome this disadvantage, a linked list can be used. Now, we will allocate storage for an element only when it is needed.

The stack is implemented as a linked list with new items added at the head of the list. When we need to pop the stack, the item at the head is removed.

We will define a **Stack** data type as a pointer to the linked list, defined by its "top" variable. So a **Stack** variable points to the variable which points to the first item in the linked list. As in the case of the array implementation, this is necessary so that changes made in the **push** and **pop** routines will be known in the calling function. We will use the following declarations:

```
typedef struct node {
  int num;
  struct node *next;
} Node, *NodePtr;

typedef struct {
  NodePtr top;
} StackType, *Stack;
```

After 36, 15, 52 and 23 (in that order) have been pushed onto a stack, **S**, we can picture it as follows. **S** is a pointer to **top** which is a pointer to the linked list of stack elements.

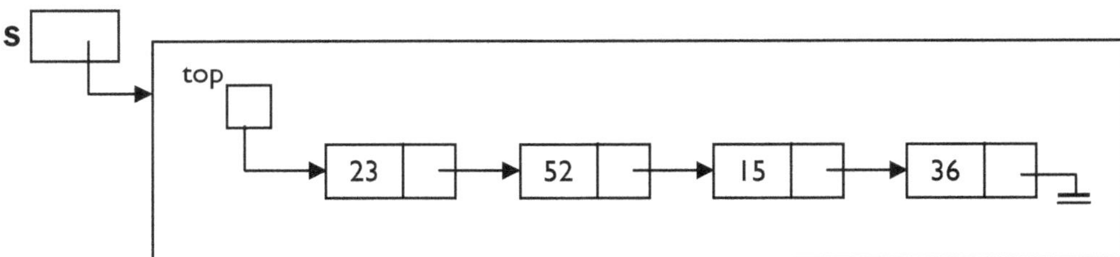


The empty stack is represented by

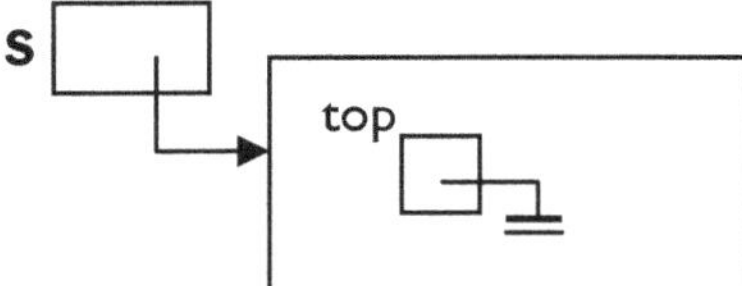

Creating an empty stack involves allocating storage for a **StackType** structure which consists of the single pointer variable, **top**, and setting **top** to **NULL**. Here is the function, **initStack**:

```
Stack initStack() {
  Stack sp = (Stack) malloc(sizeof(StackType));
  sp -> top = NULL;
  return sp;
}
```

We can test for an empty stack with

```
int empty(Stack S) {
  return (S -> top == NULL);
}
```

This simply checks if **top** is **NULL**.

To push an item onto a stack, we need to allocate storage for a node and add it to the head of the list. Here is **push**:

```
void push(Stack S, int n) {
  NodePtr np = (NodePtr) malloc(sizeof(Node));
  np -> num = n;
  np -> next = S -> top;
  S -> top = np;
}
```

To pop an item from the stack, we first check if the stack is empty. If it is, a rogue value is returned. If not, the item at the head of the list is returned and the node containing the item is deleted. Here is **pop**:

```
int pop(Stack S) {
  if (empty(S)) return RogueValue;
  int hold = S -> top -> num;
  NodePtr temp = S -> top;
  S -> top = S -> top -> next;
  free(temp);
  return hold;
}
```

Putting these functions together with **main** from Program P5.1 gives us Program P5.2 (next page) which reads a set of numbers, terminated by 0, and prints them in reverse order.

**Program P5.2**

```
#include <stdio.h>
#include <stdlib.h>
#define RogueValue -9999

typedef struct node {
  int num;
  struct node *next;
} Node, *NodePtr;

typedef struct stackType {
  NodePtr top;
} StackType, *Stack;

main() {...} //same as P5.1, page 103

Stack initStack() {
  Stack sp = (Stack) malloc(sizeof(StackType));
  sp -> top = NULL;
  return sp;
}

int empty(Stack S) {
  return (S -> top == NULL);
}

void push(Stack S, int n) {
  NodePtr np = (NodePtr) malloc(sizeof(Node));
  np -> num = n;
  np -> next = S -> top;
  S -> top = np;
}

int pop(Stack S) {
  if (empty(S)) return RogueValue;
  int hold = S -> top -> num;
  NodePtr temp = S -> top;
  S -> top = S -> top -> next;
  free(temp);
  return hold;
}
```

## 5.3 Creating a stack header file

Now that we have created a set of declarations/functions for manipulating an integer stack, we can put them together in one file so that *any* user can have access to them without having to repeat the code in their program. To illustrate, we create a file called **stack.h**, say, and put the following in it:

```
#include <stdlib.h>
#define RogueValue -9999

typedef struct node {
  int num;
  struct node *next;
} Node, *NodePtr;

typedef struct stackType {
  NodePtr top;
} StackType, *Stack;

Stack initStack() {
  Stack sp = (Stack) malloc(sizeof(StackType));
  sp -> top = NULL;
  return sp;
}

int empty(Stack S) {
  return (S -> top == NULL);
} //end empty

void push(Stack S, int n) {
  NodePtr np = (NodePtr) malloc(sizeof(Node));
  np -> num = n;
  np -> next = S -> top;
  S -> top = np;
} //end push

int pop(Stack S) {
  if (empty(S)) return RogueValue;
  int hold = S -> top -> num;
  NodePtr temp = S -> top;
  S -> top = S -> top -> next;
  free(temp);
  return hold;
} //end pop
```

Next, we put **stack.h** in the "include library" of C functions. Typically, most C compilers will have a folder called **include**. This is the same folder that contains files such as **stdio.h**, **string.h**, etc. Simply put **stack.h** in this folder[3]. Now, any program that wants to use the stack functions must contain the declaration:

```
#include <stack.h>
```

For example, Program P5.2 can now be written as Program P5.3.

**Program P5.3**

```
#include <stdio.h>
#include <stack.h>

main() {
  int n;
  Stack S = initStack();
  printf("Enter some integers, ending with 0\n");
  scanf("%d", &n);
  while (n != 0) {
    push(S, n);
    scanf("%d", &n);
  }
  printf("\nNumbers in reverse order\n");
  while (!empty(S))
    printf("%d ", pop(S));
  printf("\n");
}
```

Note how much shorter this program is, now that the stack declarations/functions are hidden away in **stack.h**.

## 5.4 A general stack type

In order to simplify our presentation, we have worked with a stack of integers. We remind you of those places in the program which are tied to the decision to use integers:

- in the declaration of **Node**, we declare an **int** called **num**;
- in **push**, we pass an **int** argument;
- in **pop**, we return an **int** result.

No changes are needed in **initStack** and **empty**.

---

[3] Some compilers may already have a file called **stack.h**. In this case, you may add your declarations to this file or just use another name for your file.

This means that if we need a stack of characters, say, we will have to change **int** to **char** in all of the above places. Similar changes will have to be made for stacks of other types.

It would be nice if we could minimize the changes needed when a different type of stack is required. We now show how this could be done.

Our first generalization lets us have a stack of *any* type, including structures. So, for instance, if we have a structure representing a fraction (page 36), we can have a stack of fractions. We can also have stacks of primitive types such as **int**, **char** and **double**. To this end, we declare a structure called **StackData**; this structure will contain the field or fields which will comprise a stack element.

Consider the following:

```
typedef struct {
  //declare all the data fields here
  char ch; //for example
} StackData;
```

Whichever kind of stack we want, we declare the data fields within the structure. In the example, above, if we want a stack of characters, we declare one field of type **char**.

Now, a linked list node will consist of two fields: a data field of type **StackData** and a field which points to the next node. Here is its declaration:

```
typedef struct node {
  StackData data;
  struct node *next;
} Node, *NodePtr;
```

The only change from before is that we use **StackData** instead of **int**.

The major change in **push** is in the function heading. We change

```
void push(Stack S, int n)
```

to

```
void push(Stack S, StackData d)
```

In the function body, we change

```
np -> num = n;
```

to

```
np -> data = d;
```

The major change in **pop** is also in the function heading. We change

```
int pop(Stack S)
```

to

```
StackData pop(Stack S)
```

In the function body, we change

```
int hold = S -> top -> num;
```

to

```
StackData hold = S -> top -> data;
```

For variation, we will write pop such that if it is called and the stack is empty, a message is printed and the program halts.

With these changes, it is now easy to change the kind of stack we want to work with. We need change only the declaration of **StackData**, including the field or fields we want for our stack elements.

To illustrate, suppose we want to read a line of data and print it reversed. We need a stack of characters. We declare **StackData** as follows:

```
typedef struct {
  char ch;
} StackData;
```

Suppose the statements in the box on the next page are stored in an "include" file, **stack.h**. The **StackData** declaration is *not* included here. This is desirable since each user may need a different type of stack and must be given the opportunity to declare whatever he wants **StackData** to be. He can do this in his own program as illustrated in Program P5.4 which reads a line of input and prints it reversed.

**Program P5.4**

```
#include <stdio.h>

typedef struct {
  char ch;
} StackData;

#include <stack.h>

main() {
  StackData temp;
  char c;
  Stack S = initStack();
  printf("Type some data and press Enter\n");
  while ((c = getchar()) != '\n') {
    temp.ch = c;
    push(S, temp);
  }
  printf("\nData in reverse order\n");
  while (!empty(S))
    putchar(pop(S).ch);
  putchar('\n');
} //end main
```

```
#include <stdlib.h>

typedef struct node {
  StackData data;
  struct node *next;
} Node, *NodePtr;

typedef struct stackType {
  NodePtr top;
} StackType, *Stack;

Stack initStack() {
  Stack sp = (Stack) malloc(sizeof(StackType));
  sp -> top = NULL;
  return sp;
}

int empty(Stack S) {
  return (S -> top == NULL);
}

void push(Stack S, StackData d) {
  NodePtr np = (NodePtr) malloc(sizeof(Node));
  np -> data = d;
  np -> next = S -> top;
  S -> top = np;
}

StackData pop(Stack S) {
  if (empty(S)) {
    printf("\nAttempt to pop an empty stack\n");
    exit(1);
  }
  StackData hold = S -> top -> data;
  NodePtr temp = S -> top;
  S -> top = S -> top -> next;
  free(temp);
  return hold;
}
```

Note the placement of **#include stack.h**—it comes *after* the declaration of **StackData**. This is necessary since there are functions/declarations in **stack.h** which make reference to **StackData**.

Note also that the stack functions work with the data type **StackData**. Even though we want a "stack of characters", a character must be stored in a **StackData** variable (**temp** is used) before it can be pushed onto the stack. Similarly, **pop** returns a **StackData** value; we must retrieve the **ch** field of the value returned to get at the character.

The following is a sample run of P5.4:

```
Type some data and press Enter
Was it a rat I saw?

Data in reverse order
?was I tar a ti saW
```

As another example, if a programmer needs to work with a stack of fractions, he can use

```
typedef struct {
  int num;
  int den;
} StackData;
```

---

### *5.4.1 Example – convert from decimal to binary*

Consider the problem of converting a positive integer from decimal to binary. We can use an integer stack, **S**, to do this using repeated division by 2 and saving the remainders. Here is the algorithm:

```
initialize S to empty
read the number, n
while (n > 0) {
  push n % 2 onto S
  n = n / 2
}
while (S is not empty) print pop(S)
```

This algorithm is implemented as Program P5.5.

Note, again, that each bit must be stored in a **StackData** variable (**temp** is used). A sample run of P5.5 is shown below:

```
Enter a positive integer: 99

Its binary equivalent is 1100011
```

**Program P5.5**

```
#include <stdio.h>

typedef struct {
  int bit;
} StackData;

#include <stack.h>

main() {
  StackData temp;
  int n;
  Stack S = initStack();
  printf("Enter a positive integer: ");
  scanf("%d", &n);
  while (n > 0) {
    temp.bit = n % 2;
    push(S, temp);
    n = n / 2;
  }
  printf("\nIts binary equivalent is ");
  while (!empty(S))
    printf("%d", pop(S).bit);
  printf("\n");
} //end main
```

## 5.5 How to convert from infix to postfix

Consider the expression: 7 + 3 * 4. What is its value? Without any knowledge about which operation should be performed first, we would probably work out the value from left to right as (7 + 3 = 10) * 4 = 40. However, normal rules of arithmetic state that multiplication *has higher precedence* than addition. This means that, in an expression like the one above, multiplication (*****) is performed before addition (**+**). Knowing this, the value is 7 + 12 = 19.

We can, of course, force the addition to be performed first by using brackets, as in (7 + 3) * 4. Here, the brackets mean that **+** is done first.

These are examples of *infix* expressions; the operator (**+**, *****) is placed *between* its operands. One disadvantage of infix expressions is the need to use brackets to override the normal *precedence rules*.

Another way of representing expressions is to use *postfix* notation. Here, the operator comes *after* its operands and there is no need to use brackets to specify which operations to perform first. For example, the postfix form of

`7 + 3 * 4` is `7 3 4 * +`

and the postfix form of

(7 + 3) * 4 is 7 3 + 4 *

One useful observation is that the operands appear in the same order in both the infix and postfix forms but operators differ in order and placement.

Why is postfix notation useful? As mentioned above, we do not need brackets to specify precedence of operators. More importantly, though, it is a convenient form for evaluating the expression.

Given the postfix form of an expression, it can be evaluated as follows:

```
initialize a stack, S, to empty
while we have not reached the end of the expression
  get the next item, x, from the expression
  if x is an operand, push it onto S
  if x is an operator, pop its operands from S, apply the operator and
        push the result onto S
endwhile
pop S; // this is the value of the expression
```

Consider the expression (7 + 3) * 4 whose postfix form is 7 3 + 4 *. It is evaluated by traversing from left to right:

- the next item is 7; push 7 onto S; S contains 7
- the next item is 3; push 3 onto S; S contains 7 3 (the top is on the right)
- the next item is +; pop 3 and 7 from S; apply + to 7 and 3, giving 10; push 10 onto S; S contains 10
- the next item is 4; push 4 onto S; S contains 10 4
- the next item is *; pop 4 and 10 from S; apply * to 10 and 4, giving 40; push 40 onto S; S contains 40
- we have reached the end of the expression; we pop S, getting 40—the result of the expression.

Note that when operands are popped from the stack, the first one popped is the second operand and the second one popped is the first operand. This does not matter for addition and multiplication, but would be important for subtraction and division. As an exercise, convert the following to postfix form and step through its evaluation using the above algorithm: (7 – 3) * (9 – 8 / 4)

---

The big question, of course, is how do we convert an infix expression to postfix? Before presenting the algorithm, we observe that it will use an "operator" stack. We will also need a "precedence table" which gives the relative precedence of the operators. Given any two operators, the table will tell us if they have the same precedence (like + and -) and, if not, which has greater precedence.

As the algorithm proceeds, it will "output" the postfix form of the given expression.

Here is the algorithm:

1. Initialize a stack of operators, S, to empty
2. Get the next item, **x**, from the infix expression; if none, go to step 8; (x is either an operand, a left bracket, a right bracket or an operator)
3. If **x** is an operand, output **x**
4. If **x** is a left bracket, push it onto S
5. If **x** is a right bracket, pop items off S and output popped items until a left bracket appears on top of S; pop the left bracket and discard
6. If **x** is an operator then

   while (S is not empty) and (a left bracket is not on top of S) and
       (an operator of equal or higher precedence than **x** is on top of S)
       pop S and output popped item
   push **x** onto S
7. Repeat from step 2.
8. Pop S and output popped item until S is empty

You are advised to step through the algorithm for the following expressions:

```
3 + 5
7 - 3 + 8
7 + 3 * 4
(7 + 3) * 4
(7 + 3) / (8 - 2 * 3)
(7 - 8 / 2 / 2) * ((7 - 2) * 3 - 6)
```

---

Let us write a program to read a simplified infix expression and output its postfix form. We assume that an operand is a single-digit integer. An operator can be one of +, –, * or /. Brackets are allowed. The usual precedence of operators apply: + and – have the same precedence which is lower than that of * and /, which have the same precedence. The left bracket is treated as an operator with very low precedence, less than that of + and –.

We will implement this as a function **precedence** which, given an operator, returns an integer representing its precedence. The actual value returned is not important as long as the relative precedence of the operators is maintained. We will use the following:

```
int precedence(char c) {
  if (c == '(') return 0;
  if (c == '+' || c == '-') return 3;
  if (c == '*' || c == '/') return 5;
}
```

The actual values 0, 3 and 5 are not important. Any values can be used as long as they represent the relative precedence of the operators.

We will need a function to read the input and return the next non-blank character. The end-of-line character will indicate the end of the expression. Here is the function (we call it **getToken**):

```
char getToken() {
  char ch;
  while ((ch = getchar()) == ' ') ; //empty body
  return ch;
}
```

The operator stack is simply a stack of characters which we will implement using

```
typedef struct {
  char ch;
} StackData;
```

Step 6 of the algorithm requires us to compare the precedence of the operator on top of the stack with the current operator. This would be easy if we can "peek" at the element on top of the stack without taking it off. To do this, we write the function, **peek**, and add it to **stack.h**, the file containing our stack declarations/ functions:

```
StackData peek(Stack S) {
  if (!empty(S)) return S -> top -> data;
  printf("\nAttempt to peek at an empty stack\n");
  exit(1);
}
```

Putting all these together, we now write Program P5.6 (shown on the next page) which implements the algorithm for converting an infix expression to postfix.

The job of reading the expression and converting to postfix is delegated to **readConvert**. This "outputs" the postfix form to a character array, **post**. So as not to clutter the code with error checking, we assume that **post** is big enough to hold the converted expression. The function returns the number of elements in the postfix expression.

The function, **printPostfix**, simply prints the postfix expression.

The following is a sample run of P5.6:

```
Type an infix expression and press Enter
(7 - 8 / 2 / 2) * ((7 - 2) * 3 - 6)

The postfix form is
7 8 2 / 2 / - 7 2 - 3 * 6 - *
```

**Program P5.6**

```
#include <stdio.h>
#include <ctype.h>
typedef struct {
  char ch;
} StackData;

#include <stack.h>

main() {
  int readConvert(char[]);
  void printPostfix(char[], int);
  char post[50];

  int n = readConvert(post);
  printPostfix(post, n);
} //end main

int readConvert(char post[]) {
  char getToken(void), token, c;
  int precedence(char);
  StackData temp;
  int j = 0;
  Stack S = initStack();
  printf("Type an infix expression and press Enter\n");
  token = getToken();
  while (token != '\n') {
    if (isdigit(token)) post[j++] = token;
    else if (token == '(') {
      temp.ch = token;
      push(S, temp);
    }
    else if (token == ')')
      while ((c = pop(S).ch) != '(') post[j++] = c;
    else {
      while (!empty(S) &&
               precedence(peek(S).ch) >= precedence(token))
        post[j++] = pop(S).ch;
      temp.ch = token;
      push(S, temp);
    }
    token = getToken();
  } //end while
  while (!empty(S)) post[j++] = pop(S).ch;
  return j; //the size of the expression
} //end readConvert
```

```
void printPostfix(char post[], int n) {
  int j;
  printf("\nThe postfix form is \n");
  for (j = 0; j < n; j++) printf("%c ", post[j]);
  printf("\n");
} //end printPostfix

char getToken() {
  char ch;
  while ((ch = getchar()) == ' ') ; //empty body
  return ch;
} //end getToken

int precedence(char c) {
  if (c == '(') return 0;
  if (c == '+' || c == '-') return 3;
  if (c == '*' || c == '/') return 5;
} //end precedence
```

Program P5.6 assumes that the given expression is a valid one. However, it can be easily modified to recognize some kinds of invalid expressions. For instance, if a right bracket is missing, when we reach the end of the expression there would be a left bracket on the stack. (If the brackets match, there would be none.) Similarly, if a left bracket is missing, when a right one is encountered and we are scanning the stack for the (missing) left one, we would not find it.

You are urged to modify P5.6 to catch expressions with mismatched brackets. You should also modify it to handle any integer operands, not just single-digit ones. Yet another modification is to handle other operations such as %, sqrt (square root), sin (sine), cos (cosine), tan (tangent), log (logarithm), exp (exponential), etc.

### *5.5.1 How to evaluate a postfix expression*

Program P5.6 stores the postfix form of the expression in a character array, **post**. We now write a function which, given **post**, evaluates the expression and returns its value. The function uses the algorithm on page 114.

We will need an *integer* stack to hold the operands and intermediate results. Recall that we needed a *character* stack to hold the operators. We can neatly work with both kinds of stacks if we declare **StackData** as:

```
typedef struct {
  char ch;
  int num;
} StackData;
```

We use the **char** field for the operator stack and the **int** field for the operand stack. Here is **eval**:

```
int eval(char post[], int n) {
  int j, a, b, c;
  StackData temp;

  Stack S = initStack();
  for (j = 0; j < n; j++) {
    if (isdigit(post[j])) {
      temp.num = post[j] - '0'; //convert to integer
      push(S, temp);
    }
    else {
      b = pop(S).num;
      a = pop(S).num;
      if (post[j] == '+') c = a + b;
      else if (post[j] == '-') c = a - b;
      else if (post[j] == '*') c = a * b;
      else c = a / b;
      temp.num = c;
      push(S, temp);
    }
  } //end for
  return pop(S).num;
} //end eval
```

We can test **eval** by adding it to P5.6 and putting its prototype in **main**, changing the declaration of **StackData** to the one above, and adding the following as the last statement in **main**:

```
printf("\nIts value is %d\n", eval(post, n));
```

The following is a sample run of the modified program:

```
Type an infix expression and press Enter
(7 - 8 / 2 / 2) * ((7 - 2) * 3 - 6)

The postfix form is
7 8 2 / 2 / - 7 2 - 3 * 6 - *

Its value is 45
```

## 5.6 Queues

A queue is a linear list in which items are added at one end and deleted from the other end. Familiar examples are queues at a bank, supermarket, a concert or a sporting event. People are supposed to join the queue at the rear and exit from the front. We would expect that a queue data structure would be useful for simulating these real-life queues.

Queues are also found inside the computer. There may be several jobs waiting to be executed and they are held in a queue. For example, several persons may each request something to be printed on a network printer. Since the printer can handle only one job at a time, the others have to be queued.

The basic operations we wish to perform on a queue are:

- add an item to the queue; we say *enqueue*
- take an item off the queue; we say *dequeue*
- check if the queue is empty
- inspect the item at the head of the queue

Like stacks, we can easily implement the queue data structure using arrays or linked lists. We will use a queue of integers for illustration purposes.

### *5.6.1 Implementing a queue using an array*

In the array implementation of a queue (of integers), we use an integer array (**QA**, say) for storing the numbers and two integer variables (**head** and **tail**, say) which indicate the item at the head of the queue and the item at the tail of the queue, respectively.

Since we are using an array, we will need to know its size in order to declare it. We will need to have some information about the problem to determine a reasonable size for the array. We will use the symbolic constant, **MaxQ**. In our implementation, the queue will be declared full if there are **MaxQ - 1** elements in it and we attempt to add another.

We use the following to define the data type **Queue**:

```
typedef struct {
  int head, tail;
  int QA[MaxQ];
} QType, *Queue;
```

Valid values for **head** and **tail** will range from 0 to **MaxQ - 1**. When we initialize a queue, we will set **head** and **tail** to 0.

We can now declare a "queue variable", **Q**, with

```
Queue Q;
```

Observe that **Queue** is declared as a *pointer* to the structure we call **QType**. So, for instance, **Q** is a pointer to a structure consisting of the variables **head** and **tail** and the array **QA**. This is necessary since **head**, **tail** and **QA** would need to be changed by the *enqueue* and *dequeue* routines and the changes known to the calling function (**main**, say). This can be achieved by passing a *pointer* to them, in effect, the **Queue** variable.

In order to work with a queue, the first task is to create an empty queue. This is done by allocating storage for a **QType**, assigning its address to a **Queue** variable and setting **head** and **tail** to 0. Later, we will see why 0 is a good value to use. We can use the following:

```
Queue initQueue() {
  Queue qp = (Queue) malloc(sizeof(QType));
  qp -> head = qp -> tail = 0;
  return qp;
}
```

In **main**, say, we can declare and initialize a queue, **Q**, with

```
Queue Q = initQueue();
```

When this statement is executed, the situation in memory can be represented by:

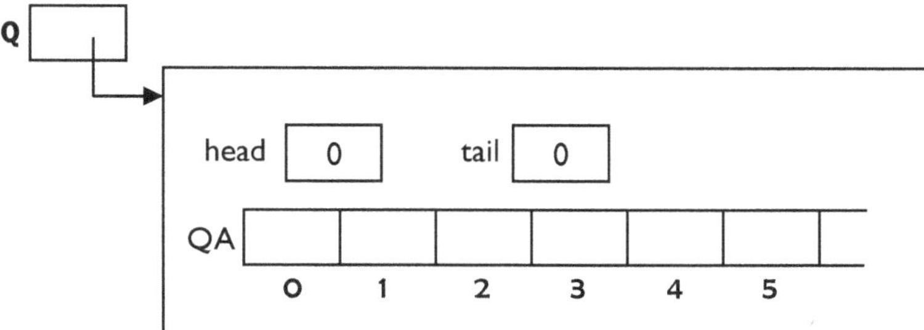


This represents the empty queue. In working with queues, we will need a function which tells us whether a queue is empty or not. We can use the following:

```
int empty(Queue Q) {
  return (Q -> head == Q -> tail);
}
```

Shortly, we will see that, given the way we will implement the *enqueue* and *dequeue* operations, the queue will be empty whenever **head** and **tail** have the same value. This value will not necessarily be 0. In fact, it may be any of the values from 0 to **MaxQ - 1**, the valid subscripts of **QA**.

Consider how we might add an item to the queue. In a real queue, a person joins at the tail. We will do the same here by incrementing **tail** and storing the item at the location indicated by **tail**.

For example, to add 36, say, to the queue, we increment **tail** to 1 and store 36 in **QA[1]**; **head** remains at 0.

If we then add 15 to the queue, it will be stored in **QA[2]** and **tail** will be 2.

If we now add 52 to the queue, it will be stored in **QA[3]** and **tail** will be 3.

Our picture in memory will look like this:

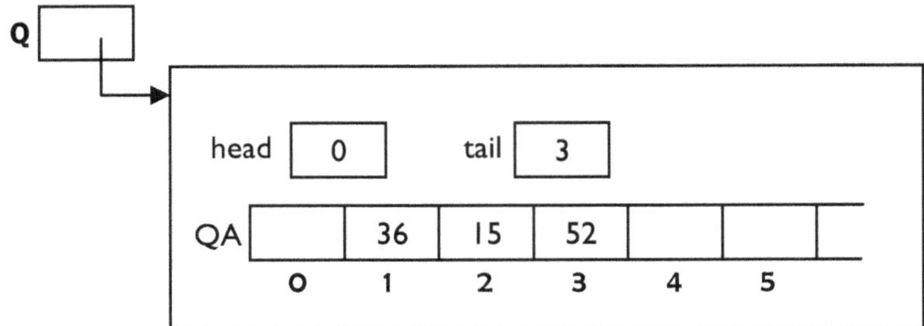


Note that **head** points "just in front of" the item which is actually at the head of the queue and **tail** points at the last item in the queue.

Now consider taking something off the queue. The item to be taken off is the one at the head. To remove it, we must *first* increment **head** and then return the value pointed to by **head**.

For example, if we remove 36, **head** will become 1 and it points "just in front of" 15, the item now at the head. Note that 36 still remains in the array but, to all intents and purposes, it is not in the queue.

Suppose we now add 23 to the queue. It will be placed in location 4 with **tail** being 4 and **head** being 1. The picture now looks like this:

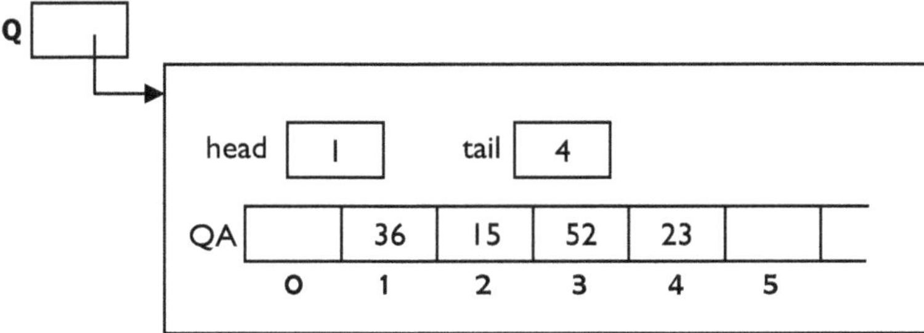


There are 3 items in the queue; 15 is at the head and 23 at the tail.

Consider what happens if we continuously add items to the queue without taking off any. The value of **tail** will keep increasing until it reaches **MaxQ - 1**, the last valid subscript of **QA**. What do we do if another item needs to be added?

We *could* say that the queue is full and stop the program. However, there are two free locations, 0 and 1. It would be better to try and use one of these. This leads us to the idea of a *circular queue*. Here, we think of the locations in the array as arranged in a circle: location **MaxQ - 1** is followed by location 0.

So if **tail** has the value **MaxQ - 1**, incrementing it will set it to 0.

Suppose we had not taken off any item from the queue. The value of **head** will still be 0. Now, what if, in attempting to add an item, **tail** is incremented from **MaxQ - 1** to 0? It now has the same value as **head**. In this situation, we declare that the queue is full.

We do this even though nothing is stored in location 0 which is, therefore, available to hold another item. The reason for taking this approach is that it simplifies our code for detecting when the queue is empty and when it is full.

To emphasize, *when the queue is declared full, it contains* ***MaxQ - 1*** *items*.

We can now write **enqueue**, a function to add an item to the queue.

```
void enqueue(Queue Q, int n) {
  if (Q -> tail == MaxQ - 1) Q -> tail = 0;
  else ++(Q -> tail);
  if (Q -> tail == Q -> head) {
    printf("\nQueue is full\n");
    exit(1);
  }
  Q -> QA[Q -> tail] = n;
} //end enqueue
```

We first increment **tail**. If, by doing so, it has the same value as **head**, we declare that the queue is full. If not, we store the new item in position **tail**.

Consider the diagram above. If we delete 15 and 52, it changes to

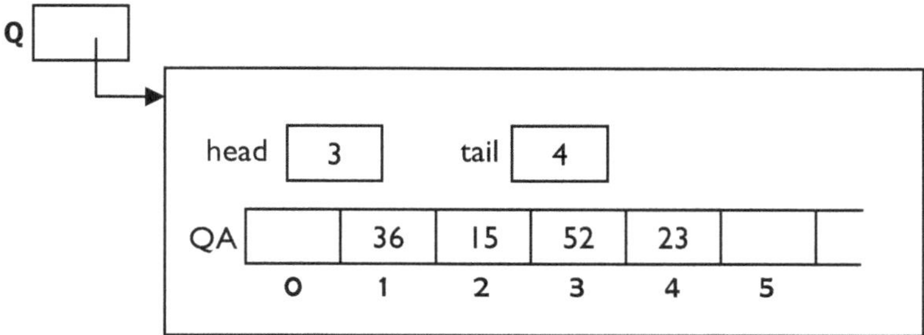


Now, **head** has the value 3, **tail** has the value 4, and there is 1 item in the queue, 23 in location 4. If we delete this last item, **head** and **tail** would both have the value 4 and the queue would be empty. This suggests that we have an empty queue when **head** has the same value as **tail**, as indicated earlier.

We can now write the function, **dequeue**, for removing an item from the queue.

```
int dequeue(Queue Q) {
  if (empty(Q)) {
    printf("\nAttempt to remove from an empty queue\n");
    exit(1);
  }
  if (Q -> head == MaxQ - 1) Q -> head = 0;
  else ++(Q -> head);
  return Q -> QA[Q -> head];
} //end dequeue
```

If the queue is empty, an error is reported and the program halted. If not, we increment **head** and return the value in location **head**. Note, again, that if **head** has the value **MaxQ - 1**, incrementing it sets it to 0.

As in the case of a stack, we can create a file, **queue.h**, and store our declarations and functions in it, so they can be used by other programs. So far, **queue.h** would contain the items shown in the box on the next page.

To test our queue operations, we write Program P5.7 which reads an integer and prints its digits in reverse order. For example, if 12345 is read, the program prints 54321. The digits are extracted, from the right, and stored in a queue. The items in the queue are taken off, one at a time, and printed.

**Program P5.7**

```
#include <stdio.h>
#define MaxQ 10
#include <queue.h>

main() {
  int n;
  Queue Q = initQueue();
  printf("Enter a positive integer: ");
  scanf("%d", &n);
  while (n > 0) {
    enqueue(Q, n % 10);
    n = n / 10;
  }
  printf("\nDigits in reverse order: ");
  while (!empty(Q))
    printf("%d", dequeue(Q));
  printf("\n");
}
```

Note the order of the header statements. The user is free to define the value of **MaxQ**; this value will be used by the declarations in **queue.h**.

```
#include <stdlib.h>

typedef struct {
  int head, tail;
  int QA[MaxQ];
} QType, *Queue;

Queue initQueue() {
  Queue qp = (Queue) malloc(sizeof(QType));
  qp -> head = qp -> tail = 0;
  return qp;
}

int empty(Queue Q) {
  return (Q -> head == Q -> tail);
}

void enqueue(Queue Q, int n) {
  if (Q -> tail == MaxQ - 1) Q -> tail = 0;
  else ++(Q -> tail);
  if (Q -> tail == Q -> head) {
    printf("\nQueue is full\n");
    exit(1);
  }
  Q -> QA[Q -> tail] = n;
}

int dequeue(Queue Q) {
  if (empty(Q)) {
    printf("\nAttempt to remove from an empty queue\n");
    exit(1);
  }
  if (Q -> head == MaxQ - 1) Q -> head = 0;
  else ++(Q -> head);
  return Q -> QA[Q -> head];
}
```

### *5.6.2 Implementing a queue using a linked list*

As with stacks, we can implement a queue using linked lists. This has the advantage of not having to decide beforehand how many items to cater for. We will use two pointers, **head** and **tail**, to point to the first and last items in the queue, respectively. The following diagram shows the data structure when four items (36, 15, 52, 23) are added to the queue:

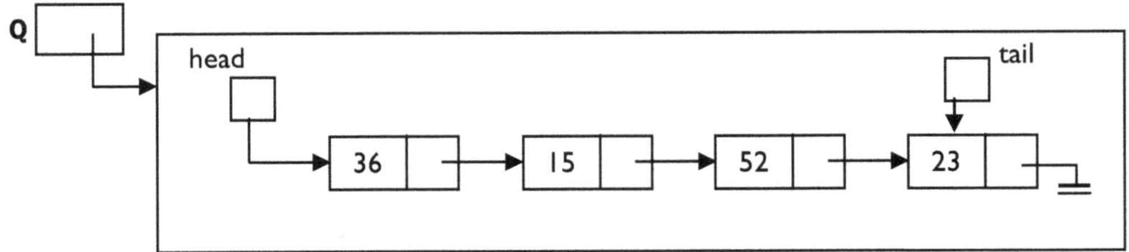


We will implement the queue so that it works with a general data type which we will store in a structure called **QueueData**. We will use the following framework:

```
typedef struct {
  //declare all the data fields here
  int num; //for example
} QueueData;
```

Whichever kind of queue we want, we declare the data fields within the structure. In the example, above, if we want a queue of integers, we declare one field of type **int**.

A linked list node will consist of two fields: a data field of type **QueueData** and a field which points to the next node. Here is its declaration:

```
typedef struct node {
  QueueData data;
  struct node *next;
} Node, *NodePtr;
```

We will define the **Queue** data type as a pointer to a structure containing two **NodePtr**s, **head** and **tail**, thus:

```
typedef struct {
  NodePtr head, tail;
} QueueType, *Queue;
```

We can declare a queue with the statement:

```
Queue Q;
```

The empty queue, **Q**, is represented by

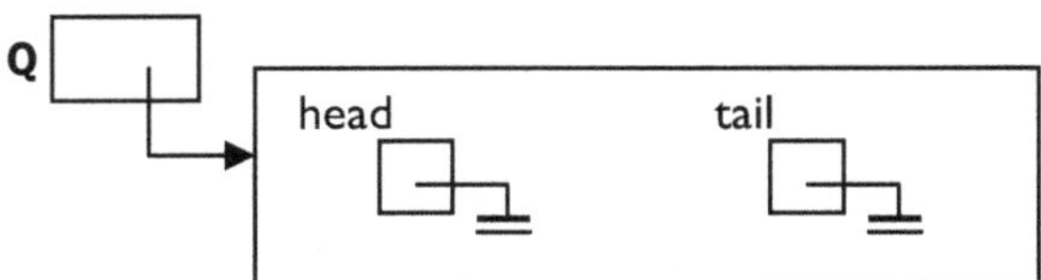


Creating an empty queue involves allocating storage for a **QueueType** structure which consists of two variables, **head** and **tail**, and setting them to **NULL**. Here is the function, **initQueue**:

```
Queue initQueue() {
  Queue qp = (Queue) malloc(sizeof(QueueType));
  qp -> head = NULL;
  qp -> tail = NULL;
  return qp;
}
```

We can test for an empty queue with

```
int empty(Queue Q) {
  return (Q -> head == NULL);
}
```

This simply checks if **head** is **NULL**.

To add an item to the queue, we need to allocate storage for a node and add it to the tail of the list. Here is **enqueue**:

```
void enqueue(Queue Q, QueueData d) {
  NodePtr np = (NodePtr) malloc(sizeof(Node));
  np -> data = d;
  np -> next = NULL;
  if (empty(Q)) {
    Q -> head = np;
    Q -> tail = np;
  }
  else {
    Q -> tail -> next = np;
    Q -> tail = np;
  }
}
```

If the queue is empty, the new item becomes the only one in the queue; **head** and **tail** are set to point to it. If the queue is not empty, the item at the tail is set to point to the new one, and **tail** is updated to point to the new one.

To take an item off the queue, we first check if the queue is empty. If it is, we print a message and end the program. If not, the item at the head of the queue is returned and the node containing the item is deleted.

If, by removing an item, **head** becomes **NULL**, it means that the queue is empty. In this case, **tail** is also set to **NULL**.

Here is **dequeue**:

```
QueueData dequeue(Queue Q) {
  if (empty(Q)) {
    printf("\nAttempt to remove from an empty queue\n");
    exit(1);
  }
  QueueData hold = Q -> head -> data;
  NodePtr temp = Q -> head;
  Q -> head = Q -> head -> next;
  if (Q -> head == NULL) Q -> tail = NULL;
  free(temp);
  return hold;
} //end dequeue
```

As before, we can store all these declarations and functions, except **QueueData**, in a file, **queue.h**, so that other programs can use them. The contents of **queue.h** are shown on the next page.

To use these functions, a user program only needs to declare what he wants **QueueData** to be. To illustrate, we rewrite Program P5.7 which reads an integer and prints its digits in reverse order. It is shown as Program P5.8.

**Program P5.8**

```
#include <stdio.h>
typedef struct {
  int num;
} QueueData;
#include <queue.h>

main() {
  int n;
  QueueData temp;
  Queue Q = initQueue();
  printf("Enter a positive integer: ");
  scanf("%d", &n);
  while (n > 0) {
    temp.num = n % 10;
    enqueue(Q, temp);
    n = n / 10;
  }
  printf("\nDigits in reverse order: ");
  while (!empty(Q))
    printf("%d", dequeue(Q).num);
  printf("\n");
}
```

queue.h

```
#include <stdlib.h>
typedef struct node {
  QueueData data;
  struct node *next;
} Node, *NodePtr;
typedef struct queueType {
  NodePtr head, tail;
} QueueType, *Queue;

Queue initQueue() {
  Queue qp = (Queue) malloc(sizeof(QueueType));
  qp -> head = NULL;
  qp -> tail = NULL;
  return qp;
} //end initQueue

int empty(Queue Q) {
  return (Q -> head == NULL);
} //end empty

void enqueue(Queue Q, QueueData d) {
  NodePtr np = (NodePtr) malloc(sizeof(Node));
  np -> data = d;
  np -> next = NULL;
  if (empty(Q)) {
    Q -> head = np;
    Q -> tail = np;
  }
  else {
    Q -> tail -> next = np;
    Q -> tail = np;
  }
} //end enqueue

QueueData dequeue(Queue Q) {
  if (empty(Q)) {
    printf("\nAttempt to remove from an empty queue\n");
    exit(1);
  }
  QueueData hold = Q -> head -> data;
  NodePtr temp = Q -> head;
  Q -> head = Q -> head -> next;
  if (Q -> head == NULL) Q -> tail = NULL;
  free(temp);
  return hold;
} //end dequeue
```

Note that the declaration of **QueueData** must come before **#include <queue.h>**. Also, since **enqueue** expects a **QueueData** argument, the digits of the integer must be stored in the **int** field of a **QueueData** variable (**temp** is used) before being passed to **enqueue**.

---

Stacks and queues are important to systems programmers and compiler writers. We have seen how stacks are used in the evaluation of arithmetic expressions. They are also used to implement the "calling" and "return" mechanism for functions. Consider the situation where function **A** calls function **C** which calls function **B** which calls function **D**. When a function "returns", how does the computer figure out where to return to? We show how a stack can be used to do this.

Assume we have the following situation:

```
function A      function B      function C      function D

    .               .               .               .
    C;              D;              B;              .
100:            200:            300:
    .               .               .               .
```

where a number, like 100, represents the "return address", the address of the next instruction to be executed when the function returns. When **A** calls **C**, the address 100 is pushed onto a stack, **S**. When **C** calls **B**, 300 is pushed onto **S**. When **B** calls **D**, 200 is pushed onto **S**. At this stage, the stack looks like this:

```
(bottom of stack) 100  300  200 (top of stack)
```

and control is in **D**. When **D** finishes and is ready to return, the address at the top of the stack (200) is popped and execution continues at this address. Note that this is the address immediately following the call to **D**.

Next, when **B** finishes and is ready to return, the address at the top of the stack (300) is popped and execution continues at this address. Note that this is the address immediately following the call to **B**.

Finally, when **C** finishes and is ready to return, the address at the top of the stack (100) is popped and execution continues at this address. Note that this is the address immediately following the call to **C**.

Naturally, queue data structures are used in simulating real-life queues. They are also used to implement queues "inside" the computer. In a multi-programming environment, several jobs may have to be queued waiting on a particular resource such as processor time or a printer.

Stacks and queues are also used extensively in working with more advanced data structures such as trees and graphs. While many of these algorithms are particularly interesting, they are beyond the scope of this book.

## Exercises 5

1. What is an *abstract data type*?
2. What is a *stack*? What are the basic operations that can be performed on a stack?
3. What is a *queue*? What are the basic operations that can be performed on a queue?
4. Modify Program P5.6 (p. 117) to recognize infix expressions with mismatched brackets.
5. Program P5.6 works with single-digit operands. Modify it to handle any integer operands.
6. Modify Program P5.6 to handle expressions with operations such as **%**, square root, sine, cosine, tangent, logarithm and exponential.
7. An integer array **post** is used to hold the postfix form of an arithmetic expression such that:

   a positive number represents an operand;

   -1 represents +;

   -2 represents -;

   -3 represents *;

   -4 represents /;

   0 indicates the end of the expression.

   Show the contents of **post** for the expression `(2 + 3) * (8 / 4) - 6`.

   Write a function **eval** which, given **post**, returns the value of the expression.
8. Write declarations/functions to implement a stack of **double** values.
9. Write declarations/functions to implement a queue of **double** values.
10. A *priority queue* is one in which items are added to the queue based on a *priority number*. Jobs with higher priority numbers are closer to the head of the queue than those with lower priority numbers. A job is added to the queue in front of all jobs of lower priority but after all jobs of greater or equal priority.

    Write declarations and functions to implement a priority queue. Each item in the queue has a job number (integer) and a priority number. Implement, at least, the following functions: (i) initialize an empty queue (ii) add a job in its appropriate place in the queue (iii) delete and dispose of the job at the head of the queue (iv) given a job number, remove that job from the queue.

    Ensure your functions work regardless of the state of the queue.
11. An input line contains a word consisting of lowercase letters only. Explain how a stack can be used to determine if the word is a palindrome.
12. Show how to implement a queue using two stacks.
13. Show how to implement a stack using two queues.
14. A stack, **S1**, contains some numbers in arbitrary order. Using another stack, **S2**, for temporary storage, show how to sort the numbers in **S1** such that the smallest is at the top of **S1** and the largest is at the bottom.

# 6 Recursion

## In this chapter, we will explain:

- what is a recursive definition
- how to write recursive functions in C
- how to convert from decimal to binary
- how to print a linked list in reverse order
- how to solve 'Towers of Hanoi'
- how to write an efficient 'power' function
- how to sort using 'merge sort'
- what are **static** variables
- how to implement 'backtracking' using recursion
- how to find a path through a maze

---

A *recursive definition* is one which is defined in terms of itself. Perhaps the most common example is the *factorial* function. The factorial of a non-negative integer, $n$, (written as $n!$) is defined as:

$$0! = 1$$
$$n! = n(n - 1)!, n > 0$$

Here, $n!$ is defined in terms of $(n - 1)!$ What is $(n - 1)!$? To find out, we must apply the definition of factorial! In this case, we have

$$(n - 1)! = 1, \text{ if } (n - 1) = 0$$
$$(n - 1)! = (n - 1)(n - 2)! \text{ if } (n - 1) > 0$$

What is 3!?

- since 3 > 0, it is 3.2!
- since 2 > 0, 2! is 2.1! and 3! is 3.2.1!
- since 1 > 0, 1! is 1.0! and 3! is 3.2.1.0!
- since 0! is 1, we have 3! is 3.2.1.1 = 6

Loosely, we say that $n!$ is the product of all integers from 1 to $n$.

Let us rewrite the definition using programming notation; we call it **fact**:

```
fact(0) = 1
fact(n) = n * fact(n - 1), n > 0
```

The recursive definition of a function consists of two parts:

- the *base* case, which gives the value of the function for a specific argument. This is also called the *anchor*, *end* case or *terminating* case and allows the recursion to terminate eventually.
- the recursive (or general) case where the function is defined in terms of itself.

Shortly, we will write **fact** as a C function. Before we do, we give a non-mathematical example of a recursive definition. Consider how you might define *ancestor*. Loosely, we can say that an ancestor is one's parent or grandparent or great-grandparent, and so on. But we can state this more precisely as follows:

> *a* is an ancestor of *b* if
> (1) *a* is a parent of *b*, or
> (2) *a* is an ancestor of *c* and *c* is a parent of *b*

(1) is the base case and (2) is the general, recursive case where *ancestor* is defined in terms of itself.

A less serious example is the meaning of the acronym LAME. It stands for LAME, Another MP3 Encoder. Expanding LAME, we get LAME, Another MP3 Encoder, Another MP3 Encoder. And so on. We can say that LAME is a recursive acronym. It's not a true recursive definition, though, since it has no base case.

## 6.1 Recursive functions in C

We have seen many examples of functions which call other functions. What we have not seen is a function which calls itself—a *recursive function*. We start off with **fact**:

```
int fact(int n) {
  if (n < 0) return 0;
  if (n == 0) return 1;
  return n * fact(n - 1);
}
```

In the last statement, we have a call to the function **fact**, the function we are writing. The function calls itself.

Consider the statement

```
int n = fact(3);
```

It is executed as follows:

- 3 is copied to a temporary location and this location is passed to **fact** where it becomes the value of **n**;
- Execution reaches the last statement and **fact** attempts to return **3 * fact(2)**. However, **fact(2)** must be calculated before the return value is known. Think of this as just a call to a function **fact** with argument 2.

- As usual, 2 is copied to a temporary location and this location is passed to **fact** where it becomes the value of **n**. If **fact** were a different function, there would be no problem. But since it's the *same* function, what happens to the first value of **n**? It has to be saved somewhere and reinstated when *this* call to fact finishes.

  The value is saved on something called the *run-time stack*. Each time a function calls itself, its arguments (and local variables, if any) are stored on the stack before the new arguments take effect. Also, for each call, new local variables are created. Thus each call has its own copy of arguments and local variables.
- When **n** is 2, execution reaches the last statement and **fact** attempts to return **2 * fact(1)**. However, **fact(1)** must be calculated before the return value is known. Think of this as just a call to a function **fact** with argument 1.
- This call reaches the last statement and **fact** attempts to return **1 * fact(0)**. However, **fact(0)** must be calculated before the return value is known. Think of this as just a call to a function **fact** with argument 0.
- At this time, the run-time stack contains the arguments 3, 2 and 1. The call **fact(0)** reaches the second statement and returns a value of 1.
- The calculation **1 * fact(0)** can now be completed, returning 1 as the value of **fact(1)**.
- The calculation **2 * fact(1)** can now be completed, returning 2 as the value of **fact(2)**.
- The calculation **3 * fact(2)** can now be completed, returning 6 as the value of **fact(3)**.

We should emphasize that this recursive version of **fact** is merely for illustrative purposes. It is not an efficient way to calculate a factorial—think of all the function calls, the stacking and unstacking of arguments, just to multiply the numbers from 1 to **n**. A more efficient function is

```
int fact(int n) {
  int f = 1;
  while (n > 0) {
    f = f * n;
    --n;
  }
  return f;
}
```

Another example of a function which can be defined recursively is the HCF (Highest Common Factor) of two positive integers, **m** and **n**.

```
hcf(m, n) is
  (1) m, if n is 0
  (2) hcf(n, m % n), if n > 0
```

If **m** = 70 and **n** = 42, we have

```
hcf(70, 42) = hcf(42, 70 % 42) = hcf(42, 28) = hcf(28, 42 % 28)
  = hcf(28, 14) = hcf(14, 28 % 14) = hcf(14, 0) = 14
```

We can write **hcf** as a recursive C function:

```
int hcf(int m, int n) {
  if (n == 0) return m;
  return hcf(n, m % n);
}
```

As a matter of interest, we can also write **hcf** as an iterative (as opposed to recursive) function, using Euclid's algorithm:

```
int hcf(int m, int n) {
  int r;
  while (n > 0) {
    r = m % n;
    m = n;
    n = r;
  }
  return m;
}
```

Effectively, this function does explicitly what the recursive function does implicitly.

---

Yet another example of a recursively defined function is that of the Fibonacci numbers. We define the first two Fibonacci numbers as `1` and `1`. Each new number is obtained by adding the previous two. So the Fibonacci sequence is: `1, 1, 2, 3, 5, 8, 13, 21`, and so on.

Recursively, we define the *n*th Fibonacci number, **F(n)**, as follows:

```
F(0) = F(1) = 1
F(n) = F(n - 1) + F(n - 2), n > 1
```

A C function to return the *n*th Fibonacci number is:

```
int fib(int n) {
  if (n == 0 || n == 1) return 1;
  return fib(n - 1) + fib(n - 2);
}
```

Again, we emphasize that while this function is neat, concise and easy to understand, it is not efficient. For example, consider the calculation of **F(5)**:

```
F(5) = F(4) + F(3) = F(3) + F(2) + F(3) = F(2) + F(1) + F(2) + F(3)
= F(1) + F(0) + F(1) + F(2) + F(3) = 1 + 1 + 1 + F(1) + F(0) + F(3)
= 1 + 1 + 1 + 1 + 1 + F(2) + F(1) =  1 + 1 + 1 + 1 + 1 + F(1) + F(0) + F(1)
= 1 + 1 + 1 + 1 + 1 + 1 + 1 + 1
= 8
```

Notice the number of function calls and additions which have to be made whereas we can calculate **F(5)** straightforwardly using only 4 additions. You are urged to write an efficient, iterative function to return the *n*th Fibonacci number.

## 6.2 Recursive decimal to binary

In Section 5.4.1, we used a stack to convert an integer from decimal to binary. We now show how to write a recursive function to perform the same task.

To see what needs to be done, suppose **n** is 13, which is 1101 in binary. Recall that **n % 2** gives us the *last* bit of the binary equivalent of **n**. If, somehow, we have a way to print all but the last bit, we can then follow this with **n % 2**. But "printing all but the last bit" is the same as printing the binary equivalent of **n/2**.

For example, 1101 is 110 followed by 1; 110 is the binary equivalent of 6, which is 13/2 and 1 is 13 % 2. So, we can print the binary equivalent of **n** as follows:

```
print binary of n / 2
print n % 2
```

We use the *same* method to print the binary equivalent of 6. This is the binary equivalent of 6/2 = 3, which is 11, followed by 6 % 2, which is 0; this gives 110.

We use the *same* method to print the binary equivalent of 3. This is the binary equivalent of 3/2 = 1, which is 1, followed by 3 % 2, which is 1; this gives 11.

We use the *same* method to print the binary equivalent of 1. This is the binary equivalent of 1/2 = 0 followed by 1 % 2, which is 1; if we "do nothing" for 0, this will give us 1.

We stop when we get to the stage where we need to find the binary equivalent of 0. This leads us to the following function:

```
void decToBin(int n) {
  if (n > 0) {
    decToBin(n / 2);
    printf("%d", n % 2);
  }
}
```

The call **decToBin(13)** will print 1101.

Note how much more compact this is than Program P5.5 (page 113). However, it is not more efficient. The stacking/unstacking that is done explicitly in P5.5 is done by the recursive mechanism provided by the language when a function calls itself. To illustrate, let us trace the call **decToBin(13)**:

- on the first call, **n** assumes the value 13;
- while the call **decToBin(13)** is executing, the call **decToBin(6)** is made; 13 is pushed onto the run-time stack and **n** assumes the value 6;
- while the call **decToBin(6)** is executing, the call **decToBin(3)** is made; 6 is pushed onto the stack and **n** assumes the value 3;
- while the call **decToBin(3)** is executing, the call **decToBin(1)** is made; 3 is pushed onto the stack and **n** assumes the value 1;
- while the call **decToBin(1)** is executing, the call **decToBin(0)** is made; 1 is pushed onto the stack and **n** assumes the value 0;
- at this stage, the stack contains 13, 6, 3, 1;
- since **n** is 0, *this* call of the function returns immediately; so far nothing has been printed;
- when the call **decToBin(0)** returns, the argument on top of the stack, 1, is reinstated as the value of **n**;
- control goes to the **printf** statement which prints 1 % 2, that is, **1**;
- the call **decToBin(1)** can now return and the argument on top of the stack, 3, is reinstated as the value of **n**;
- control goes to the **printf** statement which prints 3 % 2, that is, **1**;
- the call **decToBin(3)** can now return and the argument on top of the stack, 6, is reinstated as the value of **n**;
- control goes to the **printf** statement which prints 6 % 2, that is, **0**;
- the call **decToBin(6)** can now return and the argument on top of the stack, 13, is reinstated as the value of **n**;
- control goes to the **printf** statement which prints 13 % 2, that is, **1**;
- the call **decToBin(13)** can now return and **1101** has been printed.

We can summarize the above description as follows:

```
decToBin(13)  →  decToBin(6)
                 print(13 % 2)
              →  decToBin(3)
                 print(6 % 2)
                 print(13 % 2)
              →  decToBin(1)
                 print(3 % 2)
                 print(6 % 2)
                 print(13 % 2)
```

```
→ decToBin(0) = do nothing
  print(1 % 2) = 1
  print(3 % 2) = 1
  print(6 % 2) = 0
  print(13 % 2) = 1
```

We re-state one of the most important properties of recursive functions:

> When a function calls itself, the current arguments (and local variables, if any) are pushed onto a stack. Execution of the function takes place with the new arguments and new local variables. When execution is completed, arguments (and local variables, if any) are popped from the stack and execution resumes (with *these* popped values) with the statement following the recursive call.

Consider the following function:

```
void test(int m, int n) {
  char ch;
    .
  test(m + 1, n - 1);
  printf("%d %d", m, n);
    .
}
```

and the call **test(4, 9)**. The function executes with **m** = 4, **n** = 9 and the local variable, **ch**. When the recursive call is made,

- the values of **m**, **n** and **ch** are pushed onto a stack;
- **test** begins execution, again, with **m** = 5, **n** = 8 and a new copy of **ch**;
- whenever *this* call to **test** finishes, (perhaps even after calling itself one or more times), the stack is popped and the program resumes execution with **printf** (the statement after the recursive call) and the popped values of **m**, **n** and **ch**. In this example, 4  9 would be printed.

## 6.3 Printing a linked list in reverse order

Consider the problem of printing a linked list in reverse order.

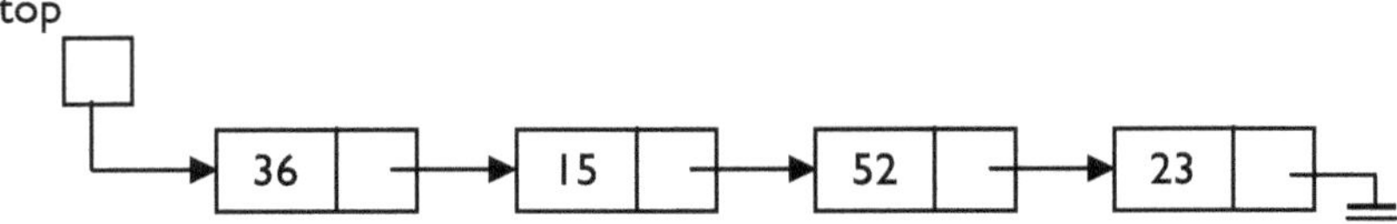


One way of doing this is to traverse the list, pushing items onto an integer stack as we meet them. When we reach the end of the list, the last number would be at the top of the stack and the first would be at the bottom. We then pop items off the stack and print each one as it is popped.

As we may expect by now, we can use recursion to perform the stacking/unstacking. We use the following idea:

```
to print a list in reverse order
  print the list, except the first item, in reverse order
  print the first item
```

Using the list, above, this says print (15 52 23) in reverse order followed by 36;

- to print (15 52 23) in reverse order, we must print (52 23) in reverse order followed by 15;
- to print (52 23) in reverse order, we must print (23) in reverse order followed by 52;
- to print (23) in reverse order, we must print nothing in reverse order followed by 23;

At the end, we would have printed: 23 52 15 36

Another way to look at this is as follows:

```
reverse(36 15 52 23)  →  reverse(15 52 23) 36
                      →  reverse(52 23) 15 36
                      →  reverse(23) 52 15 36
                      →  reverse() 23 52 15 36
                      →  23 52 15 36
```

Here is the function, assuming that the pointer to the head of the list is of type **NodePtr**, and the node fields are **num** and **next**:

```
void reverse(NodePtr top) {
  if (top != NULL) {
    reverse(top -> next);
    printf("%d ", top -> num);
  }
}
```

---

### *Comments*

The key to working out a recursive solution to a problem is to be able to express the solution in terms of itself, but on a "smaller" problem. If the problem keeps getting smaller and smaller, eventually it will be small enough that we can solve it directly.

We see this principle in both the "decimal to binary" and "print a linked list in reverse order" problems. In the first problem, the conversion of **n** is expressed in terms of **n/2**; this will, in turn, be expressed in terms of **n/4**, and so on, until there is nothing to convert. In the second problem, printing the list reversed is expressed in terms of printing a shorter list (the original list minus the first element) reversed. The list gets shorter and shorter until there is nothing to reverse.

## 6.4 Towers of Hanoi

The *Towers of Hanoi* puzzle is a classic problem that can be solved using recursion. Legend has it that, when the world was created, some high priests in the Temple of Brahma were given three golden pins. On one of the pins were placed 64 golden disks. The disks were all of different sizes with the largest at the bottom, the smallest on the top, and no disk was placed on top of a smaller one.

They were required to move the 64 disks from the given pin to another one according to the following rules:

- move one disk at a time; only a disk at the top of a pin can be moved, and it must be moved to the top of another pin;
- no disk must be placed on top of a smaller one.

When all 64 disks have been transferred, the world will come to an end.

This is an example of a problem which can be solved easily by recursion but for which a non-recursive solution is quite difficult. Let us denote the pins by *A*, *B* and *C* with the disks originally placed on *A* and the destination pin being *B*. Pin *C* is used for temporary placement of disks.

Suppose there is one disk. This can be move directly from *A* to *B*.

Next, suppose there are five disks on *A*, as shown:

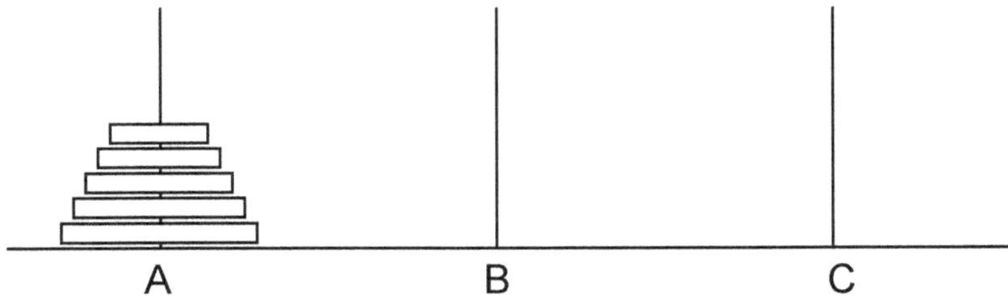


Assume we know how to transfer the top four from *A* to *C* using *B*. When this is done, we have:

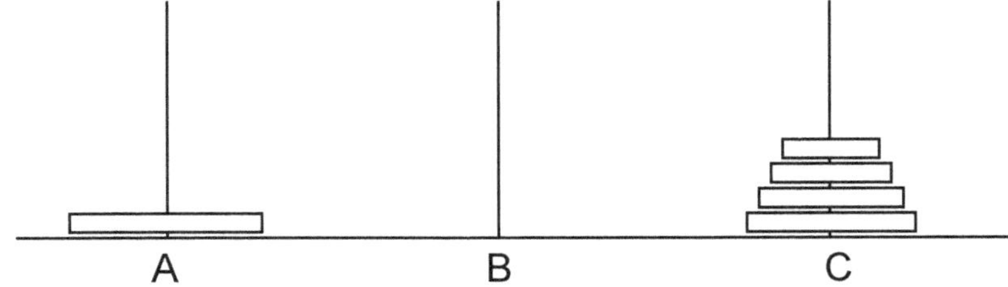

We can now move the fifth disk from *A* to *B*, giving:

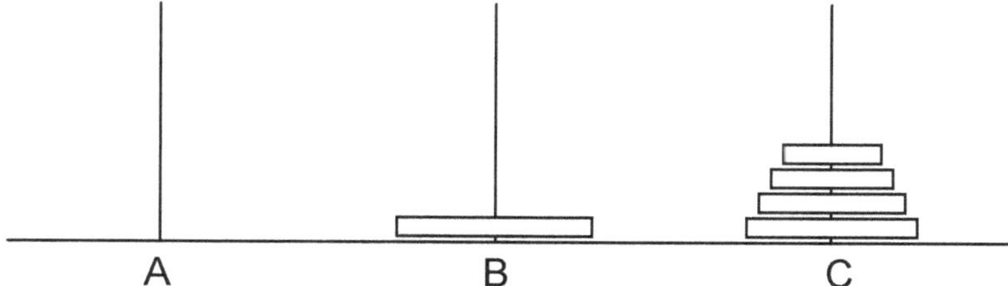


It remains only to transfer the four disks from *C* to *B* using *A*, which we assume we know how to do. When done, we will have:

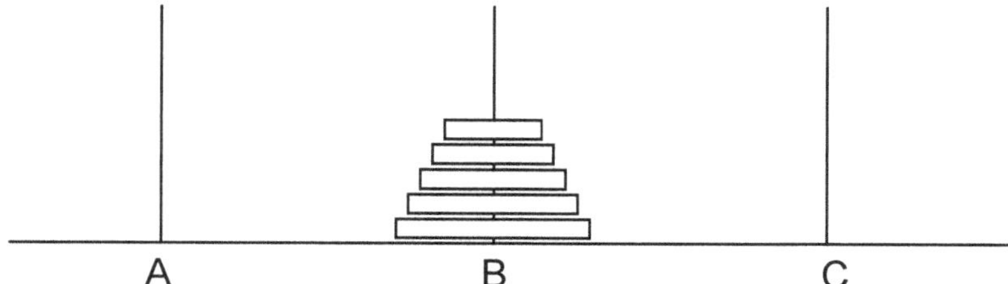


and the job is completed.

We have thus reduced the problem of transferring 5 disks to a problem of transferring 4 disks from one pin to another. This, in turn, can be reduced to a problem of moving 3 disks from one pin to another; *this* can be reduced to 2 and then to 1, which we know how to do. The recursive solution for *n* disks is:

- transfer *n* - 1 disks from *A* to *C* using *B*;
- move *n*th disk from *A* to *B*;
- transfer *n* - 1 disks from *C* to *B* using *A*.

Of course, we can use this same solution for transferring the *n* - 1 disks.

The following function transfers **n** disks from **startPin** to **endPin** using **workPin**:

```
void hanoi(int n, char startPin, char endPin, char workPin) {
  if (n > 0) {
    hanoi(n - 1, startPin, workPin, endPin);
    printf("Move disk from %c to %c\n", startPin, endPin);
    hanoi(n - 1, workPin, endPin, startPin);
  }
}
```

When called with the statement:

```
hanoi(3, 'A', 'B', 'C');  //transfer 3 disks from A to B using C
```

the function prints:

```
Move disk from A to B
Move disk from A to C
Move disk from B to C
Move disk from A to B
Move disk from C to A
Move disk from C to B
Move disk from A to B
```

How many moves are required to transfer *n* disks?

- if *n* is 1, 1 move is required; ($1 = 2^1 - 1$)
- if *n* is 2, 3 moves are required; ($3 = 2^2 - 1$)
- if *n* is 3, 7 moves (see above) are required; ($7 = 2^3 - 1$)

It appears that, for *n* disks, the number of moves is $2^n - 1$. It can be proved that this is indeed the case.

When *n* is 64, the number of moves is roughly[4]

```
16,000,000,000,000,000,000
```

using the approximation $2^{10} \approx 1000$.

Assuming the priests can move 1 disc per second, never make a mistake and never take a rest, it will take them over 500 billion years to complete the task. Rest assured that the world is not about to end any time soon!

## 6.5 The power function

Given a number, *x*, and an integer, $n \geq 0$, how do we calculate *x* raised to the power *n*, that is, $x^n$? We can use the definition that $x^n$ is *x* multiplied by itself **n - 1** times. Thus $3^4$ is $3 \times 3 \times 3 \times 3$. Here is a function which uses this method:

```
double power(double x, int n) {
   int j;
   double pow = 1.0;
   for (j = 1; j <= n; j++) pow = pow * x;
   return pow;
}
```

Note that if *n* is 0, **power** returns 1, the correct answer.

As written, this function performs *n* multiplications. However, we can write a faster function if we adopt a different approach. Supppose we want to calculate $x^{16}$. We can do it as follows:

- if we know **x8** = $x^8$, we can multiply **x8** by **x8** to get $x^{16}$, using just one more multiplication;

[4] The exact value is $2^{64} - 1 = 18{,}446{,}744{,}073{,}709{,}551{,}615$

- if we know **x4** = $x^4$, we can multiply **x4** by **x4** to get **x8**, using just one more multiplication;
- if we know **x2** = $x^2$, we can multiply **x2** by **x2** to get **x4**, using just one more multiplication;

We know **x**; therefore we can find **x2** using one multiplication; knowing **x2**, we can find **x4** using one more multiplication; knowing **x4**, we can find **x8** using one more multiplication; and knowing **x8**, we can find $x^{16}$ using one more multiplication. In all, we can find $x^{16}$ using just four multiplications.

What if **n** were 15? First, we would work out $x^{15/2}$, that is, $x^7$ (call this **x7**). We would then multiply **x7** by **x7** to give $x^{14}$. Recognizing that **n** is odd, we would then multiply this value by **x** to give the required answer. To summarize,

$$x^n = x^{n/2}.x^{n/2}, \text{ if } n \text{ is even and}$$
$$x.x^{n/2}.x^{n/2}, \text{ if } n \text{ is odd}$$

We use this as the basis for a recursive power function which calculates $x^n$ more efficiently than the function above.

```
double power(double x, int n) {
  double y;
  if (n == 0) return 1.0;
  y = power(x, n/2);
  y = y * y;
  if (n % 2 == 0) return y;
  return x * y;
}
```

As an exercise, trace the execution of the function with **n** = 5 and **n** = 6.

## 6.6 Merge sort

Consider, again, the problem of sorting a list of n items in ascending order. We will illustrate our ideas with a list of integers. In Section 1.8, we saw how to merge two sorted lists by traversing each list once. We now show how to use recursion and merging to sort a list. Consider:

```
sort a list
  sort first half of list
  sort second half of list
  merge sorted halves into one sorted list
end sort
```

Clearly, if we can sort the two halves and then merge them we will have a sorted list. But how do we sort the halves? We use the same method! For example,

```
sort first half of list
  sort first half of first half of list (one quarter of the original list)
  sort second half of first half of list (one quarter of the original list)
  merge sorted halves into one sorted list
end sort
```

And so on. For each piece we have to sort, we break it into halves, sort the halves and merge them. When do we stop using this process on a piece? When the piece consists of one element only; there is nothing to do to sort one element. We can modify our algorithm as follows:

```
sort a list
  if the list contains more than one element then
    sort first half of list
    sort second half of list
    merge sorted halves into one sorted list
  end if
end sort
```

We assume the list is stored in an array, **A**, from **A[lo]** to **A[hi]**. We can code the algorithm as a C function as follows:

```
void mergeSort(int A[], int lo, int hi) {
  void merge(int[], int, int, int);
  if (lo < hi) { //list contains at least 2 elements
    int mid = (lo + hi) / 2; //get the mid-point subscript
    mergeSort(A, lo, mid); //sort first half
    mergeSort(A, mid + 1, hi); //sort second half
    merge(A, lo, mid, hi); //merge sorted halves
  }
}
```

This assumes that **merge** is available and the statement

```
merge(A, lo, mid, hi);
```

will merge the sorted pieces in **A[lo..mid]** and **A[mid+1..hi]** so that **A[lo..hi]** is sorted. We will show how to write **merge** shortly.

But first, we show how this function sorts the following list stored in an array, **num**:

**num**

| 57 | 48 | 79 | 65 | 33 | 52 | 15 |
|---|---|---|---|---|---|---|
| 0 | 1 | 2 | 3 | 4 | 5 | 6 |

The function will be called with

```
mergeSort(num, 0, 6);
```

In the function, **num** will be known as **A**, **lo** will be 0 and **hi** will be 6. From these, **mid** will be calculated as 3, giving rise to two calls:

```
mergeSort(A, 0, 3);
mergeSort(A, 4, 6);
```

Assuming that the first will sort **A[0..3]** and the second will sort **A[4..6]**, thus:

**A**

| 48 | 57 | 65 | 79 | 15 | 33 | 52 |
|---|---|---|---|---|---|---|
| 0 | 1 | 2 | 3 | 4 | 5 | 6 |

**merge** will merge the pieces to produce

**A**

| 15 | 33 | 48 | 52 | 57 | 65 | 79 |
|---|---|---|---|---|---|---|
| 0 | 1 | 2 | 3 | 4 | 5 | 6 |

*Each* of the above calls will give rise to two further calls. The first will produce

```
mergeSort(A, 0, 1);
mergeSort(A, 2, 3);
```

and the second will produce

```
mergeSort(A, 4, 5);
mergeSort(A, 6, 6);
```

As long as **lo** is less than **hi**, two further calls will be produced. If **lo** is equal to **hi**, the list consists of one element only and the function simply returns. The following shows all the calls generated by the initial call to **mergeSort**, in the order in which they are generated:

```
mergeSort(A, 0, 6)
  mergeSort(A, 0, 3)
    mergeSort(A, 0, 1);
      mergeSort(A, 0, 0);
      mergeSort(A, 1, 1);
    mergeSort(A, 2, 3);
      mergeSort(A, 2, 2);
      mergeSort(A, 3, 3);
  mergeSort(A, 4, 6);
    mergeSort(A, 4, 5);
      mergeSort(A, 4, 4);
      mergeSort(A, 5, 5);
    mergeSort(A, 6, 6);
```

To complete the job, we need to write **merge**. We can describe **merge** as follows:

```
void merge(int A[], int lo, int mid, int hi) {
//A[lo..mid] and A[mid+1..hi] are sorted;
//merge the pieces so that A[lo..hi] are sorted
```

Note what must be done: we must merge two adjacent portions of **A** back into the *same* locations. The problem with this is that we *cannot* merge into the same locations *while the merge is being performed* since we may overwrite numbers before they are used. We will have to merge into another (temporary) array, then copy the merged elements back into the original locations in **A**.

We will use a temporary array called **T**; we just need to make sure it is big enough to hold the merged elements. This implies it must be at least as big as the array to be sorted. In **merge**, we will denote its size by the symbolic constant, **MaxSize**. Here is **merge**:

```
void merge(int A[], int lo, int mid, int hi) {
//A[lo..mid] and A[mid+1..hi] are sorted;
//merge the pieces so that A[lo..hi] are sorted
  int T[MaxSize];
  int i = lo;
  int j = mid + 1;
  int k = lo;
  while (i <= mid || j <= hi) {
    if (i > mid) T[k++] = A[j++];
    else if (j > hi) T[k++] = A[i++];
    else if (A[i] < A[j]) T[k++] = A[i++];
    else T[k++] = A[j++];
  }
  for (j = lo; j <= hi; j++) A[j] = T[j];
}
```

We use **i** to subscript the first part of **A**, **j** to subscript the second part and **k** to subscript **T**. The function merges **A[lo..mid]** and **A[mid+1..hi]** into **T[lo..hi]**.

The **while** loop expresses the following logic: as long as we haven't processed *all* the elements in *both* parts, we enter the loop. If we are finished with the first part (**i > mid**), copy an element from the second part to **T**. If we are finished with the second part (**j > hi**), copy an element from the first part to **T**. Otherwise, we copy the smaller of **A[i]** and **A[j]** to **T**.

At the end, we copy the elements from **T** to the corresponding locations in **A**.

We can test **mergeSort** with the following:

```
#include <stdio.h>
#define MaxSize 20
main() {
  void mergeSort(int[], int, int);
  int num[] = {4,8,6,16,1,9,14,2,3,5,18,13,17,7,12,11,15,10};
  int j, n = 18;
  mergeSort(num, 0, n-1);
  for (j = 0; j < n; j++) printf("%d ", num[j]);
  printf("\n\n");
}
```

When combined with **mergeSort** and **merge**, it produces the following output:

```
1 2 3 4 5 6 7 8 9 10 11 12 13 14 15 16 17 18
```

In passing, we note that merge sort is a much faster sorting method than either selection sort or insertion sort.

*Programming note*: each time we enter **merge**, storage is allocated for **T** and this storage is released when the function returns. This is so because, as declared, **T** is a local variable. If we wish, we can declare **T** as a *static* variable, thus:

```
static int T[MaxSize];
```

We simply put the word **static** before the normal declaration. We could also write

```
int static T[MaxSize];
```

Now, storage is allocated for **T** when we enter the function the first time only. It is not released when the *function* returns but remains in existence until the *program* ends. The *values* in **T** are also retained between calls to the function.

## 6.7 static variables

In general, a variable is declared to be **static** by prefixing its normal declaration with the word **static**, as in

```
static int lineCount;
```

We could also use

```
int static lineCount;
```

since the properties of a variable may be stated in any order. Initialization may be specified, as in

```
static int lineCount = 0;
```

In the absence of explicit initialization, C guarantees that **static** variables will be initialized to 0, but it is better programming practice to initialize your variables explicitly.

A **static** variable can be either (a) *internal* or (b) *external*.

### internal static

If the declaration appears inside a function, as in

```
void fun() {
  static int lineCount = 0;
      .
}
```

then the variable is known only inside the function, i.e. it is *local* to the function. Variables of the same name in other parts of the program will cause no conflict. Storage is allocated to an *internal static* variable once. If specified, initialization is done at this time. This storage (and the value it contains) is retained between calls to the function.

Thus, if the value of **lineCount** is 5 when the function returns the first time, the second call of the function can assume that the value of **lineCount** is 5. In this example, **lineCount** can be used to count the total number of lines printed by all the calls to this function.

---

### external static

If the declaration appears outside of all functions, as in

```
int fun1() {
     .
     .
}
static int lineCount = 0;
void fun2() {
     .
     .
}
```

then the variable is known from the point of declaration to the end of the file containing the declaration. In this example, **lineCount** is known to **fun2** and any functions that come after it in the file; it is *not* known to **fun1**.

If necessary, **lineCount** can be incremented by any function following the declaration, provided it is in the same file. Thus it can be used to count the total number of lines printed by all the functions which use it.

Normally, a function name is *external*, that is, it is known throughout the program, which may span several files. If we wish to restrict the scope of a function to a particular file, we can precede its normal declaration with the word **static**, as in:

```
static int fun(...)
```

Here, **fun** will be unknown outside the file in which this declaration appears.

The term **static** denotes permanence. Whether internal or external, a **static** variable is allocated storage only once, which is retained for the duration of the program. A **static** variable also affords a degree of 'privacy'. If it is internal, it is known only in the *function* in which it is declared. If it is external, it is known only in the *file* in which it is declared.

## 6.8 Counting organisms

Consider the following arrangement:

```
0 1 0 1 1 1 0
0 0 1 1 0 0 0
1 1 0 1 0 0 1
1 0 1 0 0 1 1
1 1 0 0 0 1 0
```

Assume that each `1` represents a cell of an organism; `0` means there is no cell. Two cells are *contiguous* if they are next to each other in the same row or same column. An organism is defined as follows:

- an organism contains at least one 1;
- two contiguous 1s belong to the same organism;

There are 5 organisms in the arrangement shown. Count them!

Given an arrangement of cells in a grid, we wish to write a program to count the number of organisms present.

A glance at the grid will reveal that, given a cell (`1`), the organism can extend in either of four directions. For *each* of these, it can extend in either of four directions, giving 16 possibilities. Each of these gives rise to four more possibilities, and so on. How do we keep track of all these possibilities, knowing which have been explored and which are still waiting to be explored?

The easiest way to do this is to let the recursive mechanism keep track for us.

To count the number of organisms, we need a way to determine which cells belong to an organism. To begin, we must find a `1`. Next, we must find all `1`s which are contiguous this `1`, then `1`s which are contiguous to those, and so on.

To find contiguous `1`s, we must look in four directions, North, East, South and West (in any order). When we look, there are 4 possibilities:

(1) we are outside the grid and there is nothing to do;

(2) we see a `0` and there is nothing to do;

(3) we see a `1` that has been seen previously; there is nothing to do;

(4) we see a 1 for the first time; we move into that position and look in four directions from there.

Step (3) implies that when we meet a 1 for the first time, we would need to mark it in some way so that if we come across this position later, we will know it has been met before and we will not attempt to process it again.

The simplest thing we can do is to change the value from 1 to 0; this ensures that nothing is done if this position is met again. This is fine if all we want to do is *count* the organisms. But if we also want to identify which cells make up an organism, we will have to mark it differently.

Presumably, we will need a variable which keeps count of the number of organisms. Let us call it **orgCount**. When a 1 is encountered for the first time, we will change it to **orgCount + 1**. Thus, the cells of organism 1 will be labelled 2, the cells of organism 2 will be labelled 3, and so on.

This is necessary since, if we start labelling from 1, we would not be able to distinguish between a 1 representing a not-yet-met cell and a 1 indicating a cell belonging to organism 1.

This "adding 1 to the label" is only necessary *while we are processing the grid.* When we print it, we will subtract 1 from the label so that, on output, organism 1 will be labelled 1, organism 2 will be labelled 2, and so on.

---

In writing the program, we assume that the grid data is stored in an array **G** and consists of **m** rows and **n** columns. We will use **MaxRow** and **MaxCol** to denote maximum values for **m** and **n**, respectively. Data for the program consist of values for **m** and **n**, followed by the cell data in row order. For example, data for the above grid will be supplied as:

```
5 7
0  1  0  1  1  1  0
0  0  1  1  0  0  0
1  1  0  1  0  0  1
1  0  1  0  0  1  1
1  1  0  0  0  1  0
```

We assume that the data will be read from a file, **cell.in** and output will be sent to the file **cell.out**.

The gist of the program logic is as follows:

```
scan the grid from left to right, top to bottom
when we meet a 1, we have a new organism
add 1 to orgCount
call a function findOrg to mark all the cells of the organism
```

The function, **findOrg**, will implement the four possibilities outlined above. When it sees a 1 in grid position (**i, j**), say, it will call itself recursively for each of the grid positions to the North, East, South and West of (**i, j**). All the details are shown in Program P6.1.

**Program P6.1**

```
#include <stdio.h>
#define MaxRow 20
#define MaxCol 20

int G[MaxRow][MaxCol];
int orgCount = 0;

main() {
  void findOrg(int, int, int, int);
  void printOrg(FILE *, int m, int n);
  int i, j, m, n;
  FILE * in = fopen("cell.in", "r");
  FILE * out = fopen("cell.out", "w");
  fscanf(in, "%d %d", &m, &n);
  for (i = 0; i < m; i++)
    for (j = 0; j < n; j++)
      fscanf(in, "%d", &G[i][j]);

  for (i = 0; i < m; i++)
    for (j = 0; j < n; j++)
      if (G[i][j] == 1) {
        orgCount++;
        findOrg(i, j, m, n);
      }

  printOrg(out, m, n);
} //end main

void findOrg(int i, int j, int m, int n) {
  if (i < 0 || i >= m || j < 0 || j >= n) return; //outside of grid
  if (G[i][j] == 0 || G[i][j] > 1) return; //no cell or cell already seen
  // else G[i][j] = 1;
  G[i][j]= orgCount + 1; //so that this 1 is not considered again
  findOrg(i - 1, j, m, n);
  findOrg(i, j + 1, m, n);
  findOrg(i + 1, j, m, n);
  findOrg(i, j - 1, m, n);
} //end findOrg
```

```
void printOrg(FILE * out, int m, int n) {
  int i, j;
  fprintf(out, "\nNumber of organisms = %d\n", orgCount);
  fprintf(out, "\nPosition of organisms are shown below\n\n");
  for (i = 0; i < m; i++) {
    for (j = 0; j < n; j++)
      if (G[i][j] > 1) fprintf(out, "%2d ", G[i][j] - 1);
        //organism labels are one more than they should be
      else fprintf(out, "%2d ", G[i][j]);
    fprintf(out, "\n");
  }
} //end printOrg
```

When run with the grid, above, this program produced the following output:

```
Number of organisms = 5

Position of organisms are shown below

0  1  0  2  2  2  0
0  0  2  2  0  0  0
3  3  0  2  0  0  4
3  0  5  0  0  4  4
3  3  0  0  0  4  0
```

Consider how **findOrg** identifies organism 1. In **main**, when **i** = 0 and **j** = 1, **G[0][1]** is 1 so the call **findOrg(0, 1, ...)** will be made with **G** as follows:

```
0  1  0  1  1  1  0
0  0  1  1  0  0  0
1  1  0  1  0  0  1
1  0  1  0  0  1  1
1  1  0  0  0  1  0
```

In **findOrg**, since **G[0][1]** is 1, it will be set to 2 and four calls to **findOrg** will be made as follows:

```
findOrg(-1, 1, ...); //immediate return since i < 0
findOrg(0, 2, ...); //immediate return since G[0][2] is 0
findOrg(1, 1, ...); //immediate return since G[1][1] is 0
findOrg(0, -1, ...); //immediate return since j < 0
```

All of these calls return immediately so only **G[0][1]** is marked with a 2.

Next, consider how **findOrg** identifies organism 3. In **main**, when **i** = 2 and **j** = 0, **G[2][0]** is 1 so the call **findOrg(2, 0, ...)** will be made with **G** as follows:

```
0  2  0  3  3  3  0
0  0  3  3  0  0  0
1  1  0  3  0  0  1
1  0  1  0  0  1  1
1  1  0  0  0  1  0
```

(Recall that, at this stage, the label of an organism is 1 more than the number of the organism.) For this example, we will use the notation N, E, S and W (rather than subscripts) to indicate a grid position to the North, East, South and West, respectively. At this stage, **orgCount** is 3 so that the cells will be labelled with 4.

The following are the calls generated to **findOrg** from the initial **findOrg(2, 0, ...)**.

```
findOrg(2, 0, ...) //G[2][0] is labelled with 4
  findOrg(N...) //returns immediately since G[N] is 0
  findOrg(E...) //G[E] is 1, relabelled with 4, gives rise to 4 calls
    findOrg(N...) //returns immediately since G[N] is 0
    findOrg(E...) //returns immediately since G[E] is 0
    findOrg(S...) //returns immediately since G[S] is 0
    findOrg(W...) //returns immediately since G[W] is 4
  findOrg(S...) //G[S] is 1, relabelled with 4, gives rise to 4 calls
    findOrg(N...) //returns immediately since G[N] is 4
    findOrg(E...) //returns immediately since G[E] is 0
    findOrg(S...) //G[S] is 1, relabelled with 4, gives rise to 4 calls
      findOrg(N...) //returns immediately since G[N] is 4
      findOrg(E...) //G[E] is 1, relabelled with 4, gives rise to 4 calls
        findOrg(N...) //returns immediately since G[N] is 0
        findOrg(E...) //returns immediately since G[E] is 0
        findOrg(S...) //returns immediately since G[S] is outside grid
        findOrg(W...) //returns immediately since G[W] is 4
      findOrg(S...) //returns immediately since G[S] is outside grid
      findOrg(W...) //returns immediately since G[W] is outside grid
    findOrg(W...) //returns immediately since G[W] is outside grid
  findOrg(W...) //returns immediately since G[W] is outside grid
```

When the call **findOrg(2, 0, ...)** finally returns, **G** would be changed to:

```
0  2  0  3  3  3  0
0  0  3  3  0  0  0
4  4  0  3  0  0  1
4  0  1  0  0  1  1
4  4  0  0  0  1  0
```

The third organism (labelled 4) has been identified. Note that *each* cell in the organism gave rise to 4 calls to **findOrg**.

## 6.9 Finding a path through a maze

Consider the following diagram which represents a maze:

```
##########
# #   #  #
# # # ## #
#   #    #
# ###### #
# # #S##
#     ## #
##########
```

Problem: starting at S, and moving along the open spaces, try to find a way out of the maze. The following shows how to do it with **x**s marking the path:

```
##########
# #xxx#  #
# #x#x## #
#xxx#xxxx#
#x######x#
#x# #x##xx
#xxxxx## #
##########
```

We wish to write a program which, given a maze, determines whether or not a path exists. If one exists, mark the path with **x**s.

Given any position in the maze, there are four possible directions in which one can move: North (N), East (E), South (S) and West (W). You will not be able to move in a particular direction if you meet a wall. However, if there is an open space, you can move into it.

In writing the program, we will try the directions in the order N, E, S and W. We will use the following strategy:

```
try N
if there is a wall, try E
else if there is a space, move to it and mark it with x
```

Whenever we go to an open space, we repeat this strategy. So, for instance, when we go East, if there is a space, we mark it and try the four directions *from this new position.*

Eventually, we will get out of the maze or we will reach a dead-end position. For example, suppose we get to the position marked ‘C’:

```
##########
#C#   #  #
#B# # ## #
#A  #    #
#x###### #
#x# #x##
#xxxxx## #
##########
```

There are walls in all directions except South, from which we came. In this situation, we go back to the previous position and try the next possibility from there. In this example, we go back to the position south of C (call this B).

When we were at B, we would have got to C by trying the North direction. Since this failed, when we go back to B, we will try the 'next' possibility, that is, East. This fails since there is a wall. So we try South; this fails since we have already been there. Finally, we try West which fails since there is a wall.

So, from B, we go back (we say *backtrack*) to the position from which we moved to B (call this A).

When we backtrack to A, the 'next' possibility is East. There is a space so we move into it, mark it with **x** and try the first direction (North) from there.

When we backtrack from a failed position, we must 'unmark' that position, that is, we must erase the **x**. This is necessary since a failed position will not be part of the solution path.

How do we backtrack? The recursive mechanism will take care of that for us, in a similar manner to the "counting organisms" problem. The following shows how:

```
int findPath(P) { //find a path from position P
  if P is outside the maze, return 0
  if P is at a wall, return 0
  if P was considered already, return 0
  //if we get here, P is a space we can move into
  mark P with x
  if P is on the border of the maze, we are out of the maze; return 1
  //try to extend the path to the North; if successful, return 1
  if (findPath(N)) return 1;
  //if North fails, try East, then South, then West
  //however, if North succeeds, there is no need to try other directions
  if (findPath(E)) return 1;
  if (findPath(S)) return 1;
  if (findPath(W)) return 1;
  //if all directions fail, we must unmark P and backtrack
  mark P with space
  return 0; //we have failed to find a path from P
} //end findPath
```

### *Writing the program*

First we must determine how the maze data will be supplied. In the example, above, the maze consists of 8 rows and 10 columns. If we represent each 'wall' by 1 and each 'space' by 0, the maze is represented by the following:

```
1 1 1 1 1 1 1 1 1 1
1 0 1 0 0 0 1 0 0 1
1 0 1 0 1 0 1 1 0 1
1 0 0 0 1 0 0 0 0 1
1 0 1 1 1 1 1 1 0 1
1 0 1 0 1 0 1 1 0 0
1 0 0 0 0 0 1 1 0 1
1 1 1 1 1 1 1 1 1 1
```

The start position, S, is at row 6, column 6. The first line of data will specify the number of rows and columns of the maze, and the coordinates of S. Thus, the first line of data will be:

```
8 10 6 6
```

This will be followed by the maze data, above.

When we need to mark a position with an 'x', we will use the value 2.

Our program will read data from the file **maze.in** and send output to **maze.out**. The complete program is shown as Program P6.2 (next page). When this program is run with the above data, it produces the following output:

```
##########
# #xxx#  #
# #x#x## #
#xxx#xxxx#
#x######x#
#x# #S##xx
#xxxxx## #
##########
```

**Program P6.2**

```
#include <stdio.h>
#define MaxRow 20
#define MaxCol 20

int m, n, sr, sc;
int G[MaxRow+1][MaxCol+1];

main() {
  void getData(FILE *);
  int findPath(int, int);
  void printMaze(FILE *);

  FILE * in = fopen("maze.in", "r");
```

```
    FILE * out = fopen("maze.out", "w");

    getData(in);
    if (findPath(sr, sc)) printMaze(out);
    else fprintf(out, "\nNo solution\n");

    fclose(in);
    fclose(out);
} //end main

void getData(FILE * in) {
    int r, c;
    fscanf(in, "%d %d %d %d", &m, &n, &sr, &sc);
    for (r = 1; r <= m; r++)
        for (c = 1; c <= n; c++)
            fscanf(in, "%d", &G[r][c]);
} //end getData

int findPath(int r, int c) {
    if (r < 1 || r > m || c < 1 || c > n) return 0;
    if (G[r][c] == 1) return 0; //into a wall
    if (G[r][c] == 2) return 0; //already considered

    // else G[r][c] = 0;
    G[r][c] = 2; //mark the path
    if (r == 1 || r == m || c == 1 || c == n) return 1;
    //path found - space located on the border of the maze

    if (findPath(r-1, c)) return 1;
    if (findPath(r, c+1)) return 1;
    if (findPath(r+1, c)) return 1;
    if (findPath(r, c-1)) return 1;
    G[r][c] = 0; //no path found; unmark
    return 0;
} //end findPath

void printMaze(FILE * out) {
    int r, c;
    for (r = 1; r <= m; r++) {
        for (c = 1; c <= n; c++)
            if (r == sr && c == sc) fprintf(out,"S");
            else if (G[r][c] == 0) fprintf(out," ");
            else if (G[r][c] == 1) fprintf(out,"#");
            else fprintf(out,"x");
        fprintf(out, "\n");
    }
} //end printMaze
```

## Exercises 6

1. Write an iterative function to return the *n*th Fibonacci number.
2. Print an integer with commas separating the thousands. For example, given 12058, print 12,058.
3. **A** is an array containing *n* integers. Write a recursive function to find the number of times a given integer **x** appears in **A**.
4. Write a recursive function to implement *selection sort.*
5. Write a recursive function to return the largest element in an integer array.
6. Write a recursive function to search for a given number in an **int** array.
7. Write a recursive function to search for a given number in a *sorted* **int** array.
8. What output is produced by the call **W(0)** of the following function?

```
void W(int n) {
  printf("%3d", n);
  if (n < 10) W(n + 3);
  printf("%3d", n);
}
```

9. What output is produced by the call **S('C')** of the following function?

```
void S(char ch) {
  if (ch < 'H') {
    S(++ch);
    printf("%c ", ch);
  }
}
```

10. In 9, what output would be produced if the statements within the **if** statement are interchanged?
11. In 9, what would happen if **++ch** is changed to **ch++**?
12. Write a recursive function, **length**, which, given a pointer to a linked list, returns the number of nodes in the list.
13. Write a recursive function, **sum**, which, given a pointer to a linked list of integers, returns the sum of the values at the nodes of the list.
14. Write a recursive function which, given a pointer to the head of a linked list of integers, returns 1 if the list is in ascending order and 0 if it is not.
15. What is printed by the call **fun(18, 3)** of the following recursive function?

```
void fun(int m, int n) {
  if (n > 0) {
    fun(m-1, n-1);
    printf("%d ", m);
    fun(m+1, n-1);
  }
}
```

16. What is returned by the call **test(7, 2)** of the following recursive function?

```
int test(int n, int r) {
  if (r == 0) return 1;
  if (r == 1) return n;
  if (r == n) return 1;
  return test(n-1, r-1) + test(n-1, r);
}
```

17. Write a recursive function which takes an integer argument and prints the integer with one space after each digit. For example, given `7583`, it prints `7 5 8 3 `.

18. Consider points (*m*, *n*) in the usual Cartesian coordinate system where *m* and *n* are positive *integers*. In a *north-east* path from point A to point B, one can move only *up* and only *right* (no *down* or *left* movements are allowed). Write a function which, given the coordinates of any two points A and B, returns the *number* of north-east paths from A to B.

19. The 8-queens problem can be stated as follows: place 8 queens on a chess board so that no two queens attack each other. Two queens attack each other if they are in the same row, same column or same diagonal. Clearly, any solution must have the queens in different rows and different columns.

    One approach to solving the problem is as follows. Place the first queen in the first column of the first row. Next, place the second queen so that it does not attack the first. If this is not possible, go back and place the first queen in the next column and try again.

    After the first two queens have been placed, place the third queen so that it does not attack the first two. If this is not possible, go back and place the second queen in the next column and try again. And so on.

    At each step, try to place the next queen so that it does not conflict with those already placed. If you succeed, try and place the next queen. If you fail, you must *backtrack* to the previously placed queen and try the next possible column. If all columns have been tried, you must backtrack to the queen before *this* queen and try the next column for *that* queen.

    The idea is similar to finding a path through a maze. Write a program to solve the 8-queens problem. Use recursion to implement the backtracking.

# 7 Random numbers, games and simulation

## In this chapter, we will explain:

- what are random numbers
- the difference between random and pseudo-random numbers
- how to generate random numbers on a computer
- how to write a program to play a guessing game
- how to write a program to drill a user in arithmetic
- how to write a program to play Nim
- how to simulate the collection of bottle caps to spell a word
- how to simulate queues in real-life situations
- how to estimate numerical values using random numbers

## 7.1 Random numbers

If you were to throw a 6-sided die 100 times, each time writing down the number which shows, you would have written down 100 *random* integers *uniformly distributed* in the range 1 to 6.

If you tossed a coin 144 times and, for each toss, wrote down `0` (for *heads*) or `1` (for *tails*), you would have written 144 random integers uniformly distributed in the range 0 to 1.

If you were standing by the roadside and, as vehicles passed, you noted the last two digits of the registration number, you would have noted random integers uniformly distributed in the range 0 to 99.

Spin a roulette wheel (with 36 numbers) 500 times. The 500 numbers which appear are random integers uniformly distributed in the range 1 to 36.

The word *random* implies that any outcome is completely independent of any other outcome. For instance, if a 5 showed on one throw of the die then this has no bearing on what would show on the next throw. Similarly, a 29 on the roulette wheel has no effect whatever on what number comes up next.

The term *uniformly distributed* means that all values are equally likely to appear. In the case of the die, you have the same chance of throwing a 1 or a 6 or any other number. And, in a large number of throws, each number will occur with roughly the same frequency.

In the case of a coin, if we toss it 144 times, we would expect *heads* to appear 72 times and *tails* to appear 72 times. In practice, these exact values are not normally obtained but, if the coin is a *fair* one, then the values would be close enough to the *expected* values to pass certain statistical tests. For example, 75 *heads* and 69 *tails* are close enough to the expected value of 72 to pass the required tests.

Random numbers are widely used in simulating games of chance (such as games involving dice, coins or cards), playing educational games (such as creating problems in arithmetic) and in modelling real-life situations on a computer.

For example, if we want to play a game of *Snakes and Ladders*, throwing the die is simulated by the computer *generating* a random number from 1 to 6. Suppose we want to create problems in addition for a child, using only the numbers from 1 to 9. For each problem, the computer can generate two numbers (for example, 7 and 4) in the range 1 to 9 and give these to the child to add.

But suppose we want to simulate the traffic pattern at a road intersection governed by traffic lights. We want to *time* the lights in such a way that the waiting time in both directions is as short as possible. In order to do the simulation on a computer, we will need some data as to how fast vehicles arrive at and leave the intersection. This must be done by observation in order for the simulation to be as useful as possible.

Suppose it is determined that a random number of vehicles (between 5 and 15) going in direction 1 arrive at the intersection every 30 seconds. Also, between 8 and 20 vehicles arrive every 30 seconds going in direction 2. The computer can simulate this situation as follows:

- generate a random number, **r1**, in the range 5 to 15;
- generate a random number, **r2**, in the range 8 to 20;

**r1** and **r2** are taken as the numbers of vehicles which arrive at the intersection from each direction in the first 30 seconds. The process is repeated for successive 30-second periods.

## 7.2 Random and pseudo-random numbers

The value which appears when a die is thrown has no effect on what comes up on the next throw. We say that the throws have independent outcomes and the values thrown are random integers in the range 1 to 6. But when a computer is used to generate a sequence of random numbers in a given interval, it uses an algorithm.

Normally, the next number in the sequence is generated from the previous number in a prescribed and predetermined manner. This means that the numbers in the sequence are not independent of each other, as they are when we throw a die, for instance. However, the numbers generated will pass the usual set of statistical tests for *randomness*, so, to all intents and purposes, they *are* random numbers. But, because they are generated in a very predictable manner, they are usually called *pseudo-random* numbers.

In modelling many types of situations, it does not usually matter whether we use random or pseudo-random numbers. If fact, in most applications, pseudo-random numbers work quite satisfactorily. However, consider an organization running a weekly lottery where the winning number is a 6-digit number. Should a pseudo-random number generator be used to provide the winning number from one week to the next?

Since the generator produces these numbers in a completely predetermined way, it would be possible to predict the winning numbers for weeks to come. Clearly, this is *not* desirable (unless *you* are in charge of the random number generator!). In this situation, a truly random method of producing the winning numbers is needed.

## 7.3 Generating random numbers by computer

In what follows, we make no distinction between random and pseudo-random numbers since, for most practical purposes, no distinction is necessary. Almost all programming languages provide some sort of random number generator, but there are slight differences in the way they operate.

In C, we can work with random numbers using the predefined constant **RAND_MAX** and the functions **rand** and **srand**. To use them, your program must be preceded by

```
#include <stdlib.h>
```

The value of **RAND_MAX** is the maximum possible value which can be returned by **rand**. On some systems, it is 2147483647, which is the largest signed integer representable in 32 bits. On others, it is 32767, which is the largest signed integer representable in 16 bits.

The prototype for **rand** is

```
int rand(void)
```

It returns the next random number in the series. The value is in the range 0 to **RAND_MAX**.

The prototype for **srand** is

```
void srand(unsigned int seed)
```

It uses **seed** to establish a starting point for a new series of random numbers. We say we must *seed* the random number generator. Normally, you must call **srand** to seed the generator *before* using **rand**. If you call **rand** before **srand**, it uses the value 1 as a default seed.

In practice, we would hardly ever use **rand** in the form provided. This is because, most times, we would need random numbers in a specific range (like 1 to 36, say)

rather than 0 to 32767. However, we can easily write a function which uses **rand** and **srand** to provide random numbers from **m** to **n** where **m** < **n**. Here it is:

```
int random(int m, int n) {
//returns a random integer from m to n, inclusive
  int offset = rand() / (RAND_MAX + 1.0) * (n - m + 1);
  return m + offset;
} //end random
```

Before using **random**, we must seed the generator. We can do this in **main** with:

```
srand(101); //an arbitrary integer
```

In **random**, it is important to use 1.0 instead of 1. Since **rand** returns an integer and **RAND_MAX + 1** is also an integer, if 1 is used an integer division would be performed. This would always give 0 since the maximum value of **rand** is **RAND_MAX**. The value returned by **random** would always be m.

However, using (the **double** constant) 1.0 causes **RAND_MAX + 1.0** to be evaluated as **double**, in turn causing the value returned by **rand** to be converted to **double** and a floating-point division to be performed. The value of **(n - m + 1)** is also converted to **double** and the multiplication performed. The result obtained is truncated before being assigned to the integer variable **offset**. In effect, the construct

```
rand() / (RAND_MAX + 1.0)
```

returns a random *fraction*, *f*, between 0 (inclusive) and 1 (exclusive).

To illustrate how **random** works, suppose **m** = 5 and **n** = 20. There are 20 - 5 + 1 = 16 numbers in the range 5 to 20. We calculate **offset** as follows, noting that the smallest value of *f* is 0.0 and the largest is 0.9999 (to 4 decimal places):

- *f* is multiplied by 16 to give a value from 0.0 to 15.99 (to 2 decimal places);
- when assigned to **offset** (an **int**), the fraction is discarded so **offset** assumes a value between 0 and 15;

5 is added to **offset**, giving a value between 5 and 20. *This* is the value returned by **random**.

Another reason for using 1.0 is that, on many systems, the value of **RAND_MAX** is the largest integer on the system (typically, 32767 for a 16-bit **int**). If we tried to add the *integer* 1 to it, *overflow* would occur since we would be trying to exceed the largest value which can be stored.

One final note: when we use a given seed (101, say), this determines the sequence of numbers which will be generated. If we re-run the program with the same seed, the *same* sequence will be generated. We can change the seed but this will entail changing the program. We can ask the user to enter a seed but this puts a burden on the user and may confuse her since she may not know the purpose of the number she is being asked to enter.

A common approach is to use the **time** function provided by C in **time.h**. In its simplest form, we can use

```
srand(time(0));
```

This uses the actual time at which the program is being run to seed the generator. Since this will be different each time the program is run, the sequence generated will be different.

---

### *Example*

Consider the following code which generates and prints 20 random numbers from 1 to 6:

```
#include <stdio.h>
#include <stdlib.h>
main() {
  int j, random(int, int);
  srand(101);
  for (j = 1; j <= 20; j++) printf("%2d", random(1, 6));
  printf("\n\n");
}
```

When run, it prints the following sequence of random numbers:

```
1 3 3 6 4 3 4 1 1 6 5 3 4 4 2 5 4 6 5 4
```

Each call to **random** produces the next number in the sequence. Note that the sequence may be different on another computer or on the same computer using a different compiler.

If the code is run a second time, the exact same sequence will be produced since the seed, 101, is the same.

However, if we change **srand(101)** to **srand(time(0))**, two runs of the program will produce different sequences, as shown below:

```
2 6 5 6 4 2 1 6 6 3 2 4 6 3 6 3 3 2 2 1

5 5 2 3 4 3 6 4 4 2 1 5 1 3 4 3 6 1 1 5
```

Each time the program is run, a different sequence will be generated.

Programming note: strictly speaking, in order to use the function **time**, you should have **#include <time.h>** at the head of your program. However, some compilers have a declaration for **time** in **stdlib.h** so all you need is **#include <stdlib.h>**.

## 7.4 A guessing game

To illustrate a simple use of random numbers, let us write a program to play a guessing game. The program will 'think of' a number from 1 to 100. You are required to guess the number using as few guesses as possible. The following is a sample run of the program. Underlined items are typed by the user:

```
I have thought of a number from 1 to 100.
Try to guess what it is.

Your guess? 50
Too low
Your guess? 75
Too high
Your guess? 62
Too high
Your guess? 56
Too low
Your guess? 59
Too high
Your guess? 57
Congratulations, you've got it!
```

As you can see, each time you guess, the program will tell you whether your guess is too high or too low and allow you to guess again.

The program will 'think of' a number from `1` to `100` by calling **random(1, 100)**. You will guess until you have guessed correctly or until you 'give up'. You give up by entering `0` as your guess. Program P7.1 (next page) contains all the details.

Programming note: it is a good idea to remind the user that he has the option of giving up and how to do so. To this end, the prompt can be:

```
Your guess (0 to give up)?
```

**Exercise**: modify the program to play several games in one run. After each game, ask the user if he wishes to play another.

## 7.5 Drills in addition

We wish to write a program to drill a user in simple arithmetic problems. More specifically, we want to write a program to create addition problems for a user to solve. The problems will involve the addition of two numbers. But where do the numbers come from? We will let the computer 'think up' the two numbers. By now, you should know that, in order to do this, the computer will generate two random numbers.

We also need to decide what size of numbers to use in the problems. This will determine, to some extent, how difficult the problems are going to be. We will use 2-digit numbers, that is, numbers from 10 to 99. The program can be easily modified to handle numbers in a different range.

**Program P7.1**

```
#include <stdio.h>
#include <stdlib.h>
main() {
  int answer, guess, random(int, int);

  printf("\nI have thought of a number from 1 to 100.\n");
  printf("Try to guess what it is.\n\n");

  srand(time(0));
  answer = random(1, 100);

  printf("Your guess? ");
  scanf("%d", &guess);
  while (guess != answer && guess != 0) {
    if (guess < answer) printf("Too low\n");
    else printf("Too high\n");
    printf("Your guess? ");
    scanf("%d", &guess);
  }
  if (guess == 0) printf("Sorry, answer is %d\n", answer);
  else printf("Congratulations, you've got it!\n");
} //end main

int random(int m, int n) {
//returns a random integer from m to n, inclusive
  int offset = rand() / (RAND_MAX + 1.0) * (n - m + 1);
  return m + offset;
} //end random
```

The program will begin by asking the user how many problems he wishes to be given. The user will type the amount required. He will then be asked how many attempts he wants to be given for each problem. He will enter this amount. The program then proceeds to give him the requested number of problems.

The following is a sample run of the program. Underlined items are typed by the user; everything else is typed by the computer.

```
Welcome to Problems in Addition

How many problems would you like? 3
Maximum tries per problem? 2

Problem 1, Try 1 of 2
   80 + 75 = 155
Correct, well done!
```

```
Problem 2, Try 1 of 2
   17 + 29 = 36
Incorrect, try again

Problem 2, Try 2 of 2
   17 + 29 = 46
Correct, well done!

Problem 3, Try 1 of 2
   83 + 87 = 160
Incorrect, try again

Problem 3, Try 2 of 2
   83 + 87 = 180
Sorry, answer is 170

Thank you for playing. Bye...
```

All the details are shown in Program P7.2 on the next page.

## 7.6 Nim

One version of the game called Nim is played between two people, A and B, say. Initially, there is a known number of matches (**startAmount**, say) on the table. Each player, in turn, is allowed to pick up any number of matches from 1 to some agreed maximum (**maxPick**, say). The player who picks up the last match *loses* the game. For example, if **startAmount** is 20 and **maxPick** is 3, the game may proceed as follows:

A picks up 2, leaving 18 on the table
B picks up 1, leaving 17 on the table
A picks up 3, leaving 14 on the table
B picks up 1, leaving 13 on the table
A picks up 2, leaving 11 on the table
B picks up 2, leaving 9 on the table
A picks up 1, leaving 8 on the table
B picks up 3, leaving 5 on the table
A picks up 1, leaving 4 on the table
B picks up 3, leaving 1 on the table

A is forced to pick up the last match and, therefore, loses the game.

What is the best way to play the game? Obviously, the goal should be to leave your opponent with 1 match remaining on the table. Let us call this a *losing position*. The next question to answer is: how many matches must you leave so that, no matter how many he picks up (within the rules of the game), you can leave him with 1?

**Program P7.2**

```
#include <stdio.h>
#include <stdlib.h>
main() {
  int j, try, maxTries, numProblems, answer, response;
  int num1, num2, random(int, int);

  printf("\nWelcome to Problems in Addition\n\n");
  printf("How many problems would you like? ");
  scanf("%d", &numProblems);
  printf("Maximum tries per problem? ");
  scanf("%d", &maxTries);

  srand(time(0));

  for (j = 1; j <= numProblems; j++) {
    num1 = random(10, 99);
    num2 = random(10, 99);
    answer = num1 + num2;
    for (try = 1; try <= maxTries; try++) {
      printf("\nProblem %d, Try %d of %d\n", j, try, maxTries);
      printf("%5d + %2d = ", num1, num2);
      scanf("%d", &response);
      if (response == answer) {
        printf("Correct, well done!\n");
        break;
      }
      if (try < maxTries) printf("Incorrect, try again\n");
      else printf("Sorry, answer is %d\n", answer);
    } //end for try
  } //end for j
  printf("\nThank you for playing. Bye...\n");
} //end main

int random(int m, int n) {
//returns a random integer from m to n, inclusive
  int offset = rand() / (RAND_MAX + 1.0) * (n - m + 1);
  return m + offset;
} //end random
```

In this example, the answer is 5. Whether he picks up 1, 2 or 3, you can *always* leave him with 1. If he picks up 1, you pick up 3; if he picks up 2, you pick up 2; if he picks up 3, you pick up 1. So, therefore, 5 is the next losing position.

Next question: how many matches must you leave so that, no matter how many he picks up (within the rules of the game), you can leave him with 5? The answer is 9. Try it!

And so on. Reasoning this way, we discover that 1, 5, 9, 13, 17, etc. are all losing positions. In other words, if you can leave your opponent with any of these number of matches, you can force a win.

In this example, the moment B left A with 17 matches, B was in a position from which he could not lose, unless he became careless.

In general, losing positions are obtained by adding 1 to multiples of **maxPick + 1**. If **maxPick** is 3, multiples of 4 are 4, 8, 12, 16, etc. Adding 1 gives the losing positions 5, 9, 13, 17, etc.

We will write a program in which the computer plays the best possible game of Nim. If it can force the user into a losing position, it will. If the user has forced *it* into a losing position, it will pick up a random number of matches and hope that the user makes a mistake.

If **remain** is the number of matches remaining on the table, how can the computer determine what is the best move to make?

If **remain** is less than or equal to **maxPick**, the computer picks up **remain - 1** matches, leaving the user with 1. Otherwise, we perform the calculation:

```
r = remain % (maxPick + 1)
```

If **r** is 0, **remain** is a multiple of **maxPick + 1**; the computer picks up **maxPick** matches, leaving the user in a losing position. In this example, if **remain** is 16 (a multiple of 4), the computer picks up 3, leaving the user with 13—a losing position.

If **r** is 1, the computer is in a losing position and picks up a random number of matches.

Otherwise, the computer picks up **r - 1** matches, leaving the user in a losing position. In this example, if **remain** is 18, **r** would be 2. The computer picks up 1, leaving the user with 17—a losing position.

This strategy is implemented in the function **bestPick**, part of Program P7.3 which pits the computer against a user in our version of Nim.

Note the use of the **do...while** statement for getting and validating the user's play. The general form is

```
do <statement> while (<expression>);
```

As usual, **<statement>** can be simple (one-line) or compound (enclosed in braces). The words **do** and **while**, the brackets and the semicolon are required. The programmer supplies **<statement>** and **<expression>**. A **do...while** is executed as follows:

**Program P7.3**

```
#include <stdio.h>
#include <stdlib.h>
main() {
  int remain, maxPick, userPick, compPick;
  int bestPick(int, int), min(int, int);
  printf("\nNumber of matches on the table? ");
  scanf("%d", &remain);
  printf("Maximum pickup per turn? ");
  scanf("%d", &maxPick);
  printf("\nMatches remaining: %d\n", remain);
  srand(time(0));
  while (1) { //do forever...well, until the game ends
    do {
      printf("Your turn: ");
      scanf("%d", &userPick);
      if (userPick > remain)
        printf("Cannot pick up more than %d\n", min(remain, maxPick));
      else if (userPick < 1 || userPick > maxPick)
        printf("Invalid: must be between 1 and %d\n", maxPick);
    } while (userPick > remain || userPick < 1 || userPick > maxPick);
    remain = remain - userPick;
    printf("Matches remaining: %d\n", remain);
    if (remain == 0) {
      printf("You lose!!\n");
      exit(0);
    }
    if (remain == 1) {
      printf("You win!!\n");
      exit(0);
    }
    compPick = bestPick(remain, maxPick);
    printf("I pick up %d\n", compPick);
    remain = remain - compPick;
    printf("Matches remaining: %d\n", remain);
    if (remain == 0) {
      printf("You win!!\n");  exit(0);
    }
    if (remain == 1) {
      printf("I win!!\n");  exit(0);
    }
  } //end while(1)
} //end main
```

```
int bestPick(int remain, int maxPick) {
  int random(int, int);
  if (remain <= maxPick) return remain - 1; //put user in losing position
  int r = remain % (maxPick + 1);
  if (r == 0) return maxPick; //put user in losing position
  if (r == 1) return random(1, maxPick); //computer in losing position
  return r - 1; //put user in losing position
} //end bestPick

int min(int a, int b) {
  if (a < b) return a;
  return b;
} //end min

int random(int m, int n) {
//returns a random integer from m to n, inclusive
  int offset = rand() / (RAND_MAX + 1.0) * (n - m + 1);
  return m + offset;
} //end random
```

(1) **<statement>** is executed;

(2) **<expression>** is then evaluated; if it is true (non-zero), repeat from (1). If it is false (zero), execution continues with the statement, if any, after the semicolon.

As long as **<expression>** is true, **<statement>** is executed. It is important to note that because of the nature of the construct, **<statement>** is *always executed at least once*. This is particularly useful in a situation where we *want* **<statement>** to be executed at least once. In this example, we need to prompt the user at least once for his play, hence the use of **do...while**.

A sample run of P7.3 is shown on the next page.

We note, in passing, that it would be useful to provide instructions for the game when it is run.

## 7.7 Non-uniform distributions

So far, the random numbers we have generated have been *uniformly distributed* in a given range. So that, for instance, when we generated numbers from 10 to 99, each number in that range had the same chance of being generated. Similarly, the call **random(1, 6)** will generate each of the numbers 1 to 6 with equal probability.

Now suppose we want the computer to "throw" a 6-sided die. Since the computer can't physically throw the die, it has to simulate the process of throwing. What is the purpose of throwing the die? It is simply to come up with a random number from 1 to 6. As we have seen, *this* the computer knows how to do.

```
Number of matches on the table? 30
Maximum pickup per turn? 5

Matches remaining: 30
Your turn: 2
Matches remaining: 28
I pick up 3
Matches remaining: 25
Your turn: 3
Matches remaining: 22
I pick up 3
Matches remaining: 19
Your turn: 6
Invalid: must be between 1 and 5
Your turn: 1
Matches remaining: 18
I pick up 5
Matches remaining: 13
Your turn: 4
Matches remaining: 9
I pick up 2
Matches remaining: 7
Your turn: 9
Cannot pick up more than 5
Your turn: 2
Matches remaining: 5
I pick up 4
Matches remaining: 1
I win!!
```

If the die is ‘fair’, then each of the faces has the same chance of showing. To simulate the throwing of such a die, all we have to do is generate random numbers uniformly distributed in the range 1 to 6. We can do this with **random(1, 6)**.

Similarly, when we toss a ‘fair’ coin, *heads* and *tails* both have the same chance of showing. To simulate the tossing of such a coin on a computer, all we have to do is generate random numbers uniformly distributed in the range 1 to 2. We can let 1 represent *heads* and 2 represent *tails*.

In general, if all possible occurrences of an event (like throwing a fair die) are equally likely, we can use uniformly distributed random numbers to simulate the event. However, if all occurrences are not equally likely, how can we simulate such an event?

To give an example, consider a *biased* coin which comes up *heads* twice as often as *tails*. We say that the probability of *heads* is 2/3 and the probability of *tails* is 1/3. To simulate such a coin, we generate random numbers uniformly distributed in the range 1 to 3. If 1 or 2 occurs, we say that *heads* was thrown; if 3 occurs, we say that *tails* was thrown.

Thus, to simulate an event which has a non-uniform distribution, we convert it to one in which we can use uniformly distributed random numbers.

For another example, suppose that, for any day of a given month (June, say), we know that the:

probability of sun = 4/9
probability of rain = 3/9
probability of overcast = 2/9

and only these conditions are possible. We can simulate the weather for June as follows:

```
for each day in June
  r = random(1, 9)
  if (r <= 4) "the day is sunny"
  else if (r <= 7) "the day is rainy"
  else "the day is overcast"
endfor
```

We note, in passing, that we can assign *any* 4 numbers to 'sunny', any other 3 to 'rainy' and the remaining 2 to 'overcast'.

---

### 7.7.1 Collecting bottle caps

The maker of a popular beverage is running a contest in which you must collect bottle caps to spell the word M-A-N-G-O. It is known that in every 100 bottle caps, there are 40 As, 25 Os, 15 Ns, 15 Ms and 5 Gs. We wish to write a program to perform 20 simulations of the collection of bottle caps until we have enough caps to spell M-A-N-G-O. For each simulation, we want to know how many caps were collected. We also want to know the average number of bottle caps collected per simulation.

The collection of a bottle cap is an event with non-uniform distribution. It is easier to collect an A than a G. To simulate the event, we can generate random numbers uniformly distributed in the range 1 to 100. To determine which letter was collected, we can use:

```
c = random(1, 100)
if (c <= 40) we have an A
else if (c <= 65) we have an O
else if (c <= 80) we have an N
else if (c <=95) we have an M
else we have a G
```

In this example, if we wish, we can scale everything by a factor of 5 and use:

```
c = random(1, 20)
if (c <= 8) we have an A
else if (c <= 13) we have an O
else if (c <= 16) we have an N
else if (c <=19) we have an M
else we have a G
```

Either version will work fine for this problem.

The gist of the algorithm for solving this problems is as follows:

```
totalCaps = 0
for sim = 1 to 20
  capsThisSim = perform one simulation
  print capsThisSim
  add capsThisSim to totalCaps
endfor
print totalCaps / 20
```

The logic for performing one simulation is as follows:

```
numCaps = 0
while (word not spelt) {
  collect a cap and determine the letter
  mark the letter collected
  add 1 to numCaps
}
return numCaps
```

We will use an array **cap[5]** to hold the status of each letter: **cap[0]** for A, **cap[1]** for O, **cap[2]** for N, **cap[3]** for M and **cap[4]** for G. A value of 0 indicates that the corresponding letter has not been collected. When we collect an N, say, we set **cap[2]** to 1; similarly for the other letters. We have collected each letter at least once when all the elements of **cap** are 1.

All these details are incorporated in Program P7.4, shown on the next page. When run, this program produced the following output:

```
Simulation  Caps collected

     1           10
     2           10
     3           22
     4           12
     5           36
     6            9
     7           15
     8            7
     9           11
    10           70
    11           17
    12           12
    13           27
    14           10
    15            6
    16           25
    17            8
    18            7
    19           39
    20           71

Average caps per simulation: 21
```

The results range from as few as 6 caps to as many as 71. Sometimes you get lucky, sometimes you don't.

**Program P7.4**

```
#include <stdio.h>
#include <stdlib.h>
#define MaxSim 20
#define MaxLetters 5
main() {
  int sim, capsThisSim, totalCaps = 0, doOneSim();

  srand(time(0));
  printf("\nSimulation  Caps collected\n\n");
  for (sim = 1; sim <= MaxSim; sim++) {
    capsThisSim = doOneSim();
    printf("%6d %13d\n", sim, capsThisSim);
    totalCaps += capsThisSim;
  }
  printf("\nAverage caps per simulation: %d\n", totalCaps/MaxSim);
} //end main

int doOneSim() {
  int j, cap[MaxLetters], numCaps = 0, mango(int []), random(int, int);
  for (j = 0; j < MaxLetters; j++) cap[j] = 0;
  while (!mango(cap)) {
    int c = random(1, 20);
    if (c <= 8) cap[0] = 1;
    else if (c <= 13) cap[1] = 1;
    else if (c <= 16) cap[2] = 1;
    else if (c <= 19) cap[3] = 1;
    else cap[4] = 1;
    numCaps++;
  }
  return numCaps;
} //end doOneSim

int mango(int cap[]) {
  int j;
 for (j = 0; j < MaxLetters; j++)
    if (cap[j] == 0) return 0;
  return 1;
} //end mango

int random(int m, int n) {
//returns a random integer from m to n, inclusive
  int offset = rand() / (RAND_MAX + 1.0) * (n - m + 1);
  return m + offset;
} //end random
```

## 7.8 Simulation of real-life problems

The computer can be used to answer certain questions about many real-life situations by using *simulation*. The process of simulation allows us to consider different solutions to a problem. This enables us to choose, with confidence, the best alternative for a given situation.

However, before the computer simulation is done, we need to collect data to enable the simulation to be as realistic as possible. For example, if we wish to simulate the serving of customers at a bank, we would need to know (or at least estimate):

- the time, *t1*, between arrivals of customers in the queue
- the time, *t2*, to serve a customer

Of course, *t1* could vary greatly. It would depend, for instance, on the time of the day; at certain times, customers arrive more frequently than at other times. Also, different customers have different needs, so *t2* would vary from one customer to the next. However, by observing the system in operation for a while, we can usually make assumptions like:

- *t1* varies randomly between 1 and 5 minutes
- *t2* varies randomly between 3 and 10 minutes

Using these assumptions, we can do the simulation to find out how the queue length varies when there are 2, 3, 4, ..., etc. service counters. We assume that there is one queue; the person at the head of the queue goes to whichever counter first becomes available. In practice, a bank usually assigns more counters at peak periods than at slow periods. In this case, we can do the simulation in two parts, using the assumptions which apply for each period.

Other situations in which a similar method of simulation applies are:

- checkout counters at supermarkets or stores; we are normally interested in a compromise between the number of checkout counters and the average queue length. The fewer counters we have, the longer will be the queue. However, more counters mean more machines and more employees. We want to find the best compromise between the cost of operation and service to customers.
- gasoline stations; how many pumps will best serve the needs of the customers?
- queues at traffic lights; what is the best 'timing' of the lights so that the average length of the queues in all directions is kept to a minimum? In this case, we would need to gather data such as:
  (i) how often do cars arrive from direction 1, and from direction 2? The answer to this might be something like:

  between 5 and 15 cars arrive every minute from direction 1;
  between 10 and 30 cars arrive every minute from direction 2.

(ii) how fast can cars leave in direction 1, and in direction 2? The answer might be:

20 cars can cross the intersection in direction 1 in 30 seconds;
30 cars can cross the intersection in direction 2 in 30 seconds.

We assume, in this simple situation, that turning is not allowed.

## 7.9 Simulating a queue

Consider the situation at a bank or supermarket checkout, where customers arrive and must queue for service. Suppose there is one queue but several counters. If a counter is free, the person at the head of the queue goes to it. If all counters are busy, the customers must wait; the person at the head of the queue goes to the first available counter.

To illustrate, suppose there are two counters; we denote them by C1 and C2. To perform the simulation, we need to know the frequency with which customers arrive and the time it takes to serve a customer. Based on observation and experience, we may be able to say that:

- the time between customer arrivals varies randomly from 1 to 5 minutes
- the time to serve a customer varies randomly from 3 to 10 minutes

In order for the simulation to be meaningful, this data must be close to what occurs in practice. As a general rule, a simulation is only as good as the data on which it is based.

Suppose we begin at 9:00 a.m. We can simulate the arrival of the first 10 customers by generating 10 random numbers from 1 to 5, thus:

```
3 1 2 4 2 5 1 3 2 4
```

This means that the first customer arrives at 9:03, the second at 9:04, the third at 9:06, the fourth at 9:10, and so on.

We can simulate the service time for these customers by generating 10 random numbers from 3 to 10, thus:

```
5 8 7 6 9 4 7 4 9 6
```

This means that the first customer spends 5 minutes at the teller, the second spends 8 minutes, the third spends 7 minutes, and so on.

The following table shows what happens to these 10 customers.

| Customer | Arrives | Start Service | Counter | Service Time | Departs | Wait Time |
|---|---|---|---|---|---|---|
| 1 | 9:03 | 9:03 | C1 | 5 | 9:08 | 0 |
| 2 | 9:04 | 9:04 | C2 | 8 | 9:12 | 0 |
| 3 | 9:06 | 9:08 | C1 | 7 | 9:15 | 2 |
| 4 | 9:10 | 9:12 | C2 | 6 | 9:18 | 2 |
| 5 | 9:12 | 9:15 | C1 | 9 | 9:24 | 3 |
| 6 | 9:17 | 9:18 | C2 | 4 | 9:22 | 1 |
| 7 | 9:18 | 9:22 | C2 | 7 | 9:29 | 4 |
| 8 | 9:21 | 9:24 | C1 | 4 | 9:28 | 3 |
| 9 | 9:23 | 9:28 | C1 | 9 | 9:37 | 5 |
| 10 | 9:27 | 9:29 | C2 | 6 | 9:35 | 2 |

- The first customer arrives at 9:03 and goes straight to C1. His service time is 5 minutes so he will leave C1 at 9:08.
- The second customer arrives at 9:04 and goes straight to C2. His service time is 8 minutes so he will leave C2 at 9:12.
- The third customer arrives at 9:06. At this time, both C1 and C2 are busy so he must wait. C1 will be the first to become free at 9:08. This customer will begin service at 9:08. His service time is 7 minutes so he will leave C1 at 9:15. This customer had to wait in the queue for 2 minutes.
- The fourth customer arrives at 9:10. At this time, both C1 and C2 are busy so he must wait. C2 will be the first to become free at 9:12. This customer will begin service at 9:12. His service time is 6 minutes so he will leave C2 at 9:18. This customer had to wait in the queue for 2 minutes.

And so on. Work through the rest of the table to make sure you understand how those values are obtained.

Also observe that once the tellers started serving, they had no 'idle' time. As soon as one customer left, another was waiting to be served.

---

### *Programming the simulation*

We now show how to write a program to produce the above table. First we observe that it is no more difficult to write the program for several counters than it is for two. Hence, we will assume that there are **n** (**n** < 10) counters.

We will use an array **depart[10]** such that **depart[j]** will hold the time at which counter **j** will next become free. We will not use **depart[0]**. If we need to handle more than 9 counters, we just need to increase the size of **depart**.

Suppose the customer at the head of the queue arrives at **arriveTime**. He will go to the first free counter. Counter **j** is free if **arriveTime** is greater than or equal to

**depart[j]**. If no counter is free, he must wait. He will go to the counter with the lowest value in the array **depart**; suppose this is **depart[m]**. He will begin service at a time which is the later of **arriveTime** and **depart[m]**.

The program begins by asking for the number of counters and the number of customers to be simulated. The simulation starts from time 0 and all times are relative to this. The details are shown in Program P7.5.

**Program P7.5**

```
#include <stdio.h>
#include <stdlib.h>
#define MaxCounters 9
main() {
  int random(int, int), smallest(int[], int, int), max(int, int);
  int depart[MaxCounters + 1];
  int j, m, n, numCust, arriveTime, startServe, serveTime, waitTime;

  printf("\nHow many counters? ");
  scanf("%d", &n);
  printf("\nHow many customers? ");
  scanf("%d", &numCust);

  for (j = 1; j <= n; j++) depart[j] = 0;
  srand(time(0));
  printf("\n               Start        Service       Wait\n");
  printf("Customer Arrives Service Counter  Time  Departs Time\n\n");
  arriveTime = 0;
  for (j = 1; j <= numCust; j++) {
    arriveTime += random(1, 5);
    m = smallest(depart, 1, n);
    startServe = max(arriveTime, depart[m]);
    serveTime = random(3, 10);
    depart[m] = startServe + serveTime;
    waitTime = startServe - arriveTime;
    printf("%5d %8d %7d %6d %7d %8d %5d\n",
      j, arriveTime, startServe, m, serveTime, depart[m], waitTime);
  } //end for
} //end main

int smallest(int list[], int lo, int hi) {
//returns the subscript of the smallest value in list
  int j, k = lo;
  for (j = lo + 1; j <= hi; j++)
    if (list[j] < list[k]) k = j;
  return k;
} //end smallest
```

```
int max(int a, int b) {
  if (a > b) return a;
  return b;
} //end max

int random(int m, int n) {
//returns a random integer from m to n, inclusive
  int offset = rand() / (RAND_MAX + 1.0) * (n - m + 1);
  return m + offset;
} //end random
```

A sample run of P7.5 is shown below:

```
How many counters? 2

How many customers? 10

                  Start          Service          Wait
Customer Arrives Service Counter  Time   Departs Time

    1        3       3      1       8       11     0
    2        7       7      2       9       16     0
    3       10      11      1       9       20     1
    4       11      16      2       4       20     5
    5       14      20      1       5       25     6
    6       19      20      2       9       29     1
    7       23      25      1       7       32     2
    8       26      29      2       8       37     3
    9       29      32      1       7       39     3
   10       33      37      2       6       43     4
```

As you can see, the waiting time is reasonably short. However, if you run the simulation with 25 customers, you will see that the waiting time increases appreciably. What if we added added another counter? With simulation, it's easy to test the effect of this without actually having to buy another machine or hire another employee.

In this case, all we have to do is enter 3 and 25 for the number of counters and customers, respectively. When we do, we will find that there is very little waiting time. We urge you to experiment with different data—counters, customers, arrival times, service times—to see what happens.

**Exercise**: modify the program to calculate the average waiting time for customers and the total idle time for each counter.

## 7.10 Estimating numerical values using random numbers

We have seen how random numbers can be used to play games and simulate real-life situations. A less obvious use is to estimate numerical values which may be difficult or cumbersome to calculate. We will show how to use random numbers to estimate the square root of a number and $\pi$ (pi).

### *Estimating* $\sqrt{5}$

We use random numbers to estimate the square root of 5 based on the following:

- $\sqrt{5}$ is between 2 and 3.
- $x$ is less than $\sqrt{5}$ if $x^2$ is less than 5.
- random numbers, with fractions, between 2 and 3 are generated. A count is kept of those numbers which are less than $\sqrt{5}$.
- let **maxCount** be the total amount of random numbers generated between 2 and 3. The user will supply **maxCount**.
- let **amountLess** be the count of those numbers less than $\sqrt{5}$.
- an approximation to $\sqrt{5}$ is given by $2 + \frac{\text{amountLess}}{\text{maxCount}}$

To understand the idea behind the method, consider the line segment between 2 and 3 and let the point **r** represent the square root of 5.

If we imagine the line between 2 and 3 completely covered with dots, we would expect that the number of dots between 2 and **r** would be proportional to the length of that segment. In general, the number of dots falling on any line segment would be proportional to the length of that segment—the longer the segment, the more dots will fall on it.

Now, each random number between 2 and 3 represents a dot on that line. We would expect that the more numbers we use, the more accurate would be our statement that the length of the line between 2 and **r** is proportional to the amount of numbers falling on it and, hence, the more accurate our estimate.

Program P7.6 (shown on the next page) calculates an estimate for $\sqrt{5}$ based on the above method.

When run with 1000 numbers, this program gave 2.234 as the square root of 5. The value of $\sqrt{5}$ is 2.236 to 3 decimal places.

**Program P7.6**

```
#include <stdio.h>
#include <stdlib.h>
main() {
  int j, maxCount, amountLess;
  double r;

  printf("\nHow many numbers to use? ");
  scanf("%d", &maxCount);

  srand(time(0));
  amountLess = 0;
  for (j = 1; j <= maxCount; j++) {
    r = 2 + rand() / (RAND_MAX + 1.0);
    if (r * r < 5) ++amountLess;
  }
  printf("\nAn approximation to the square root of 5 is %5.3f\n",
          2 + (double) amountLess / maxCount);
} //end main
```

## *Estimating π*

Consider the following diagram of a circle within a square:

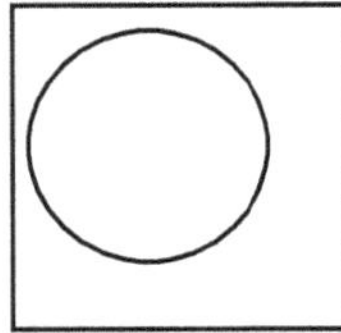

If you close your eyes and keep stabbing at the diagram repeatedly with a pencil, you may end up with something like the following (considering only the dots which fall within the diagram):

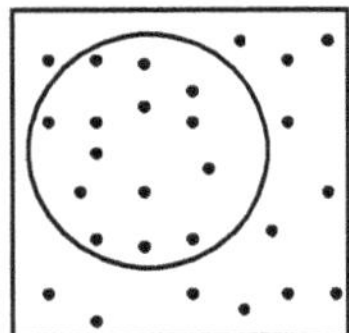

Note that some dots fall inside the circle and some fall outside the circle. If the dots were made ‘at random’, it seems reasonable to expect that the number of dots inside the circle is proportional to the area of the circle—the larger the circle, the more dots will fall inside it.

Based on this, we have the following approximation:

$$\frac{\textit{area of circle}}{\textit{area of square}} = \frac{\textit{number of dots inside circle}}{\textit{number of dots inside square}}$$

Note that the number of dots inside the square also includes those inside the circle. If we imagine the entire square filled with dots, then the above approximation will be quite accurate. We now show how to use this idea to estimate $\pi$.

Consider the following:

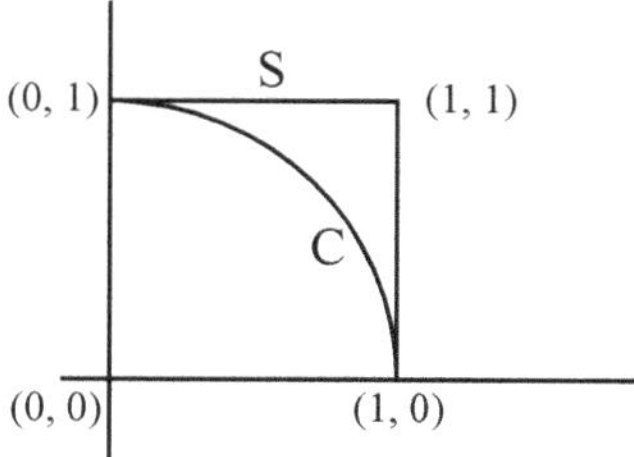


C is a quarter circle of radius 1; S is a square of side 1

Area of C = $\frac{\pi}{4}$ Area of S = 1

A point (x, y) within C satisfies $x^2 + y^2 \leq 1, x \geq 0, y \geq 0$

A point (x, y) within S satisfies $0 \leq x \leq 1, 0 \leq y \leq 1$

Suppose we generate two random fractions, that is, two values between 0 and 1; call these values *x* and *y*.

Since $0 \leq x \leq 1$ and $0 \leq y \leq 1$, it follows that the point $(x, y)$ lies within S. This point will also lie within C if $x^2 + y^2 \leq 1$.

If we generate *n* pairs of random fractions, we have, in fact, generated *n* points within S. For each of these points, we can determine whether or not the point lies with C. Suppose *m* of these *n* points fall within C. From our discussion above, we can assume that the following approximation holds:

$$\frac{\textit{area of C}}{\textit{area of S}} = \frac{m}{n}$$

The area of C is $\frac{\pi}{4}$ and the area of S is 1. So we have

$$\frac{\pi}{4} = \frac{m}{n}$$

Hence $\pi = \frac{4m}{n}$

Based on the above, we write Program P7.7 to estimate $\pi$.

**Program P7.7**

```
#include <stdio.h>
#include <stdlib.h>
main() {
  int j, inS, inC = 0;
  double x, y;

  printf("\nHow many numbers to use? ");
  scanf("%d", &inS);

  srand(time(0));
  for (j = 1; j <= inS; j++) {
    x = rand() / (RAND_MAX + 1.0);
    y = rand() / (RAND_MAX + 1.0);
    if (x * x + y * y <= 1) inC++;
  }
  printf("\nAn approximation to pi is %5.3f\n", 4.0 * inC / inS);
}
```

The value of $\pi$ to 3 decimal places is 3.142. When run with 1000 numbers, this program gave 3.132 as an approximation to $\pi$. When run with 2000 numbers, it gave 3.140 as the approximation.

## Exercises 7

1. Write a program to request two numbers, *m* and *n*, and print 25 random numbers from *m* to *n*.
2. Explain what you need to do so that the program in 1 will produce different numbers each time it is run for the same values of *m* and *n*.
3. Modify Program P7.2 to incorporate a scoring system. For example, for 2 attempts at a problem, you can give 2 points for a correct answer on the first attempt and 1 point for a correct answer on the second attempt.
4. Modify Program P7.2 to give a user problems in subtraction.
5. Modify Program P7.2 to give a user problems in multiplication.
6. Rewrite Program P7.2 so that it presents the user with a menu which allows him to choose what kinds of problems he gets (addition, subtraction or multiplication).
7. Write a program to simulate 1000 throws of a die and determine the number of 1s, 2s, 3s, 4s, 5s and 6s which show. Write the program (a) without using an array (b) using an array.
8. Write a program to simulate the weather for 60 days using the probabilities on page 173.
9. In the manufacture of electric bulbs, the probability that a bulb is defective is 0.01. Simulate the manufacture of 5000 bulbs, indicating how many are defective.

10. A die is weighted such that 1s and 5s come up twice as often as any other number. Simulate 1000 throws of this die, indicating the frequency with which each number occurs.
11. One-Zero is a game which can be played among several players using a 6-sided die. On his turn, a player can throw the die as many times as he wishes. His score for that turn is the sum of the numbers he throws *provided he does not throw* a 1. If he throws a 1, his score is 0. Suppose a player decides to adopt the strategy of ending his turn after 7 throws. (Of course, if he throws a 1 before the 7th throw, he must end his turn). Write a program to play 10 turns using this strategy. For each turn, print the score obtained. Also, print the average score for the 10 turns.

    Generalize the program to request values for **numTurns** and **maxThrowsPerTurn** and print the results as above.
12. Write a program to simulate the game of *Snakes and Ladders*. The board consists of 100 squares. Snakes and ladders are input as ordered pairs of numbers, *m* and *n*. For example, the pair `17 64` means that there is a ladder from 17 to 64 and the pair `99 28` means that there is a snake from 99 to 28.

    Simulate the playing of 20 games, each game lasting a maximum of 100 moves. Print the number of games which were completed in the 100 moves, and the average number of moves per game for completed games.
13. Write a program to play a modified game of Nim (page 167) in which there are two heaps of matches and a player, on his turn, may choose from either one. However, in this case, a player *wins* if he picks up the last match.
14. Using the traffic lights data on page 176, write a program to simulate the situation at the lights for a 30-minute period. Print the number of cars in each queue each time the light changes.
15. Write a program to estimate the square root of 59.
16. Write a program to read a positive integer *n* and estimate the square root of *n*.
17. Write a program to read a positive integer *n* and estimate the cube root of *n*.
18. Write a program to simulate the collection of bottle caps to spell A-P-P-L-E. In every 100 caps, A and E occur 40 times each, P and L occur 10 times each. Do 50 simulations and print the average number of caps per simulation.
19. The Lotto requires one to pick 7 numbers from the numbers 1 to 40. Write a program to randomly generate and print 5 sets of 7 numbers each (one set per line). No number is to be repeated in any of the sets, that is, exactly 35 of the 40 numbers must be used. If a number (*p*, say) is generated which has been used already, the first unused number after *p* is used. (Assume that 1 follows 40). For example, if 15 is generated but has been used already, 16 is tried but if this has been used, 17 is tried, and so on, until an unused number is found.
20. A function $f(x)$ is defined for $0 \le x \le 1$, and such that $0 \le f(x) < 1$ for all $0 \le x < 1$. Write a program to estimate the integral of $f(x)$ from 0 to 1. Hint: estimate the area under the curve by generating points $(x, y)$, $0 \le x < 1$, $0 \le y < 1$.
21. A gambler pays $5 to play the following game. He throws two 6-sided dice. If the sum of the two numbers thrown is even, he loses his bet. If the sum is odd, he draws a card from a standard pack of 52 playing cards. If he draws an ace, 3, 5, 7 or 9, he is paid the value of the card plus $5 (ace counts as 1). If he draws any other card, he loses. Write a program to simulate the playing of 20 games and print the average amount won by the gambler per game.

# 8 Working with files

## In this chapter, we will explain:

- how to read data from a file
- how to send output to a file
- the difference between text files and binary files
- how to write a program to compare two text files
- how to perform input/output with binary files
- how to work with a binary file of records
- what are random access files
- how to create and retrieve records from random access files
- what are indexed files
- how to update a random access file using an index

Almost anything we need to store on a computer must be stored in a file. We use text files for storing the kinds of documents we create with a text editor or word processor. We use binary files for storing photographic image files, sound files, video files and files of 'records'. In this chapter, we show how to create and manipulate text and binary files. We also explain how to work with that most versatile kind of file—a random access file.

So far, our programs have read data from the standard input stream (the keyboard) and written output to the standard output stream (the screen). We now explain how to read data from a file and send output to a file.

## 8.1 Reading data from a file

Suppose we want to be able to read data from the file, **input.txt**. The first thing we need to do is declare an identifier called a "file pointer". This can be done with the statement

```
FILE * in;    // read as "file pointer in"
```

The word **FILE** must be spelt as shown, with all uppercase letters. The spaces before and after * may be omitted. So you could write **FILE* in**, **FILE *in** or even **FILE*in**. We have used the identifier **in**; any other will do, such as **inf**, **infile**, **inputFile**, **payData**.

The second thing we must do is associate the file pointer **in** with the file **input.txt** and tell C we will be reading data from the file. This is done using the function **fopen**, as follows:

```
in = fopen("input.txt", "r");
```

This tells C to "open the file **input.txt** for reading": **"r"** indicates reading. We will use **"w"** if we want the file to be opened for "writing", that is, to receive output. If we wish, we could combine the two statements into one, with:

```
FILE * in = fopen("input.txt", "r");
```

Once this is done, a "data pointer" will be positioned at the beginning of the file. This pointer indicates the position in the file from which C will start looking for the next data item. As items are read, the pointer moves through the file. You can imagine it always being positioned just after the last item read.

We can now write statements which will read data from the file. We will see how shortly.

It is up to us to ensure that the file exists and contains the appropriate data. If not, we will get an error message such as "File not found". If we need to, we can specify the *path* to the file.

Suppose the file is located at: **C:\testdata\input.txt**.

We can tell C we will be reading data from the file with:

```
FILE * in = fopen("C:\\testdata\\input.txt", "r");
```

Recall that the escape sequence \\ is used to represent \ within a string. If the file is on a diskette, we can use:

```
FILE * in = fopen("A:\\input.txt", "r");
```

## *fscanf*

We use the statement (more precisely, the function) **fscanf** to read data from the file. It is used in exactly the same way as **scanf** except that the first argument is the file pointer **in**. For example, if **num** is **int**, the statement

```
fscanf(in, "%d", &num);
```

will read an integer from the file **input.txt** (the one associated with **in**) and store it in **num**. Note that the argument is the *file pointer* and *not* the name of the file. When we have finished reading data from the file, we should *close* it. This is done with **fclose**, as follows:

```
fclose(in);
```

There is one argument, the file pointer (not the name of the file). This statement breaks the association of the file pointer **in** with the file **input.txt**. If we need to, we could now link the identifier **in** with another file (**payData.txt**, say) using:

```
in = fopen("payData.txt", "r");
```

Note that we do not repeat the **FILE *** part of the declaration, since **in** has already been declared as **FILE ***. Subsequent **fscanf(in, ...)** statements will read data from the file **payData.txt**.

### *Finding the average of some numbers in a file*

To illustrate the use of **fscanf**, let us write Program P8.1 to read several numbers from a file and find their average. Suppose the file is called **input.txt** and contains several positive integers with 0 indicating the end, for example,

```
24 13 55 32 19 0
```

Program P8.1 shows how to define the file as the place from which the data will be read and how to find the average.

**Program P8.1**

```
//read numbers from a file and find their average; 0 ends the data
#include <stdio.h>
main() {
  FILE * in = fopen("input.txt", "r");
  int num, sum = 0, n = 0;
  fscanf(in, "%d", &num);
  while (num != 0) {
    n = n + 1;
    sum = sum + num;
    fscanf(in, "%d", &num);
  }
  if (n == 0) printf("\nNo numbers entered\n");
  else {
    printf("\n%d numbers were entered\n", n);
    printf("The sum is %d\n", sum);
    printf("The average is %3.2f\n", (double) sum/n);
  }
  fclose(in);
} //end main
```

If the data file contains

```
24 13 55 32 19 0
```

the output will be

```
5 numbers were supplied
The sum is 143
The average is 28.60
```

The numbers in the file could be supplied in "free format"—any amount could be put on a line. For example, the sample data could have been typed on one line as above or as follows:

```
24   13
55 32
         19 0
```

or

```
24   13
55
   32 19
 0
```

or

```
24
13
55
32
19
0
```

**File cannot be found**: when you try to run this program, it may not run properly because it cannot find the file **input.txt**. This may be because the compiler is looking for the file in the wrong place. Some compilers expect to find the file in the same folder/directory as the program file. Others expect to find it in the same folder/directory as the compiler.

Try placing **input.txt** in each of these folders, in turn, and run the program. If this does not work then you will need to specify the complete path to the file in the **fopen** statement. For example, if the file is in the folder **data** which is in the folder **CS10E** which is on the **C:** drive, you will need to use the statement:

```
FILE * in = fopen("C:\\CS10E\\data\\input.txt", "r");
```

## 8.2 Sending output to a file

We have just seen how to read data from a file. We now show you how you can send output to a file.

This is important because when we send output to the screen, it is lost when we exit the program or when we switch off the computer. If we need to save our output, we must write it to a file. Then the output is available as long as we wish to keep the file.

The process is similar to reading from a file. We must declare a "file pointer" (we will use **out**) and associate it with the actual file (**output.txt**, say) using **fopen**. This can be done with

```
FILE * out = fopen("output.txt", "w");
```

This tells C to "open the file **output.txt** for writing"; **"w"** indicates writing. When this statement is executed, the file **output.txt** is created if it does not already exist. If it exists, its contents are destroyed. In other words, whatever you write to the file will *replace* its original contents. Be careful that you do not open for writing a file whose contents you wish to keep.

### *fprintf*

We use the statement (more precisely, the function) **fprintf** to send output to the file. It is used in exactly the same way as **printf** except that the first argument is the file pointer **out**. For example, if **sum** is **int** with value 143, the statement

```
fprintf(out, "The sum is %d\n", sum);
```

will write

```
The sum is 143
```

to the file **output.txt**.

Note that the argument is the *file pointer* and *not* the name of the file.

When we have finished writing output to the file, we must *close* it. This is especially important for output files since, the way some compilers operate[5], this is the only way to ensure that all output is sent to the file. We close the file with **fclose**, as follows:

```
fclose(out);
```

There is one argument, the file pointer (not the name of the file). This statement breaks the association of the file pointer **out** with the file **output.txt**. If we need to, we could now link the identifier **out** with another file (**payroll.txt**, say) using:

```
out = fopen("payroll.txt", "w");
```

Note that we do not repeat the **FILE *** part of the declaration, since **out** has already been declared as **FILE ***. Subsequent **fprintf(out, ...)** statements will send output to the file **payroll.txt**.

For example, in P8.1, we can send the output to the file **output.txt** by replacing the **printf** statements with **fprintf**, thus:

```
if (n == 0) fprintf(out, "No numbers entered\n");
else {
  fprintf(out, "%d numbers were entered\n", n);
  fprintf(out, "The sum is %d\n", sum);
  fprintf(out, "The average is %3.2f\n", (double) sum/n);
}
```

As explained above, you can, if you wish, specify the complete path to your file in the **fopen** statement. For instance, if you want to send the output to a diskette, you can use

```
FILE * out = fopen("a:\\output.txt", "w");
```

[5] For instance, they send output to a temporary buffer in memory and only when the buffer is full is it sent to the file. If you do not close the file, some output may be left in the buffer and never sent to the file.

## 8.3 Text and binary files

A *text* file is a sequence of characters organized into lines. Conceptually, we think of each line as being terminated by a newline character. However, depending on the host environment, certain character translations may occur. For example, if we wrote the newline character `\n` to a file, it could be translated into two characters—a carriage return and a line-feed character.

Thus, there is not necessarily a one-to-one correspondence between characters written and those stored on an external device. Similarly, there may not be a one-to-one correspondence between the number of characters stored in a file and the number read.

A *binary* file is simply a sequence of bytes, with *no* character translations occurring on input or output. Thus there *is* a one-to-one correspondence between what is read or written and what is stored in the file.

Apart from possible character translations, there are other differences between text and binary files. To illustrate, if an integer is stored in 2 bytes (16 bits); the number `3371` is stored as `00001101 00101011`.

If we were to write this number to a text file, it would be written as the character '3', followed by the character '3', followed by '7', followed by '1', occupying 4 bytes in all. However, we could simply write the two bytes 'as is' to a binary file.

Even though we could still think of them as a sequence of two 'characters', the values they contain may not represent any valid characters. In this case, the decimal values of the two bytes are `13` and `43` which, interpreted as two ASCII characters, are the carriage return character (CR) and `'+'`.

Another way to look at it is that, in general, each byte in a text file contains a human-readable character whereas, in general, each byte in a binary file contains an arbitrary bit pattern. Binary files are important for writing data directly from its internal representation to an external device, usually a disk file.

The standard input and output are considered text files. A disk file may be created as a text file or as a binary file. We will see how to do so shortly.

## 8.4 Internal vs external file name

The usual way of using a computer is via its operating system. We normally create and edit files using a word processor or a text file editor. When we create a file, we give it a name which we use whenever we need to do anything with the file. This is the name by which the file is known to the operating system.

We will refer to such a name as an *external* file name. (The term *external* is used here to mean 'external to a C program'.) When we are writing a program, we may want to specify, say, the reading of data from a file. The program will need to use a file name but, for several reasons, this name should not be an external file name. The major reasons are:

- The file to be read may not have been created as yet.
- If the external name is tied to the program, the program will be able to read a file with that name only. If the data is in a file with a different name, either the program will have to be changed or the file renamed.
- The program will be less portable since different operating systems have different file-naming conventions. A valid external file name on one system may be invalid on another one.

For these reasons, a C program uses an *internal* file name—this is the file pointer referred to earlier. For instance, when we write

```
FILE * in = fopen("input.txt", "r");
```

we associate the internal name, **in**, with the external file, **input.txt**. This is the only statement which mentions the external file name. The rest of the program is written in terms of **in**. Of course, we can be even more flexible and write:

```
FILE * in = fopen(fileName, "r");
```

and, when the program is run, supply the name of the file in **fileName**, as with

```
printf("Enter file name: ");
gets(fileName);
```

---

## 8.5 fopen and fclose

In this section, we take a closer look at **fopen** and **fclose**.

The standard function **fopen** returns a pointer to a **FILE**, and its prototype is declared in **stdio.h** as:

```
FILE *fopen(char name[], char mode[]);
```

or

```
FILE *fopen(char *name, char *mode);
```

or

```
FILE *fopen(char *, char *);
```

Both parameters are strings (or, more accurately, character pointers). The first specifies an external file name and the second specifies the manner in which the file is to be used, for example, whether text or binary or whether for reading or writing. The valid modes are as follows:

| | |
|---|---|
| "r" | open text file for reading; file must exist. |
| "w" | create text file for writing; if file exists, its contents are destroyed, otherwise it is created, if possible. |
| "a" | open text file for appending (writing at the end). If file does not exist, it is created, if possible; some systems may report error. |

"r+" open text file for both reading and writing; file must exist.
"w+" create text file for both reading and writing; if file exists, its contents are destroyed, otherwise it is created, if possible.
"a+" open text file for reading and appending; if the file exists, its contents are retained. If file does not exist, it is created, if possible; some systems may report error.

A file opened for reading ("**r**" or "**r+**") must exist. If it doesn't, then **fopen** returns **NULL**. As indicated above, certain modes (e.g., "**w**" or "**a**") require that a file be created. If it cannot be created (for example, the user may have exceeded his allotted disk space or the disk may be write-protected), then **fopen** returns **NULL**. If the external file exists, then opening it for 'writing' causes the old contents to be destroyed.

If a file is opened with "**a**" or "**a+**", all write operations occur at the end of the file. This holds even if the file pointer is repositioned with **fseek** or **rewind** (page 202). When a write operation is about to occur, the file pointer is positioned at the end of the file. This ensures that existing data cannot be overwritten.

When "**b**" is added to the above modes, the files are treated as binary, rather than text. Thus the following are also valid modes:

"rb" open binary file for reading; file must exist.
"wb" create binary file for writing; if file exists, its contents are destroyed, otherwise it is created, if possible.
"ab" open binary file for appending (writing at the end). If file does not exist, it is created, if possible; some systems may report error.
"rb+" open binary file for both reading and writing; file must exist.
"wb+" create binary file for both reading and writing; if file exists, its contents are destroyed, otherwise it is created, if possible.
"ab+" open binary file for reading and appending; if the file exists, its contents are retained. If file does not exist, it is created, if possible; some systems may report error.

Observe that the basic modes are reading ("**r**"), writing ("**w**") and appending ("**a**"). Adding "**+**" allows both reading and writing, and adding "**b**" specifies that the file is to be treated as a binary file. The modes "**rb+**", "**wb+**" and "**ab+**" could also be written as "**r+b**", "**w+b**" and "**a+b**", respectively.

Consider the statement:

```
FILE *inPay = fopen("payrollNov.txt", "r");
```

This says to open the external file **payrollNov.txt** for reading. If such a file does not exist, an error results and **fopen** returns **NULL**. If the file exists, then **fopen** returns the address of the place in memory where information about the file would be kept.

In the example, this address is assigned to **inPay**, thus establishing a connection between the external file name **payrollNov.txt** and the internal name **inPay**. Subsequent accesses to the external file are done via the internal name only. Once the file has been opened, we can read data from it using **fscanf**, say. For example, the statement:

```
fscanf(inPay, "%s %f %f", name, &hours, &rate);
```

says to read values for **name, hours** and **rate** from the file associated with **inPay**. We use **fscanf** in exactly the same way as **scanf**, except that the first argument is now a file pointer.

When we are finished using the file, we must *close* it. This is done via the standard function **fclose**. The above file may be closed with

```
fclose(inPay);
```

In the example, this statement severs the association between the internal name **inPay** and the external file **payrollNov.txt**. If required, the name **inPay** can now be used with another external file.

It is important to close all files before your program terminates. Failure to do so could result in output being lost or a file becoming corrupted.

As used above, the name of the external file **payrollNov.txt** is tied to the program, since it is used in the **fopen** statement. If the data to be processed is in another file **payrollDec.txt**, say, then the statement to open the file must be changed to:

```
FILE *inPay = fopen("payrollDec.txt", "r");
```

or the name of the file must be changed to **payrollNov.txt**, which may not be desirable.

A more flexible approach is to let the user supply the name of the external file at run time. For instance, if **payFile** is an array of characters large enough to hold the name of the file, then we can use:

```
printf("Enter payroll data file name: ");
gets(payFile);
inPay = fopen(payFile, "r");
```

Just in case the user types the file name incorrectly or forgot to create the file, we can use the fact that **fopen** will return **NULL** to check for this, as in:

```
do {
  printf("Enter payroll data file name: ");
  gets( payFile);
  inPay = fopen(payFile, "r");
  if (inPay == NULL) printf("File does not exist\n");
} while (inPay == NULL);
```

Now, exit from the **do...while** takes place only when an existing file name is entered. As usual, the assignment and test of **inPay** (against **NULL**) can be done in one statement:

```
if ((inPay = fopen(payFile, "r")) == NULL) printf("File does not exist\n");
```

To pursue the example, suppose we want to write the payroll report onto an external file called **payReportNov.txt**. Suppose **outPay** is declared as:

```
FILE *outPay;
```

then the statement:

```
outPay = fopen("payReportNov.txt", "w");
```

will associate the internal name **outPay** with the file, **payReportNov.txt**. Output can then be sent to the file using **fprintf**, say, as in:

```
fprintf(outPay, "Name: %s,  Net pay: $%7.2f\n", name, salary);
```

**fprintf** is identical to **printf**, except that the first argument is now a file pointer, indicating where the output is to be sent.

As above, it is best to let the user supply the name of the file at run time and to use a character array variable as the first argument to **fopen**.

## 8.6 getc and putc

We have used **getchar** to read a character from the standard input and **putchar** to send a character to the standard output. To read a character from a named file, we use **getc**, as in:

```
ch = getc(filePtr);
```

where **ch** is an **int** and **filePtr** is the pointer to the file from which characters are being read. To write a character to a file, we can use **putc**, as in:

```
putc(ch, filePtr);
```

Note that the file pointer is the *second* argument to **putc**.

In C, the file pointers **stdin** and **stdout** are predefined to point to the standard input and output, respectively. Thus,

**getchar()** is equivalent to **getc(stdin)**

and

**putchar(ch)** is equivalent to **putc(ch, stdout)**.

## 8.7 feof and ferror

When data is being read from a file, several possible conditions can arise.

1. The data could be read successfully.
2. An attempt may be made to read beyond the end of the file.

3. A 'read error' could occur; for example, the disk may be damaged.

The functions which read data return **EOF** if an attempt has been made to read beyond the end of the file. However, many of these functions also return **EOF** if an error is encountered (for example, trying to write to a file opened for reading only). How can a program determine which condition obtained?

The function **feof** can be used to check the end-of-file condition on a file. Its prototype is

```
int feof(FILE *fp);
```

The argument to **feof** is a file pointer (**fp**, say). It returns non-zero (true) if the end of the file linked to **fp** has been reached; otherwise, it returns zero (false). For example, to copy a file (associated with **fp**) to the standard output, we could use:

```
while (!feof(fp)) putchar(getc(fp));
```

Of course, the code could also be written as (**ch** is an **int**):

```
while ((ch = getc(fp)) != EOF) putchar(ch);
```

Testing for end-of-file with **EOF** is fine for text files. This is because C guarantees that the (integer) value of **EOF** is different from that of any other character. Thus **EOF** could be returned only when the end of the file is actually reached.

Unfortunately, the same does not hold for binary files. This is because a binary file consists of arbitrary bit patterns (as opposed to bit patterns representing characters). Thus it is entirely possible that the value of an arbitrary byte could be the same as the value of **EOF**. Testing such a byte against **EOF** would lead to the erroneous conclusion that the end of the file had been reached. For binary files, therefore, the safest way to test for end-of-file is to use the function **feof**.

The function **ferror** accepts a file pointer (**fp**, say) and returns non-zero (true) if an error occurred during the last file operation attempted; otherwise, it returns zero (false). Its prototype is:

```
int ferror(FILE *fp);
```

and can be used as in the following example (**chFile** is a **FILE ***):

```
fscanf(chFile, "%d %f", &age, &allowance); // int age; float allowance;
if (ferror(chFile)) fprintf(stderr, "Error reading age, allowance\n");
```

Since the error indication (for a given file) could be set by any file operation, it is important to test for it immediately after a given operation. If this is not done, an error may be lost. For example, suppose two **scanf**s are done and then **ferror** is called. If it returns true, we would not know whether the error was due to the first or the second call to **scanf**.

## 8.8 fgets and fputs

These are two standard functions which can be used with arbitrary files: **fgets** is used to read an entire string (up to, and including, the next newline) and **fputs** is used to output a string which may or may not contain a newline.

The prototype of **fgets** is:

```
char *fgets(char line[], int max, FILE *infile);
```

The character array **line** must have at least **max** elements. Characters are read from **infile** and stored in **line** until 'newline' is encountered or **max - 1** characters have been stored, whichever comes first. If 'newline' is encountered and **max - 1** characters have not yet been stored, **\n** is added to **line**. In either case, **line** is terminated with **\0**.

If at least one character (other than **\0**) is stored in **line**, **fgets** returns **line** (which is, in effect, a pointer to the characters stored). If end-of-file is encountered and no characters have been stored in **line**, **fgets** returns **NULL**. If an error occurs, **fgets** also returns **NULL**. Since **NULL** is returned for both end-of-file and error conditions, the functions **feof** and/or **ferror** must be used to determine which one occurred. Note that the file pointer is the *last* argument, not the first as in **fscanf** or **fprintf**.

**fgets** is useful for reading strings which may contain blanks or tabs. Recall that the **%s** option of **fscanf** cannot be used to read a string containing blanks or tabs.

The prototype for **fputs** is:

```
void fputs(char string[], FILE *outFile);
```

**string** contains the string (properly terminated by **\0**) to be written to **outFile**. It may contain *any* characters, including newlines. The terminating **\0** is not written. If successful, **fputs** returns a non-negative value; if unsuccessful, it returns **EOF**.

---

### *Example – comparing two files*

This example uses **fgets** to compare two files, printing the first lines, if any, where they differ.

Program P8.2 (next page) reads lines from both files (using **fgets**) until a mismatch is found or one of the files comes to an end. It also illustrates one way of verifying the file name that a user enters, using the function **getFileName**.

If the first file contains

```
one and one are two
two and two are four
three and three are six
four and four are eight
five and five are ten
six and six are twelve
```

**Program P8.2**

```
#include <stdio.h>
#define MaxName 20
#define MaxLine 101
main() {
  char name1[MaxName], name2[MaxName];
  char line1[MaxLine], line2[MaxLine];
  FILE *file1, *file2, *getFileName(char *, char *);
  char *eof1, *eof2;

  int lineNum = 0;
  file1 = getFileName("First file?", name1);
  file2 = getFileName("Second file?", name2);

  while (((eof1 = fgets(line1, MaxLine, file1)) != NULL) &&
        ((eof2 = fgets(line2, MaxLine, file2)) != NULL) &&
        (strcmp(line1, line2) == 0))
    lineNum++;
  // at this stage, linenum is the number of matching lines found
  if (eof1 == NULL) //first file ended
    if (fgets(line2, MaxLine, file2) == NULL) //second also ended
      printf("\nFiles are identical\n\n");
    else  //first file ended, second file not ended
      printf("\n%s, with %d line(s), is a subset of %s\n",
              name1, lineNum, name2);
  else if (eof2 == NULL)  //first file not ended, second file ended
      printf("\n%s, with %d line(s), is a subset of %s\n",
              name2, lineNum, name1);
  else { // mismatch found
    printf("\nThe files differ at line %d\n", ++lineNum);
    printf("The lines are \n%s\n and \n%s\n", line1, line2);
  }
  fclose(file1);  fclose(file2);
} //end main

FILE * getFileName(char *prompt, char *name) {
//store the filename in 'name' and return the pointer to the file
  FILE *filePtr;
  do {
    printf("%s ", prompt); gets(name);
    if ((filePtr = fopen(name, "r")) == NULL)
      printf("File does not exist or access denied\n");
  } while (filePtr == NULL);
  return filePtr;
} //end getFileName
```

and the second file contains

```
one and one are two
two and two are four
three and three are six
four and four are eight
this is the fifth line
six and six are twelve
```

the program will print

```
The files differ at line 5
The lines are
five and five are ten
 and
this is the fifth line
```

The following points are for noting:

- The maximum length of the file name catered for is **MaxName – 1**.
- The maximum line length (including **\n**) catered for is **MaxLine – 1**.
- The file name is read using **gets**, so it may contain blanks. With **gets**, **\n** is never part of the string returned.
- In the interest of brevity and simplicity, we assume that no errors in reading the files occur—the files are read until one or the other comes to an end. To cater for errors, we could use **ferror** to determine if a reading error caused **fgets** to return **NULL**. Alternatively, we could use **feof** to determine if the end-of-file was actually reached.

## 8.9 Input/output for binary files

As mentioned before, a binary file contains data in a form which corresponds exactly with the internal representation of the data. For example, if a **float** variable occupies 4 bytes of memory, writing it to a binary file simply involves making an exact copy of the 4 bytes. On the other hand, writing it to a text file causes it to be converted to character form and the characters obtained are stored in the file.

Normally, a binary file can be created only from within a program and its contents can be read only by a program. Listing a binary file, for example, only produces 'garbage' and, sometimes, generates an error. Compare a text file which can be created by typing into it and whose contents can be listed and read by a human. However, a binary file does have the following advantages:

- data can be transferred to and from a binary file much faster than for a text file since no data conversions are necessary; the data is read and written 'as is'.
- the values of data types such as arrays and structures can be written to a binary file. For a text file, individual elements must be written.
- data stored in a binary file usually occupies less space than the same data stored in a text file. For example, the integer –25367 (six characters) occupies 6 bytes in a text file but only 2 bytes in a binary file.

C provides the functions **fread** and **fwrite** for use on binary files.

### 8.9.1 fread and fwrite

Consider the problem of reading integers from the standard input and writing them, in their internal form, to a (binary) file. Assume that the numbers are to be stored in the external file, **num.bin**. This can be done with Program P8.3:

**Program P8.3**

```
#include <stdio.h>
  main() {
    FILE *intFile;
    int num;
    if ((intFile = fopen("num.bin", "wb")) == NULL) {
      printf("Cannot open file\n");
      return;
    }
    while (scanf("%d", &num) == 1)
      fwrite(&num, sizeof(int), 1, intFile);
    fclose (intFile);
  } //end main
```

The program reads data from the standard input until an invalid integer is read or end-of-file is met (for instance, if a user types **Ctrl-z**).

In P8.3, **num.bin** is opened with **"wb"** which means 'open a binary file for writing'. If the file cannot be opened, a message is printed and the program is stopped. (A **return** statement in **main** returns control to the operating system.)

In the statement:

```
fwrite(&num, sizeof(int), 1, intFile);
```

- **&num** specifies the starting address of the item(s) to be written;
- **sizeof(int)** specifies the size of each item to be written;
- **1** specifies that one item is to be written;
- **intFile** specifies the file to which the items are to be written.

In general, **fwrite** writes a specified number of items to a binary file. Its prototype is (think of **size_t** as **int**):

```
size_t fwrite(void *buffer, size_t unitSize, size_t numItems, FILE *fp);
```

where

- **buffer** is the starting address of the item(s) to be written;
- **unitSize** is the size of each item;
- **numItems** is the number of items to be written;

- **fp** is the file pointer.

**fwrite** returns the number of full items written; this could be less than **numItems** if an error occurs. We usually specify **unitSize** using the **sizeof** operator. This is particularly useful for structures as well as to ensure portability. As another example, if **poly** is a **double** array of size 20, then:

```
fwrite(poly, sizeof(double), 20, fp);
```

writes the entire array to the file specified by **fp**. Recall that an array name is a synonym for the address of its first element.

Given the declaration:

```
struct child {
   char name[20];
   int age;
   char gender;
   double allowance;
} sassy;
```

we could write the entire structure **sassy** to a file with:

```
fwrite(&sassy, sizeof(struct child), 1, fp);
```

If **class** is an array of structures defined as:

```
struct child class[100];
```

then the 100 structure elements could be written to a file with:

```
fwrite(class, sizeof(struct child), 100, fp);
```

---

The function **fread** has the same format as **fwrite**, and is used for reading a specified number of items from a binary file. Its prototype is:

```
size_t fread(void *buffer, size_t unitSize, size_t numItems, FILE *fp);
```

where

- **buffer** is the address where the items read are to be stored;
- **unitSize** is the size of each item;
- **numItems** is the number of items to be written;
- **fp** is the file pointer.

**fread** returns the number of full items actually read; this could be less than **numItems** if an error occurs or if the end of the file is reached before **numItems** are read. The functions **feof** or **ferror** may be used to distinguish between a read error and an end-of-file condition.

Program P8.4 reads the file of integers created above and prints them on the standard output. The file is opened with **"rb"** which means 'open a binary file for reading'. Each time a number is read, the return value of **fread** should be **1**; if it isn't, then either the end-of-file was reached or an error occurred.

**Program P8.4**

```
#include <stdio.h>
main() {
  FILE *intFile;
  int num;
  if ((intFile = fopen("num.bin", "rb")) == NULL) {
    printf("Cannot open file\n");
    return;
  }
  while (fread(&num, sizeof(int), 1, intFile) == 1)
    printf("%d\n", num);
  if (feof(intFile)) printf("\nEnd of list\n");
  else printf("\nError reading file\n");
  fclose(intFile);
} //end main
```

## 8.10 Random access files

In the normal mode of operation, data is read from a file in the order in which it is stored. When a file is opened, one can think of an imaginary pointer positioned at the beginning of the file. (This is not to be confused with the data type **FILE *** discussed previously.) As items are read from the file, this pointer moves along by the number of bytes read. Put another way, this pointer indicates where the next read (or write) operation would occur.

Normally, this pointer is moved implicitly by a read or write operation. However, C provides facilities for moving the pointer explicitly to any position in the file. We discuss the functions **rewind** and **fseek**. While **rewind** can be used on either text or binary files, **fseek** is recommended for use with binary files only. For a text file, character translations would cause **fseek** to give unexpected results.

### *8.10.1* rewind and fseek

The function **rewind** positions the pointer at the beginning of the file. Its prototype is:

```
void rewind(FILE *fp);
```

**rewind** does not return a value. If the end-of-file or error condition was set for a file, a call to **rewind** clears the condition.

The function **fseek** allows more flexible movement within a file. Its prototype is:

```
int fseek(FILE *fp, long offset, int origin);
```

and it moves the file pointer to a position which is **offset** bytes from **origin**. If successful, **fseek** returns **zero**; otherwise, it returns non-zero.

**origin** must be one of the following predefined constants (defined in **stdio.h**):

| | |
|---|---|
| **SEEK_SET** | beginning of the file |
| **SEEK_CUR** | current position of file pointer |
| **SEEK_END** | end of the file |

**offset** is a long integer; if the actual argument is not **long**, then the function prototype causes automatic coercion to **long**. For example,

```
fseek(intFile, 32, SEEK_SET);
```

moves the file pointer to a position which is 32 bytes from the beginning of the file, that is, to the beginning of the 33rd byte. Since 32 is an **int**, it is automatically converted to **long int** before being passed to **fseek**. We could also have used **32L**.

One of the most common uses of **fseek** is to retrieve the records of a file in random order. This is illustrated by the next example.

Consider the declaration:

```
struct partRecord {
  char partNum[7];  // part number
  char name[25];    // name of part
  int amtInStock;   // quantity in stock
  double unitPrice; // unit selling price
};
```

and suppose we want to create a file containing the records for several parts. The data for each part will be read from a text file, **parts.txt**, stored in a temporary structure and then written, as one unit, to a binary file.

Suppose that a part number is a six-character string (e.g. PKL070) and a part name is a maximum of 24 characters long. (The extra character declared is used for storing **\0**.) For simplicity, we assume that a part name does not contain any spaces. Some sample data are shown below:

```
PKL070 Park-Lens 8 6.50
BLJ375 Ball-Joint 12 11.95
FLT015 Oil-Filter 23 7.95
DKP080 Disc-Pads 16 9.99
GSF555 Gas-Filter 9 4.50
```

Program P8.5 (next page) reads the data and stores it in a binary file, **parts.bin**. The data are stored in the same order as in the text file.

The program confirms that a given part record has been written successfully to the parts file by checking the return value of **fwrite**. If successful, **fwrite** should return **1**, in this example. Note the specification **%lf** (percent ell f) for reading a value into a **double** variable.

**Program P8.5**

```
#include <stdio.h>

typedef struct partRecord {
  char partNum[7];
  char name[25];
  int amtInStock;
  double unitPrice;
} PartRecord;

main() {
  FILE *ftxt, *fbin;
  PartRecord part;

  if ((ftxt = fopen("parts.txt", "r")) == NULL) {
    printf("Cannot open parts file\n");
    return;
  }

  if ((fbin = fopen("parts.bin", "wb")) == NULL) {
    printf("Cannot create file\n");
    return;
  }

  while (fscanf(ftxt, "%s %s %d %lf", part.partNum, part.name,
                        &part.amtInStock, &part.unitPrice) == 4)
    if (fwrite(&part, sizeof(PartRecord), 1, fbin) != 1) {
      printf("Error in writing file\n");
      return;
    }

  fclose(ftxt);
  fclose(fbin);
} //end main
```

---

To understand how **fseek** may be used on the binary parts file, think of the records as being numbered consecutively from 1 and suppose that each record is 40 bytes long. The records are stored in the file starting at byte 0.

Record 1 occupies bytes 0 – 39;
Record 2 occupies bytes 40 – 79;
Record 3 occupies bytes 80 – 119;

and, in general,

Record $n$ starts at byte number $(n - 1)*40$ and occupies the next 40 bytes.

Now, suppose we want to read record $n$; we must

1. position the file pointer at the beginning of the *n*th record;
2. read a number of bytes equal to the size of a record.

This can be done with:

```
fseek(fbin, (n - 1) *sizeof(PartRecord), SEEK_SET);
fread(&part, sizeof(PartRecord), 1, fbin);
```

As usual, we could check the return values to ensure successful completion of the operations. Program P8.6 requests a record number, reads the record from the file and prints the record information on the screen. It assumes that the record number supplied is a valid one.

**Program P8.6**

```
#include <stdio.h>

typedef struct partRecord {
  char partNum[7];
  char name[25];
  int amtInStock;
  double unitPrice;
} PartRecord;

main() {
  FILE *fbin;
  PartRecord part;
  int n;

  if ((fbin = fopen("parts.bin", "rb")) == NULL) {
    printf("Cannot open file\n");
    return;
  }
  printf("Enter record number: ");
  scanf("%d", &n);
  while (n != 0) {
    fseek(fbin, (n - 1) * sizeof(PartRecord), SEEK_SET);
    fread(&part, sizeof(PartRecord), 1, fbin);

    printf("\nPart number: %s\n", part.partNum);
    printf("Part name: %s\n", part.name);
    printf("Amount in stock: %d\n", part.amtInStock);
    printf("Price: $%3.2f\n\n", part.unitPrice);

    printf("Enter record number: ");
    scanf("%d", &n);
  }
  fclose(fbin);
} //end main
```

If **parts.bin** was created using the sample data on page 203, the following is a sample run of P8.6:

```
Enter a record number: 3
Part number: FLT015
Part name: Oil-Filter
Amount in stock: 23
Price: $7.95

Enter a record number: 1
Part number: PKL070
Part name: Park-Lens
Amount in stock: 8
Price: $6.50

Enter a record number: 4
Part number: DKP080
Part name: Disc-Pads
Amount in stock: 16
Price: $9.99

Enter a record number: 0
```

## 8.11 Indexed files

The above showed how to retrieve a part record given the record number. But this is not the most natural way to retrieve records. More likely than not, we would want to retrieve records based on some *key*, in this case, the part number. It is more natural to ask, "How many of BLJ375 do we have?" rather than "How many of record 2 do we have?". The problem then is how to retrieve a record given the part number.

One approach is to use an *index*. Just as a book index lets us quickly locate information in a book, a file index enables us to quickly find records in a file. The index is created as the file is loaded. Later on, it must be updated as records are added to, or deleted from, the file. In our example, an index entry will consist of a part number and a record number.

We will use the following declaration for an index entry:

```
struct indexEntry {
  char partNum[7];
  int recNum;
};
```

and an array of such structures will be used to hold the entire index. For example, if we want to cater for up to 100 items, we could use:

```
struct indexEntry index[100];
```

The index will be kept in order by part number. Let us illustrate how to create an index for the following records:

```
PKL070 Park-Lens     8  6.50
BLJ375 Ball-Joint   12 11.95
FLT015 Oil-Filter   23  7.95
DKP080 Disc-Pads    16  9.99
GSF555 Gas-Filter    9  4.50
```

We assume that the records are stored in the file in the order shown. When the first record is read and stored, the index will contain:

```
PKL070     1
```

meaning that the record for PKL070 is record number 1 in the parts file. After the second record is read and stored, the index will be:

```
BLJ375   2
PKL070   1
```

since the index is in order by part number. After the third record is read and stored, the index will be:

```
BLJ375   2
FLT015   3
PKL070   1
```

After the fourth record is read and stored, the index will be:

```
BLJ375   2
DKP080   4
FLT015   3
PKL070   1
```

and after the fifth record is read and stored, the index will be:

```
BLJ375   2
DKP080   4
FLT015   3
GSF555   5
PKL070   1
```

Program P8.7 illustrates how an index can be created as described above.

**Program P8.7**

```
#include <stdio.h>
#include <stdlib.h>
#include <string.h>

#define PartNumSize 6
#define MaxName 24
#define MaxRecords 100

typedef struct partRecord {
  char partNum[PartNumSize + 1];
  char name[MaxName + 1];
  int amtInStock;
  double unitPrice;
} PartRecord;
```

```
typedef struct indexEntry {
  char partNum[PartNumSize + 1];
  int recNum;
} IndexEntry;

main() {
  IndexEntry index[MaxRecords + 1];
  void createMaster(char *, IndexEntry[], int);
  void saveIndex(char *, IndexEntry[], int);
  createMaster("parts.bin", index, MaxRecords);
  saveIndex("index.bin", index, MaxRecords + 1);
} //end main

void createMaster(char *fileName, IndexEntry index[], int maxRecords) {
// stores records in 'fileName'; caters for maxRecords index entries;
// sets index[0].recNum to the number of index entries actually used
  FILE *ftxt, *fbin;
  PartRecord part;
  IndexEntry newEntry;
  int searchResult, search(char[], IndexEntry[], int);
  int numRecords = 0;

  if ((ftxt = fopen("parts.txt", "r")) == NULL) {
    printf("Cannot open parts file\n"); return;
  }

  if ((fbin = fopen("parts.bin", "wb")) == NULL) {
    printf("Cannot create file\n");
    return;
  }

  while (fscanf(ftxt, "%s %s %d %lf", part.partNum, part.name,
                              &part.amtInStock, &part.unitPrice) == 4) {
    searchResult = search(part.partNum, index, numRecords);
    if (searchResult > 0)
      printf("Duplicate part: %s ignored\n", part.partNum);
    else { //this is a new part number
      if (numRecords == maxRecords) {
        printf("Too many records: only %d allowed\n", maxRecords);
        exit(1);
      }
      //the index has room; shift entries to accommodate new part
      int j;
      for (j = numRecords; j >= -searchResult; j--)
          index[j + 1] = index[j];
      strcpy(index[-searchResult].partNum, part.partNum);
      index[-searchResult].recNum = ++numRecords;
```

```
      if (fwrite(&part, sizeof(PartRecord), 1, fbin) != 1) {
        printf("Error in writing file\n"); exit(1);
      }
      printf("%s %-11s %2d %5.2f\n", part.partNum, part.name,
                                    part.amtInStock, part.unitPrice);
    }
  }
  index[0].recNum = numRecords;
  fclose(fbin);
} //end createMaster

int search(char key[], IndexEntry list[], int n) {
//searches list[1..n] for key. If found, it returns the location; otherwise
//it returns the negative of the location in which key should be inserted.
  int lo = 1;  int hi = n;
  while (lo <= hi) {     // as long as more elements remain to consider
    int mid = (lo + hi) / 2;
    int cmp = strcmp(key, list[mid].partNum);
    if (cmp == 0) return mid;  // search succeeds
    if (cmp < 0) hi = mid - 1;  // key is 'less than' list[mid].partNum
    else lo = mid + 1;          // key is 'greater than' list[mid].partNum
  }
  return -lo;                   // key not found; insert in location lo
} //end search

void saveIndex(char *fileName, IndexEntry index[], int max) {
//save the index in fileName; max is the size of index.
  FILE *indexFile;
  if ((indexFile = fopen(fileName, "wb")) == NULL) {
    printf("Cannot create file %s. Index not saved\n", fileName);
    exit(1);
  }
  fwrite(&max, sizeof(int), 1, indexFile);  //save the index size first
  fwrite(index, sizeof(IndexEntry), max, indexFile); //save the index
  fclose(indexFile);
} //end saveIndex
```

When a part number is read, we look for it in the index. Since the index is kept in order by part number, we search it using a binary search. If the part number is present, it means the part has been stored already so this record is ignored. If it is not present, this is a new part so its record is stored in the parts file, **parts.bin**, provided we have not already stored **MaxRecords** records.

A count is kept (in **numRecords**) of the number of records read. The part number and the record number are then inserted in the proper place in the **index** array.

When all the records have been stored, the index is saved in another file, **index.bin**. The value of **MaxRecords** is the first value sent to the file. This is followed by **index[0]** to **index[MaxRecords]**. Remember that **index[0].recNum** contains the value of **numRecords**.

Given that **parts.txt** contains:

```
PKL070 Park-Lens 8 6.50
BLJ375 Ball-Joint 12 11.95
PKL070 Park-Lens 8 6.50
FLT015 Oil-Filter 23 7.95
DKP080 Disc-Pads 16 9.99
GSF555 Gas-Filter 9 4.50
FLT015 Oil-Filter 23 7.95
```

P8.7 prints the following:

```
PKL070 Park-Lens    8  6.50
BLJ375 Ball-Joint  12 11.95
Duplicate part: PKL070 ignored
FLT015 Oil-Filter  23  7.95
DKP080 Disc-Pads   16  9.99
GSF555 Gas-Filter   9  4.50
Duplicate part: FLT015 ignored
```

---

Next, we write a program which tests our index by first retrieving it from the file. The user is then asked to enter part numbers, one at a time. For each, it searches the index for the part number. If it finds it, the index entry will indicate the record number in the parts file. Using the record number, the part record is retrieved. If the part number is not found in the index, then there is no record for that part. The program is shown as P8.8.

**Program P8.8**

```
#include <stdio.h>
#include <string.h>
#define PartNumSize 6
#define MaxName 24
#define MaxRecords 100
typedef struct partRecord {
  char partNum[PartNumSize + 1];
  char name[MaxName + 1];
  int amtInStock; double unitPrice;
} PartRecord;
typedef struct indexEntry {
  char partNum[PartNumSize + 1];
  int recNum;
} IndexEntry;

main() {
  FILE *partFile;
  IndexEntry index[MaxRecords + 1];
```

```
  void retrieveIndex(char *, IndexEntry[]);
  void retrieveRecords(IndexEntry[], FILE *);

  if ((partFile = fopen("parts.bin", "rb")) == NULL) {
    printf("Cannot open file\n");  return;
  }
  retrieveIndex("index.bin", index);
  retrieveRecords(index, partFile);
  fclose(partFile);
} //end main

void retrieveRecords(IndexEntry index[], FILE *pf) {
  char pnum[PartNumSize * 2]; //to cater for extra characters typed
  PartRecord part;

  int numRecords = index[0].recNum;
  printf("\nEnter a part number (E to end): ");
  scanf("%s", pnum);
  while (strcmp(pnum, "E") != 0) {
    int n = search(pnum, index, numRecords);
    if (n < 0) printf("Part not found\n");
    else {
      fseek(pf, (index[n].recNum - 1)*sizeof(PartRecord), SEEK_SET);
      fread(&part, sizeof(PartRecord), 1, pf);
      printf("\nPart number: %s\n", part.partNum);
      printf("Part name: %s\n", part.name);
      printf("Amount in stock: %d\n", part.amtInStock);
      printf("Price: $%3.2f\n", part.unitPrice);
    }
    printf("\nEnter a part number (E to end): ");
    scanf("%s", pnum);
  } //end while
} //end retrieveRecords

void retrieveIndex(char *fileName, IndexEntry index[]) {
  FILE *indexFile;
  int maxRecords;

  if ((indexFile = fopen(fileName, "rb")) == NULL){
    printf("cannot open index file.\n");  exit(1);
  }
  fread(&maxRecords, sizeof(int), 1,indexFile);
  fread(index, sizeof(IndexEntry), maxRecords, indexFile);
  fclose(indexFile);
} //end retrieveIndex

//function search from page 209 goes here
```

The following is a sample run of P8.8:

```
Enter a part number (E to end): DPK080
Part number: DKP080
Part name: Disc-Pads
Amount in stock: 16
Price: $9.99

Enter a part number (E to end): GSF555
Part number: GSF555
Part name: Gas-Filter
Amount in stock: 9
Price: $4.50

Enter a part number (E to end): PKL060
Part not found

Enter a part number (E to end): PKL070
Part number: PKL070
Part name: Park-Lens
Amount in stock: 8
Price: $6.50

Enter a part number (E to end): E
```

If required, we could use the index to print the records in order by part number. We simply print the records in the order in which they appear in the index. For example, using our sample data, we have the index:

```
BLJ375   2
DKP080   4
FLT015   3
GSF555   5
PKL070   1
```

If we print record 2, followed by record 4, followed by record 3, followed by record 5, followed by record 1, we would have printed them in ascending order by part number. This can be done with the following code (**n** is **int**):

```
for (n = 1; n <= numRecords; n++) {
  fseek(partFile, (index[n].recNum - 1)*sizeof(PartRecord), SEEK_SET);
  fread(&part, sizeof(PartRecord), 1, partFile);
  printf("%s %-11s %2d %5.2f\n", part.partNum, part.name,
                     part.amtInStock, part.unitPrice);
}
```

## 8.12 Updating a random access file

The information in a file is not usually static. It must be updated from time to time. For our parts file, we may want to update it to reflect the new 'quantity in stock' as items are sold or to reflect a change in price. We may decide to stock new parts so we must add records to the file, and we may discontinue selling certain items so their records must be deleted from the file.

Adding new records is done in a similar manner to loading the file in the first place. We can delete a record logically by marking it as deleted in the index, or simply removing it from the index. Later, when the file is reorganized, the record could be deleted physically (that is, not present in the new file). But how can we *change* the information in an existing record? To do this, we must:

- locate the record in the file;
- read it into memory;
- change the desired fields;
- write the updated record to the *same position* in the file from which it came.

This requires that our file be opened for both reading and writing. Assuming that the file already exists, it must be opened with mode **"rb+"**. We explain how to update a record whose part number is stored in **key**.

First we search the index for **key**. If it is not found, no record exists for this part. Suppose it is found in location **k**. Then **index[k].recNum** gives its record number (**n**, say) in the parts file. We then proceed as follows (omitting error checking in the interest of clarity):

```
fseek(partFile, (n - 1) * sizeof(PartRecord), SEEK_SET);
fread(&part, sizeof(PartRecord), 1, partFile);
```

The record is now in memory in the structure variable **part**. Suppose we need to subtract **amtSold** from the amount in stock. This could be done with:

```
if (amtSold > part.amtInStock)
  printf("Cannot sell more than you have: ignored\n");
else part.amtInStock -= amtSold;
```

Other fields (except the part number, since this is used to identify the record) could be updated similarly. When all changes have been made, the updated record is in memory in **part**. It must now be written back to the file in the same position from which it came. This could be done with:

```
fseek(partFile, (n - 1) * sizeof(PartRecord), SEEK_SET);
fwrite(&part, sizeof(PartRecord), 1, partFile);
```

Note that we must call **fseek** again since, after the previous **fread**, the file is positioned at the beginning of the *next* record. We must re-position it at the beginning of the record just read. The net effect is that the updated record overwrites the old one.

Program P8.9 (next page) updates the **amtInStock** field of records in the parts file. The user is asked to enter a part number and the amount sold. The program searches the index for the part number using a binary search. If found, the record is retrieved from the file, updated in memory, and written back to the file. This is repeated until the user enters a dummy part number **"E"**.

**Program P8.9**

```
#include <stdio.h>
#include <string.h>
#define PartNumSize  6
#define MaxName  24
#define MaxRecords 100
typedef struct partRecord {
  char partNum[PartNumSize + 1];
  char name[MaxName + 1];
  int amtInStock;
  double unitPrice;
} PartRecord;
typedef struct indexEntry {
  char partNum[PartNumSize + 1];
  int recNum;
} IndexEntry;
main() {
  FILE *partFile;
  IndexEntry index[MaxRecords + 1];
  void retrieveIndex(char *, IndexEntry[]);
  void updateRecord(int, FILE *);
  int search(char[], IndexEntry[], int);
  char pnum[PartNumSize + 1];
  if ((partFile = fopen("parts.bin", "rb+")) == NULL) {
    printf("Cannot open file\n");
    return;
  }
  retrieveIndex("index.bin", index);
  int numRecords = index[0].recNum;
  printf("\nEnter a part number (E to end): ");
  scanf("%s", pnum);
  while (strcmp(pnum, "E") != 0) {
    int n = search(pnum, index, numRecords);
    if (n < 0) printf("Part not found\n");
    else updateRecord(index[n].recNum, partFile);
    printf("\nEnter a part number (E to end): ");
    scanf("%s", pnum);
  } // end while
  fclose(partFile);
} //end main
```

```
void updateRecord(int n, FILE *pf) {
//update record n in file pf
  PartRecord part;
  int amtSold;

  fseek(pf, (n - 1) * sizeof(PartRecord), SEEK_SET);
  fread(&part, sizeof(PartRecord), 1, pf);
  printf("Enter amount sold: ");
  scanf("%d", &amtSold);
  if (amtSold > part.amtInStock)
    printf("You have %d: cannot sell more, ignored\n", part.amtInStock);
  else {
    part.amtInStock -= amtSold;
    printf("Amount remaining: %d\n", part.amtInStock);
    fseek(pf, (n - 1) * sizeof(PartRecord), SEEK_SET);
    fwrite(&part, sizeof(PartRecord), 1, pf);
    printf("%s %-11s %2d %5.2f\n", part.partNum, part.name,
                                   part.amtInStock, part.unitPrice);
  } //end if
} //end updateRecord

//retrieveIndex and search go here
```

The following is a sample run of P8.9:

```
Enter part number (E to end): BLJ375
Enter amount sold: 2
Amount remaining: 10
BLJ375 Ball-Joint  10 11.95

Enter part number (E to end): BLJ375
Enter amount sold: 11
You have 10: cannot sell more, ignored

Enter part number (E to end): DKP080
Enter amount sold: 4
Amount remaining: 12
DKP080 Disc-Pads   12  9.99

Enter part number (E to end): GSF55
Part not found

Enter part number (E to end): GSF555
Enter amount sold: 1
Amount remaining: 8
GSF555 Gas-Filter   8  4.50

Enter part number (E to end): E
```

## Exercises 8

1. What is the difference between a file opened with "r+" and one opened with "w+"?
2. Write a program to determine if two binary files are identical. If they are different, print the first byte number at which they differ.
3. Write a program to read a (binary) file of integers, sort the integers and write them back to the same file. Assume that all the numbers can be stored in an array.
4. Repeat (3) but assume that only 20 numbers can be stored in memory (in an array) at any one time. Hint: you will need to use at least 2 additional files for temporary output.
5. Write a program to read two sorted files of integers and merge the values to a third sorted file.
6. Write a program to read a text file and produce another text file in which all lines are less than some given length. Make sure and break lines in sensible places, for example, avoid breaking words or putting isolated punctuation marks at the beginning of a line.
7. What is the purpose of creating an index for a file?

   The following are some records from an employee file. The fields are employee number (the key), name, job title, telephone number, monthly salary and tax to be deducted.

   ```
   STF425, Julie Johnson, Secretary, 623-3321, 2500, 600
   COM319, Ian McLean, Programmer, 676-1319, 3200, 800
   SYS777, Jean Kendall, Systems Analyst, 671-2025, 4200, 1100
   JNR591, Lincoln Kadoo, Operator, 657-0266, 2800, 700
   MSN815, Camille Kelly, Clerical Assistant, 652-5345, 2100, 500
   STF273, Anella Bayne, Data Entry Manager, 632-5324, 3500, 850
   SYS925, Riaz Ali, Senior Programmer, 636-8679, 4800, 1300
   ```

   a. How can a record be retrieved given the record number?
   b. How can a record be retrieved given the key of the record?
   c. As the file is loaded, create an index in which the keys are in the order given. How is such an index searched for a given key?
   d. As the file is loaded, create an index in which the keys are sorted. Given a key, how is the corresponding record retrieved?

   Discuss what changes must be made to the index when records are added to and deleted from the file.
8. For the 'parts file' application discussed in this chapter, write functions for (i) adding new records and (ii) deleting records.

# Index

www.ingramcontent.com/pod-product-compliance
Lightning Source LLC
Chambersburg PA
CBHW080406060326
40689CB00019B/4151
* 9 7 8 1 4 3 8 2 7 5 5 7 4 *